THE EVERYTHING.
GUIDE TO NARCISSISTIC PERSONALITY DISORDER

Dear Reader,

Imagine you say something that seems completely innocent, even lighthearted. "Hmm, next time I put the Macintosh or Golden Delicious apples on my list for you, I'll have to specify large apples, not small," you say with a laugh. But he doesn't laugh. He scowls and begins a defensive tirade about how what he did was right. Did you accuse? Blame? Put down? Of course not!

You ask her, "The appointment is for 9:30?" and she replies, "No, it's 9:00," trying to remain calm because she'd already given you two long explanations of how and why the time changed in the space of three days. "How is it that you don't listen to me?" She collapses inside herself, thinking, "I can't connect, he claims he loves me but he only remembers what he says, and it's usually wrong or twisted."

Communication, interactions, and day-to-day living with narcissists or those with NPD is anywhere from difficult and confusing to frustrating and damaging, and it is persistent. If you are dealing with someone with NPD regularly—a partner, sibling, relative, friend, coworker, or boss—life will be a continuing mess of often impossible and damaging behaviors and interchanges. Typical and regular behaviors can include explosions and tirades of belittling, blame, and verbal abuse, leaving you feeling helpless to know what or how to say the next thing, feeling hurt and even damaged that this person does not seem to care about hearing you, listening to you, or paying attention to you, your feelings, or your ideas.

Each situation is a little different, but in this book you will find great ideas and valuable tools from our personal and professional experiences, along with heartfelt concern for you, so you can gain the knowledge and understanding you need to make your life and your relationships with narcissists or those with NPD better and more fulfilling.

Cynthia Lechan Goodman, MEd

Barbara Leff, LCSW

Welcome to the EVERYTHING® Series!

These handy, accessible books give you all you need to tackle a difficult project, gain a new hobby, comprehend a fascinating topic, prepare for an exam, or even brush up on something you learned back in school but have since forgotten.

You can choose to read an Everything® book from cover to cover or just pick out the information you want from our four useful boxes: e-questions, e-facts, e-alerts, and e-ssentials.

We give you everything you need to know on the subject, but throw in a lot of fun stuff along the way, too.

We now have more than 400 Everything® books in print, spanning such wide-ranging categories as weddings, pregnancy, cooking, music instruction, foreign language, crafts, pets, New Age, and so much more. When you're done reading them all, you can finally say you know Everything®!

QUESTION

Answers to common questions

FACT

Important snippets of information

ALERT

Urgent warnings

ESSENTIAL

Quick handy tips

PUBLISHER Karen Cooper

DIRECTOR OF ACQUISITIONS AND INNOVATION Paula Munier

MANAGING EDITOR, EVERYTHING® SERIES Lisa Laing

COPY CHIEF Casey Ebert

ASSISTANT PRODUCTION EDITOR Melanie Cordova

ACQUISITIONS EDITOR Kate Powers

ASSOCIATE DEVELOPMENT EDITOR Hillary Thompson

EDITORIAL ASSISTANT Ross Weisman

EVERYTHING® SERIES COVER DESIGNER Erin Alexander

LAYOUT DESIGNERS Erin Dawson, Michelle Roy Kelly, Elisabeth Lariviere, Denise Wallace

Visit the entire Everything® series at www.everything.com

THE EVERYTHING®

GUIDE TO

NARCISSISTIC PERSONALITY DISORDER

Professional, reassuring advice for coping with the disorder—at work, at home, and in your family

Cynthia Lechan Goodman, MEd and Barbara Leff, LCSW

Adams Media

New York London Toronto Sydney New Delhi

To my beloved son Brett Jay Leff, whose loving
understanding supported my work. —B.L.

To my loving husband Steve, who crosses the bridges
to learn about my world and opens himself up to
courageously learn about his own world. —C.G.

Adams Media
An Imprint of Simon & Schuster, Inc.
100 Technology Center Drive
Stoughton, MA 02072

For information about special discounts for bulk purchases, please contact Simon & Schuster Special Sales at 1-866-506-1949 or business@simonandschuster.com.

The Simon & Schuster Speakers Bureau can bring authors to your live event. For more information or to book an event contact the Simon & Schuster Speakers Bureau at 1-866-248-3049 or visit our website at www.simon-speakers.com.

Manufactured in the United States of America

15 2023

Library of Congress Cataloging-in-Publication Data has been applied for.

ISBN 978-1-4405-2881-1
ISBN 978-1-4405-2968-9 (ebook)

This book is intended as general information only, and should not be used to diagnose or treat any health condition. In light of the complex, individual, and specific nature of health problems, this book is not intended to replace professional medical advice. The ideas, procedures, and suggestions in this book are intended to supplement, not replace, the advice of a trained medical professional. Consult your physician before adopting any of the suggestions in this book, as well as about any condition that may require diagnosis or medical attention. The author and publisher disclaim any liability arising directly or indirectly from the use of this book.

Contents

11 Tools and Coping Techniques / 117

12 Understanding Megalomania / 133

13 Narcissism and Depression / 141

14 Changing Perspectives of the Relationships / 149

15 The Digital Narcissist / 165

16 If You Believe Someone Needs Help with NPD / 177

Acknowledgments

With love and thankfulness for Charlotte Goodman, the most quintessential mother-in-law and best friend, for her understanding of the inevitable mistakes of parenting and for her model of never-ending unlimited support, thoughtfulness, recognition, generosity, and love for both her sons and her daughters-in-law.

With heartfelt gratitude to Ziva Avramovich, clinical and geriatric therapist, whose words allow the possibilities for individuals and couples to find bridges of connections to each other, building on learning, understanding, and love.

With love forever to my devoted family, for always being there with unlimited support for me, for recognizing and encouraging my talents, and for instilling in me the respect, compassion, and empathy for the uniqueness of others.

With the deepest level of thankfulness for the loving, supportive friendship of forty years of Frank Cannavo, LCSW, whose natural compassion, empathy, patience, and appreciation of others have helped to heal many.

With the utmost appreciation for my editor, Kate Powers, who has the gift of knowing, and the skills to shape words to allow another person's writing abilities and ideas to shine through clearly, and simply, from the heart and soul.

With enduring gratitude to Rabbi Allan Tuffs, who officiated at my marriage and rededication of marriage, for his spiritual leadership, and friendship that has supported the loving growth and bonds of my family.

The Top 10 Signs of Narcissistic Personality Disorder

1. A need to feel superior to others; belittles and demeans others in this regard

2. Little or no empathy or compassion for the feelings, thoughts, or opinions of others

3. Always preoccupied with his own problems or thoughts

4. Shows little or no respect for authority and/or has little concern for morals

5. Extremely sensitive to any kind of criticism

6. Exploitative and vain toward all in order to provide a sense of power, exceptionalism, or feeling better than others

7. Prone to explosive fits of rage

8. Extreme jealousy

9. Lacks the ability to admit when wrong

10. Distorts and lies to support her own interests, perceptions, and goals

Introduction

> *He seeks, is sought, he burns and he is burnt.*
> *And how he kisses the deceitful fount;*
> *and how he thrusts his arms to catch the neck*
> *that's pictured in the middle of the stream!*
> *Yet never may he wreathe his arms around*
> *that image of himself.*

THIS PASSAGE IS FROM Ovid's *Metamorphoses: Echo and Narcissus*, which tells the tale of a beautiful young Greek boy who fell in love with his own reflection, leading to his own destruction. This classic parable of the dangers of self-love gave us the terms "narcissist" and "narcissism." As you may have guessed, it was Sigmund Freud in the mid-1900s who actually introduced these terms into the psychological texts. But since then a lot has been learned about narcissism. Today, more than ever, there are still many myths and misunderstandings about the emotional disorder. Questions are now on everyone's mind about our friends, neighbors, family, and adored and admired celebrities.

- Is my husband or wife a narcissist?
- Is narcissism really a personality disorder?
- Is narcissism always a bad thing?
- Isn't a little narcissism necessary for success?
- Aren't all celebrities basically narcissistic?
- What should we do about a potential narcissist at home, at work, or in the family?

These are just some of the questions and controversies this book will explore, along with helpful tips and resources on how to identify the signs and symptoms of narcissistic personality disorder (NPD), and how to deal with the effects of narcissism in your personal and professional relationships.

According to researchers at San Diego State University, we may be living with an "epidemic of narcissism" in the youth of America. The researchers concluded that permissive parenting, celebrity culture, and the Internet may have all contributed. *ABC News 20/20* recently ran an episode titled "The Rise of Narcissism in America." In her book based on the San Diego State study, psychologist Jean M. Twenge, PhD, wrote that there has been a 67 percent increase in narcissism over the past two decades, and she estimated 10 percent of the overall population suffers from narcissism as full-blown NPD.

This means it is likely that you may be loving, living with, or working with someone who has some degree of NPD. That situation can be frustrating, unsettling, and even damaging to relationships. But take comfort in the knowledge that you are not alone in this situation. This book will give you all the information and tools you need to know where, when, how, and why narcissism may be affecting your life. And it will show you the many ways you can help yourself and anyone you may know, love, or live with.

From Greek mythology to modern psychology, our understanding of narcissists and narcissism has come a long way. For many years, narcissism was considered untreatable. But over the course of the last four decades, mental health professionals have begun to identify successful treatment procedures and management tools for narcissists and their families.

CHAPTER 1

The Basics of Narcissistic Personality Disorder (NPD)

Of course, there is nothing wrong with feeling good about yourself. Everyone wants to see their success and talents noticed by loved ones and others around them. But it is time for concern when such self-importance gets out of control: where self-love becomes so strong that there is no compassion for others. This can lead to abuse or other harmful and unpleasant behaviors, and is how narcissistic personality disorder becomes a serious problem for those that have it—and for their friends and families.

The History Behind the Disorder

In December 2010, the *New York Times* reported that the American Psychiatric Association might drop NPD as a recognized personality disorder in the next edition of the *Diagnostic and Statistical Manual of Mental Disorders* (DSM), the American Psychiatric Association's standard reference for classification of mental disorders in the United States. Does this mean that narcissists can breathe a sigh of relief and say, "See, I told you there was nothing wrong with me?" Hardly, although they would certainly be the first ones to want to.

The truth is that narcissism and narcissists have been around for far longer than the official diagnosis of NPD, and their immature behaviors create many challenges for themselves and those around them.

FACT

There are no poor narcissists, or at least very few of them. Narcissism seems to be a condition of the privileged. In their book *Personality Disorders in Modern Life*, Theodore Millon and Roger Davis state that pathological narcissism was a condition of the royals and the wealthy. Today, it seems be rampant in powerful and prosperous nations such as the United States. People in less advantaged nations are too busy just trying to survive to be arrogant and grandiose.

The word "narcissism" comes from the Greek myth of *Echo and Narcissus*. Echo was a wood nymph who fell in love with the incredibly beautiful and vain young man, Narcissus. He ignored her love, and she died of a broken heart. The gods took pity on Echo and were angered by Narcissus's pride and vanity. They made him live alone and never know human love. One day, while bending into a pool for a drink, he fell in love with his own reflection. He never left it, and died beside the pool.

The British psychologist Havelock Ellis was the first to use the story of Narcissus in 1898 to describe pathological self-absorption. Other psychologists soon picked up the terms "narcissist" and being "narcissistic." The words came into everyday use after the father of psychoanalysis Sigmund Freud wrote a paper titled "On Narcissism: An Introduction" in 1914.

Currently the Fourth Edition of the *Diagnostic and Statistical Manual of Mental Disorders* (DSM-IV), and its later revision, the DSM-IV-TR (Text Revised), which is what mental health professionals use to diagnose mental disorders, lists narcissistic personality disorder as one of the ten identified personality disorders. As a group, the book describes a personality disorder as something that involves repeated behavior over a long period of time and leads to trouble at work, at home, or in social situations.

Different Expressions of NPD

So what is narcissism? As with the boy in the myth, there is an obsession with oneself. But it is much more than high self-esteem, or being egotistical, conceited, or full of oneself—all of which could be unattractive attitudes and tough on a relationship. True narcissism involves a pumped-up ego, as well as an almost maniacal pursuit of gratification, praise, and ambition.

Those with any degree of NPD can be vain, smug, and arrogant, and do appear to have higher-than-usual self-esteem. But, most of the time, inwardly, narcissists are very insecure, with little real self-worth. They feed their belief in their own importance from the admiration of others. This is what is called narcissistic supply—and if that sounds like a drug, for the narcissist it is. Narcissists are addicted to the need for confirmation of their belief in their own superiority. Narcissists also typically have a lack of empathy, which means they couldn't care less about the feelings of those around them.

There are different levels of narcissism. In fact, it could be said that we might all have a little bit of narcissist in us. It has even been said that some narcissism is necessary just to get by in today's world. Maybe a little bit of egotism can be a good thing, but when it comes to full NPD, behaviors are always destructive.

The psychological criteria for narcissistic personality disorder are:

- The narcissist cannot put things in perspective, and situations are blown way out of proportion.

- The narcissist has little or no empathy and cannot identify with the feelings or thoughts of another person.
- The narcissist is preoccupied with his own problems.
- The narcissist does not respect authority and has little concern for morals.
- The narcissist feels inferior, and will try to be seen as superior.
- The narcissist is extremely sensitive to any kind of criticism.
- The narcissist is often an exhibitionist and needs sexual admiration.
- The narcissist is exploitative, vain, and not self-sufficient.

All cases of NPD show these traits to some degree, but there are some different types of narcissists to watch for.

Since the 1950s there has been a dramatic increase in people with narcissism. As the numbers of narcissists increased, therapists started noticing some differences between the types of narcissism. The first way that narcissists were divided into different types was based on age. Splitting narcissists into age groups was done because narcissistic tendencies in children are a learned behavior, and can usually be unlearned. Full-blown NPD is believed to exist only in adults, and needs to be treated differently. There have been many other ways introduced to classify types of narcissistic behavior. The official diagnoses of narcissistic personality disorder did not appear until 1980.

Other than the age distinction, other kinds of narcissists include:

- **The Craving Narcissist:** Despite the typical inflated ego of NPD, craving narcissists are extremely needy and emotionally clingy, or demanding of love and attention of those around them.
- **The Paranoid Narcissist:** Paranoid narcissists are the opposite of craving narcissists. Inwardly the paranoid narcissist is filled with self-loathing and projects that outward, usually driving people away from them with maniacal jealousy and extreme sensitivity to criticism.
- **The Manipulative Narcissist:** This is the type of narcissist that actually enjoys influencing and manipulating others. The manipulative narcissist feeds her need for power by intimidating others, usually through bullying, lies, and manipulation.
- **The Phallic Narcissist:** Those in this group are almost exclusively males. They are not only in love with themselves but also with their

body image. The phallic narcissist struts like a rooster. They are aggressive, athletic exhibitionists who enjoy showing off their muscles, clothes, and other aspects of what they perceive as their superior manhood.

QUESTION

What is narcissistic supply?
Narcissists need a source of "narcissistic supply" from people in their environment just like a baby needs someone else to bring it food. These love addicts will try to influence their source of supply by every means possible. The "supply" for narcissists is love, praise, and attention from those around them that fuel their behaviors.

Grandiosity is the single most significant trait of a narcissistic personality. Grandiosity is not the same as pridefulness or ordinary boasting; it implies self-aggrandizement that has little or no basis in reality. If a person goes on and on about being the MVP of his college basketball team at a cocktail party, it may be ill-mannered boasting or conceit, which can be incredibly annoying and self-serving, but it is not narcissistic if it is true. On the other hand, if someone made the same type of claim, but was actually a bench-warmer or never even played on the team, that is being grandiose.

Millon's Subtypes

Theodore Millon, an American psychotherapist well known for his ground-breaking work in identifying personality disorders, added these additional subtypes of narcissists:

- **The Unprincipled Narcissist:** This narcissism is characterized by pathological lying and deliberate deception to obtain narcissistic supply. Millon's unprincipled narcissist is a con man, an abuser, deceptive and unscrupulous.
- **The Amorous Narcissist:** The key feature of amorous narcissism is an obsession with erotica and seduction. A subtype of the manipulative

narcissist, the amorous narcissist uses sex and sex appeal as a tool and a weapon for control and power. He does not restrict his perceived power of seduction to members of the opposite sex, but believes his superhuman charisma can influence the same sex as well.

- **The Compensatory Narcissist:** Uses narcissistic supply to compensate for deep and overwhelming feelings of inadequacy and low self-esteem. According to Millon, the compensatory narcissist "seeks to create an illusion of superiority and to build up an image of high self-worth."
- **The Elitist Narcissist:** Millon's elitist narcissist has all of the characteristics of the phallic narcissist, but is not exclusively male.
- **The Fanatic Narcissist:** Fanatic narcissists believe they are gods, but are very paranoid. They try to fight very poor self-esteem with extreme delusions of grandeur.

No matter what you call it, narcissism remains very difficult to treat. People who suffer from it in any form rarely seek out or enter therapy on their own. After all, not only do they think that there is nothing wrong with them, they think they are superior to the therapist!

Drug and Alcohol Abuse

Narcissists are dependent by nature. They depend on others to feed their inflated views of themselves. They crave idolization by others like a physical addiction. It is not surprising then that often narcissists fall easily into other dependencies, including gambling, compulsive shopping, workaholism, alcoholism, and drug addiction. The narcissist, like all other addicts, gets pleasure from the behaviors and actions that feed his narcissistic supply. When that falls short, he seeks a similar high from other sources such as sex or drugs and alcohol.

Drugs and alcohol can give pleasure and can provide anyone with a way to withdraw from the pressures of reality. Sufferers of NPD will take drugs and drink to support their inflated self-image and to help them escape when reality does not match up to their world view.

For narcissists, drugs and alcohol became a way to shield themselves from the harsh reality of a world where they are not the center of the universe; where they have faults, failures, and limitations just like everyone else. Drugs and alcohol also provide a way for people with NPD to cut themselves off from what they consider to be the inferior crowd around them.

Compulsory, even risky and dangerous behaviors such as drug and alcohol abuse are also part of the narcissist's false view of his superhuman ability to handle them. A narcissistic drug addict or alcoholic will deny strongly that he has a problem, possibly even more than the abuser without NPD. Narcissists maintain the grandiose view that they are in control of the addiction and can quit anytime they want to. They feel they are exempt from conventional laws regarding the use of illicit substances, as well as immune to the natural laws of damaging effects on the body.

Narcissists easily fall prey to drug abuse and alcoholism because:

- Drugs and alcohol provide feelings of power and well-being.
- Drugs and alcohol can make them feel whole.
- Taking drugs and abusing alcohol is a totally selfish and self-indulgent act.
- Narcissists require a high level of stimulation.

ALERT

Individuals with NPD prefer drugs that stimulate their inflated sense of self and provide euphoria and feelings of vitality, and fight feelings of depression and low self-esteem. Cocaine provides all of these, and cocaine abuse is very common among narcissists.

Narcissists are the emotional equivalent of an alcoholic. As with alcoholics or drug addicts, their needs are insatiable. There is often a big gap between reality and grandiosity in narcissists, or the distance between the false image they project and the painful truth. Drug and alcohol abuse by people with NPD is a way to self-medicate and deal with the pain caused by this gap.

Narcissists' addictions serve deep emotional needs. Drug abuse and alcoholism in narcissists cannot be treated without also treating the underlying NPD.

Eating Disorders

Eating disorders are closely linked to narcissistic tendencies. People suffering from eating disorders are obsessed with body image. The most common eating disorders are bulimia (binge eating and purging), anorexia (not eating), and purging (eating very little and forcing regurgitation), all of which are impulsive, compulsive behaviors. Narcissists are reckless and impulsive, and can develop eating disorders for the same reasons they become alcoholics or drug abusers—their desire to exert some power or influence over an aspect of their lives.

A study published in the *International Journal of Eating Disorders* compared eighty-four women diagnosed with eating disorders with seventy non-eating-disordered women for core elements of NPD, such as entitlement and grandiosity. The eating-disordered group scored significantly higher than the other women on the measures of narcissism. The study concluded that narcissistic traits are particularly relevant in understanding the treatment of eating disorders.

Full-blown NPD is not a common diagnosis in people with eating disorders; however, a large percentage of patients with eating disorders have narcissistic issues. Consider the original myth of Narcissus. Narcissus did not actually fall in love with *himself*, but with his *reflection*. He did not know that the unobtainable image he could never reach out and grasp was himself. This is just like the person with an eating disorder who is in love with an image in the mirror that she can never hope to obtain.

Relationship Issues

In the narcissist's worldview, like the death of Narcissus at the side of his own reflection, all human relationships are doomed from the start. This strong belief usually comes from some kind of early childhood trauma or negative experience that caused feelings of humiliation, betrayal, or abandonment.

Even though this belief may have been formed many years ago, to the narcissist any emotional interaction—any connection that requires an emotional commitment—is bound to end badly. That means that getting attached to a particular home, a career, a job—even an *idea*—is considered by a narcissist to be just as bad as getting attached to people. That is why the narcissist avoids any kind of intimacy. He may surround himself with people to feed his narcissistic supply, but he cannot make any real friendships, or truly love, or express any real feelings of commitment or attachment.

It is extremely difficult to be in any kind of relationship with a narcissist. A narcissist basically lives in a bubble, surrounded by his own reflection. Try as you might, you cannot enter that bubble, which leaves you stuck outside, feeling alone, hurt, and frustrated.

ALERT

Narcissistic supply has a "trigger." Supply is "triggered" by whatever it is that causes the source of narcissistic supply to give to the narcissist what he wants to feed his false self-image. Publicity is a trigger of narcissistic supply because it makes people pay attention to the narcissist. Narcissists may resort to almost anything to gain attention and trigger narcissistic supply.

In any kind of relationship a narcissist is unable to develop any sense of security, or any real pleasure for that matter. Narcissists will only invest emotionally in the one thing they feel in full control of—themselves.

The Nature of the Beast

The big problem with narcissists is that they can't or won't change their ways, even when it causes problems at work, at home, or when people complain about the way they act. When it comes to most emotional disorders, you may have heard that the first step in getting help is admitting there is a problem. The nature of narcissism makes it impossible for the person with NPD to admit he has a problem. Narcissists will always blame other people for the stress they feel, and for the problems around them, when it is really caused by their own behavior.

CHAPTER 2

CHAPTER 2
Symptoms and Behaviors of NPD

Remember the "terrible twos"? How everything was "I want!" and "Me! Me! Me!"? And when that didn't happen, remember the resulting tantrums? Fortunately, most of us grow out of that kind of behavior eventually—but not narcissists. They are usually stuck there, and the destructive behaviors that those around them have to deal with are a lot like a two-year-old's, only now often fueled by adult-sized rage and cruelty.

Causes and Risk Factors

As with many emotional disorders, there is not one specific cause for NPD. But just as there is a chance you can get a chill and catch a cold if you run outside naked on a cold, rainy day, there are factors that can put someone at greater risk for developing narcissistic behaviors.

As with most mental illnesses, the roots of NPD are very complex. The likelihood of developing narcissism is linked to childhood events and dysfunctional parenting. Interestingly enough, too much pampering, as well as neglect and abuse, are both associated with the development of NPD and narcissistic tendencies. Recent thinking also points to genetics and the connection between a person's brain and behavior.

Statistically, more men than women suffer from NPD. Full-blown NPD rarely is seen in children or adolescents. NPD usually does not show up until adulthood. Research continues to look at the risk factors that may increase the chances of developing a problem with narcissism.

For some time, experts believed one of the main influences of narcissistic behavior was excessive praise to children, or "overindulgent" parenting. Constant praise and admiration by parents under certain conditions could lead to a pathologically inflated sense of self. Today, however, it is believed that parental neglect is more likely responsible for NPD. Neglect does not have to be just the obvious physical abandonment. Emotional neglect by parents can sometimes take on many not-so-noticeable forms.

Studies have found that rates of NPD are higher for young adults, and for those who were separated, divorced, or widowed, than for those never married. Significant cultural differences have also been found, with black men and black and Hispanic women showing higher rates of NPD than Hispanic men and whites of both genders.

We are all born as narcissists. Naturally, as infants and toddlers with our parents catering to our every whim, we *are* the center of the universe. Our parents are godlike mythical figures, awesomely powerful, whose job is to protect and feed us. This is "primary narcissism." In a healthy environment, children gradually lose these childish views and grasp reality. Healthy emotional development is a process of coming to grips with the disappointments of the real world. But if something goes wrong with this process, then primary narcissism may never go away.

Risk factors for the development of NPD can include:

- Parents that ignore their child's fears and needs
- Parents that belittle childhood fears, or say they are signs of weakness, especially in male children
- General lack of affection, and not enough positive praise during childhood
- Neglect and other kinds of emotional abuse in childhood
- Inconsistent or unreliable caregiving from parents
- Imitation of manipulative behaviors learned from parents

Children, especially male children, who are made to believe, usually by their fathers, that to show vulnerability is unacceptable and unmanly, can lose their empathy and compassion for others. To be superheroic in their fathers' eyes, such children may cover up their emotional needs. The covers can be grandiose, egotistical behaviors that make them seem emotionally bulletproof. Such coverup behaviors can lead to NPD later in life.

As with other personality disorders, NPD develops as a type of defense mechanism. The idea basically goes like this: Human beings grow, or develop emotionally, just like trees do. When a tree comes upon an obstacle, it will grow around it. The branches then are often twisted, gnarled, and ugly, but the obstacle is gotten around, and growth continues. Personality disorders, while sometimes twisted and ugly like those branches, are a means of survival.

Warning Signs and Red Flags

People with NPD usually have an overinflated sense of their own importance and an overwhelming hunger for admiration and the approval of others. Showing little or no regard for other people's feelings often fuels their belief in their own superiority. But buried beneath this outer skin of ultra-confidence often lies a fragile person who has trouble accepting even the slightest criticism.

It may seem as if the characteristics of NPD are nothing more than being strong-willed, being overconfident, or just being someone with very strong self-esteem. But narcissistic personality disorder crosses the line of positive self-assuredness. It goes down the dark path of a person thinking so highly of herself that the self is put on a pedestal, believing that all others are beneath her. People with healthy self-confidence, on the other hand, do not have to build themselves up by breaking others down.

QUESTION

How can my mother be narcissistic? She talks about *me* all the time!
Narcissistic parents may seem like they are emotionally invested in their children because they constantly brag about them to others. But to the narcissist, her children are not sources of pride but narcissistic supply. Bragging about her child's accomplishments is just a way to emphasize her own image of superiority.

It may not be as easy to recognize a narcissist as you might think. Narcissists are, by their very nature, masters of disguise and deceit. They hide behind a mask of false self-image. There continues to be ongoing debate about what defines full-blown NPD. But here are some telltale behaviors to look for:

- Does your partner try to cut you off from, or limit your contacts with, your friends and relatives?
- Is he extremely jealous? Does he often invent relationships and suspect you of infidelities with friends, coworkers, or acquaintances?
- Is she belittling?
- Does he resort to verbal or physical abuse?
- Does she punish you?
- Has she suddenly withdrawn emotionally?
- Does he lack the ability to admit when he's wrong?
- Does he try to control your time?
- Has she ever resorted to self-mutilation?
- Does she threaten or otherwise try to intimidate you?
- Does he purposefully destroy your things?

- Does she claim to know your feelings and motivations "better than you do"?

QUESTION

I suspect someone I know may be a narcissist. How can I be certain? One way to know is to watch his behavior in a group setting. See if he continuously puts himself at the center of attention. See if he regularly interrupts and has to bring the focus of the conversation back to himself. Look for continual signs of actions and behaviors that are clearly bids for attention.

Your Own Sense of Self

Another red flag or way to tell if you are living with a narcissist whose behavior is damaging the relationship is to look at your own behaviors. How do you feel? Are you on your guard often? Do you alter your behavior to keep your partner happy, even if you are betraying your own desires and needs? Is your relationship one-sided? Do you find yourself constantly walking on eggshells?

Take a good look at the mirror of your own behavior. Do you like what you see? Do you feel like the same person you were when you first entered into this relationship? This is a difficult question if you are dealing with a relative or a family member. But in those cases, ask yourself: Am I happier when I'm free of this person? Does being around this person bring me down?

If you live with a true narcissist long enough, chances are you will start to believe her belittling and begin to develop feelings of inadequacy. This can occur consciously or subconsciously. You may not have had such a negative self-image before living with the narcissist. But after being browbeaten over the years, you may be left with the psychological equivalent of a very bad taste in your mouth. Do you find yourself filled with many negative feelings that you did not have before? Feelings that make you feel like you are not you? Day-in and day-out interaction with a narcissistic partner may be to blame.

Narcissists love to play the blame game. Narcissists often internalize failure, and their first reaction to any kind of failure is usually to feel shame, rather than guilt, responsibility, or determination to improve for next time. Shame is something narcissists seek to avoid, so they blame someone else for their failures. It cannot possibly be their fault that they have failed; the blame lies with the coworker who didn't help, the teacher who has never liked them, the partners who never believed in them in the first place; the list goes on and on.

ALERT

Don't expect a narcissist to thank you. People with narcissistic personality disorder often demand that others provide them with comfort and gifts, and satisfy other needs, but they usually will not acknowledge or appreciate such actions with thanks. The narcissist may even mock and demean both gift and giver.

A change in your own self-image often leads to another powerful emotion when you are around a partner with NPD: fear. You walk around in constant fear of saying or doing the wrong thing, until you get to the point where you watch your every move. This kind of fear may not allow you to be true to yourself, and can cause you to further behave in uncharacteristic ways or ways that make you feel uncomfortable.

This is one of the more complex issues when living with a narcissist. People do have some negative feelings about themselves to some degree, whether in a relationship with a narcissist or not. But narcissists are manipulators and abusers; they can sense weakness in another person like a lion stalking prey. Narcissists like to feed on the negative self-images of those around them and exaggerate those negative images that others may have of themselves. They can exploit their partner's shortcomings, gorging on the resulting narcissistic supply like emotional vampires.

Symptoms

People with NPD usually come across as conceited, egotistical, and arrogant. Narcissists can monopolize conversations. Narcissists can belittle others, looking down on friends, relatives, and coworkers. They usually show very little compassion for the feelings of others, or very little interest in the thoughts of others.

Narcissists usually walk around with feelings of entitlement. They have been described as emotionally immature. When they do not get the things they think they are entitled to, they may react violently, even throwing temper tantrums and giving the silent treatment, like a child.

They tend to be vain and obsessed with status symbols, and often feel they have to drive the best cars, belong to the best clubs, and live in the best neighborhoods. But beneath all of this surface bravado often lies very fragile self-esteem. Most narcissists have trouble handling even the slightest criticism.

For all of their self-perceived power, narcissists are often lazy. Many may take the easy route by preferring fantasylands to reality, grandiose self-concepts over realistic self-evaluations, sexual fantasies to mature adult relationships, and daydreams to real-life achievements.

These are all general behaviors that you might see in a person with NPD. Here is another way to look at some of the specific symptoms:

- If someone believes she is better than everyone else, she might be a narcissist.
- If he constantly fantasizes about power and success, he might be a narcissist.
- If he exaggerates or lies about achievements or talents, he might be a narcissist.
- If she demands constant praise and admiration, she might be a narcissist.
- If he believes he is special and beyond legal or moral consequences, he might be a narcissist.
- If she fails to recognize other people's feelings, she might be a narcissist.
- If he expects others to always go along with his ideas and plans, he might be a narcissist.

- If she enjoys taking advantage of or manipulating others, she might be a narcissist.
- If he is jealous of others, while thinking that others are jealous of him, he might be a narcissist.
- If she sets ridiculously unrealistic goals, she might be a narcissist.
- If he thinks emotions are a sign of weakness, he might be a narcissist.

Most narcissists usually only put emotional investment into one thing: their false self-image. If a narcissist seems to value another person, it is probably only because that person has something to offer, some way to feed his unquenchable thirst for narcissistic supply. To a person with NPD, other people are often servants or useful tools. If a narcissist has someone in his life who constantly praises him and showers him with compliments, it's only natural that he will want to keep this person around to feed his narcissistic supply. But it's unlikely that the narcissist genuinely cares for this person. In fact, this other individual probably gets the worst of the narcissist's cruel attitude and mistreatment.

Another way to spot a narcissist? Trust your gut feelings. There may not be a way to explain it, but when it comes to narcissists, you just may know one when you see one. You probably will feel uneasy in the presence of a narcissist for no apparent reason. Do you ever have this experience when you meet someone, and no matter how charming, intelligent, thought-provoking, or charismatic he seems, some little bell goes off that tells you something is wrong? What you might be instinctively recognizing is the narcissist's inability to really care about you.

When to See a Psychologist or Psychotherapist

Getting people who show these signs and symptoms of NPD to see a therapist is very challenging. They will probably think there is nothing wrong with them. Or even if they realize they have a problem, they will not accept that even a trained professional knows more about how to help them than they know how to help themselves. But a narcissist has great difficulties trying to treat or help herself—it's like trying to pull yourself up out of quicksand by your own hair.

You will recognize that it is time for someone exhibiting the signs of narcissism to seek help when her behaviors are causing problems at work and at home. People wrestling with NPD may do everything they can to appear in control. But they also may be moving in and out of depression, having trouble with personal relationships, losing friends, or missing work or school. If any of these things are happening when combined with the signs and symptoms described, it may be time to seek professional help.

There also are other complications or conditions that can appear along with NPD. If a person is exhibiting any of the following, along with any of the other symptoms described, it's time to get professional help:

- Substance abuse
- Alcohol abuse
- Depression
- Suicidal thoughts or behavior
- Eating disorders, including anorexia, bulimia, or purging

It is the nature of the disorder that people with narcissistic tendencies, let alone full-blown NPD, will usually not seek help until they have reached some major crisis in their lives, such as losing their business, a job, or their family. Even then, they usually won't recognize that it was their narcissism that brought on the crisis. They seek to place the blame elsewhere. However, if you are going to get a narcissist to agree to seek help, this is likely one time it can happen.

Can a narcissist be cured? As with many conditions, diseases, or disorders, it depends on a lot of things. With time, therapy can tackle the more destructive aspects of this disorder. The right kind of counseling can help; a person with NPD can get used to living with the condition, learn how to accept it, and learn how to live a more meaningful and productive life.

Remember that the narcissist in your life is driven by a need to succeed, to be the best, and to be better than everyone around her. Learning to live with this disorder and putting her life and relationships back on track can be the greatest accomplishment any narcissist can achieve.

Tests and Diagnosis

There is no x-ray machine or blood test that can detect narcissism. The only way for a clinician to diagnose NPD is through observation of the signs, behaviors, and symptoms. There are tools available that can aid the mental health professional. He may use a questionnaire and other proven methods of psychological evaluation to make a diagnosis.

One such tool widely used for clinical diagnosis of NPD and other personality disorders is known as the Millon™ Clinical Multiaxial Inventory, or MCMI™, currently in its third edition (MCMI-III™). Based on the work of personality disorder researcher Theodore Millon, the MCMI is a diagnostic test that provides a scale for assessing personality traits, including narcissism. The test is made up of 175 true-false questions, which take the average person about thirty minutes to complete. The MCMI is generally recognized as one of the most well researched measures of personality disorders available to clinicians today.

ALERT

While there are no medical tests that can diagnose NPD, a person may be given or sent for a physical exam as part of a diagnostic evaluation, just to rule out any kind of physical problem or injury that could be causing symptoms of NPD.

According to the *Diagnostic and Statistical Manual of Mental Disorders*, in order for a clinician to make an official diagnosis of NPD, a patient must present five or more of the following personality traits:

- He has a grandiose sense of self-importance (exaggerates accomplishments and demands to be considered superior without real evidence of achievement).
- He lives in a dream world of exceptional success, power, beauty, genius, or "perfect" love.
- He thinks of himself as "special," or privileged, and that he can only be understood by other special or high-status people.
- He demands excessive amounts of praise or admiration from others.
- He feels entitled to automatic deference, compliance, or favorable treatment from others.
- He is exploitative toward others and takes advantage of them.

- He lacks empathy and does not recognize or identify with others' feelings.
- He is frequently envious of others or thinks that they are envious of him.
- He has an attitude or frequently acts in haughty or arrogant ways.

Living with someone with NPD or recognizing some signs or symptoms in yourself can be very scary. But by reaching out for help from a trusted healthcare provider or mental health professional, you can begin to turn things around.

Varieties of Personality Disorders

CHAPTER 3

Comparing NPD to Other Personality Disorders

You can't compare apples to oranges, but you can compare NPD to other personality disorders. One of the reasons that there has been so much debate over whether or not narcissism even qualifies as a personality disorder is because its risk factors, causes, and symptoms can often overlap or occur with other emotional illnesses.

Varieties of Personality Disorders

What exactly is a personality disorder? There remains a lot of controversy over the answer to that question, especially regarding official clinical diagnosis. But one thing is clear about narcissistic and other personality behaviors: They are repetitive and destructive.

What is personality?
In psychological terms, personality is the unique set of behaviors, character traits, styles, and patterns that make up who people are. Personality affects how people see the world and create a place in it. Thoughts, attitudes, and feelings toward people and things are a part of personality.

A healthy personality is defined by two things:

- The ability to deal acceptably with the everyday stresses of life
- The capability of forming healthy relationships with friends, family, and coworkers

According to the Mayo Clinic, a personality disorder is defined as a kind of emotional illness in which individuals have trouble understanding the realities of the world around them and difficulties relating to situations, to others, and even to themselves.

Personality disorders have been defined in many ways and placed in many different types of categories. These categories are commonly called clusters, and most personality disorders fall into three clusters:

- **Cluster A:** This can be described as consistent and odd, abnormal, or eccentric behaviors that are damaging.
- **Cluster B:** This can be described as consistent and overly dramatic, highly emotional, "high-strung," or erratic behaviors that are damaging.

- **Cluster C:** This can be described as consistent and fearful or anxious behaviors that are damaging.

Cluster B Personality Disorders

NPD belongs in the Cluster B disorders. Cluster B disorders are the most commonly diagnosed personality disorders. Here are the other Cluster B disorders:

- Histrionic Personality Disorder
- Borderline Personality Disorder
- Antisocial Personality Disorder

There may be many factors that can contribute to the development of personality disorders. Individuals classified as having one of the Cluster B personality disorders typically appear to be erratic and dramatic in their behavior. Usually, symptoms of the Cluster B disorders show up during adolescence, but most often are not actually diagnosed until adulthood. Often in cases of Cluster B disorders, there is evidence of some form of abuse as a child. Abuse in this context can be physical, sexual, or emotional.

QUESTION

How do I recognize a personality disorder?
Personality disorders involve deeply ingrained, inflexible, unhealthy patterns of relating, perceiving, and thinking that become serious enough to affect relationships and day-to-day living. The important aspect of what makes a personality disorder is a *pattern of repeated behavior or thinking*. It has to be a consistent way of behaving, not just a few isolated incidents.

Another way to think of personality is, "Who am I?" Narcissists do not really have an authentic personality because they are wrapped up in the false ones that they project. If they take away the praise, the inflated self-image, and the toys and belongings, who are they?

Histrionic Personality Disorder

The main trait of someone with histrionic personality disorder (HPD) is to behave melodramatically, or over the top. Think of the drama queen—but in overdrive! People with HPD have a personality based on theatrical and over-exaggerated behavior, constantly displaying an excessive level of emotion.

Like narcissists, histrionics can crave the limelight and may need to seek constant attention and approval. Similar to those with NPD, people suffering from HPD can tend to monopolize conversations and use grandiose language. Also like narcissists, people with HPD can sometimes be manipulative. But unlike narcissists, it is in a "why me?" kind of way, or an attempt to draw sympathy, because to most histrionics even negative attention is better than no attention at all.

Some of the signs to look for in a person with histrionic personality disorder that may distinguish it from NPD could include:

- Dressing provocatively and/or being excessively seductive or flirtatious, especially in inappropriate situations
- Having rapid mood swings
- Acting very dramatically as if he is performing on stage
- Being overly concerned with appearance
- Being bored by routines and becoming frustrated easily, often starting things and failing to finish them
- Acting rashly without thinking
- Threatening or attempting suicide, or faking illness to get attention

Borderline Personality Disorder

People with borderline personality disorder (BPD) are emotionally unstable in many ways. A person with BPD may have trouble with interpersonal relationships, may show extreme swings of behavior and mood, and may have problems with self-image.

Extremely sudden mood changes and very stormy relationships, along with unpredictable behaviors and self-destructive actions, are typical characteristics of someone with BPD. Unlike the narcissist who believes he knows who he is (although that view is a false hyperinflated one), those with

BPD often have trouble with any kind of sense of identity or self. Many times people with BPD fail to perceive any gray areas; they tend to think in absolutes. All things and all people are either all good or all bad.

Relationships with people with BPD are very often intense and at the same time unstable. A narcissist rarely forms any kind of bond with a partner, but a person with BPD may form a very strong, almost obsessive attachment to one person, only to just as quickly break it off over the slightest perceived insult. It is believed that fears of abandonment caused by early childhood trauma can lead to an unnatural dependency on others in people with BPD.

It is common for many people with BPD to self-mutilate or to attempt suicide to manipulate others and gain attention. BPD seems to occur more often in women than in men.

Other behaviors that can be common in people with BPD include:

- Acting impulsively
- Often feeling bored or feeling empty inside
- Having fits of intense and inappropriate anger

BPD is considered the most serious of the four currently recognized Cluster B personality disorders, as people with BPD can be violent and very self-destructive. Those with the disorder are also likely to suffer from other emotional problems that can severely impact their lives and the lives of those around them, such as substance abuse, eating disorders, compulsive sex, anxiety disorders, and depression.

ESSENTIAL

Like NPD, there is no known specific cause for borderline personality disorder. It is believed that BPD is the result of a combination of biological and psychological factors.

In other words, people with BPD are likely born with a predisposition of developing the disorder, which is then triggered by trauma, stress, or other factors.

Antisocial Personality Disorder

People who have antisocial personality disorder (ASPD) are very difficult to deal with. They act however they want to and feel the normal rules of society do not apply to them. They can be rude, impulsive, irresponsible, and very self-centered. These are qualities that reflect narcissism to some degree; however, in the person with ASPD, any attention they get is usually negative attention. Unlike narcissists, those with ASPD tend to push people away from them, or keep them close only out of fear. Unlike narcissists who are often leaders with great responsibility, such as running major corporations, those with ASPD are most often belligerent and irresponsible, and often have run-ins with the law. They can be very aggressive and physically abusive in relationships.

Persons with ASPD can be totally disrespectful of other people's feelings and hurt people emotionally and even physically, often showing no signs of remorse whatsoever. However, like people with NPD, those with ASPD are often at high risk for alcoholism and substance abuse, because they feel that such indulgences relieve their tension, irritability, and boredom.

ALERT

It is important to note that personality disorders, especially all of those that are considered Cluster B, do not exist in a vacuum. They all overlap and interrelate. Diagnosing personality disorders is not an exact science. Rarely is someone clearly suffering from NPD without any of the symptoms of BPD, HPD, or ASPD, and vice versa.

People with ASPD are what used to be called sociopaths. It is believed there is a very thin line between ASPD and NPD, and that ASPD is really just a less inhibited or even more over-the-top form of NPD, more similar to the classical description of manipulative narcissism, or Theodore Millon's unprincipled narcissist subcategory.

Dissociative Identity Disorder

Though not a Cluster B disorder, dissociative identity disorder (DID), previously called multiple personality disorder, is sometimes confused with narcissism. Dissociative identity disorder is still more commonly known to many laypeople as multiple personality disorder. The famous case of Sybil brought multiple personality disorder to light. People with DID develop these multiple personalities as alter egos to escape from the harshness of a traumatic reality. These so-called alters are sometimes compared to, or confused with, the image of the false self of narcissists.

But there is a very distinct difference. The false self of the narcissist is not an alternative self existing side by side with the true self, as do the separate multiple personalities of a person with DID. Narcissists believe the false self *is* their true self; there is no separation from it.

On the other hand, the person with DID often is not even aware of all of her different alters. These alters are each distinct, with different names, various ages, sometimes even different genders. Each alter has a distinct personality, one or more of which may in fact be a narcissist.

According to therapists, individuals with DID usually have an innocent host personality who was spared from the abuse that gave rise to her alternate personalities. The host personality is the entity that people with DID most often identify as "me." It is the host personality who is, on the surface, reacting with the real world most of the time. The alters take over from the host in response to perceived threats or to protect the host from further abuse.

Narcissism as the Basis for All Personality Disorders

One of the reasons why the American Psychiatric Association is considering dropping NPD as a separate diagnostic category of personality disorders is because there is growing belief that there is a degree of narcissism underlying all of the Cluster B personality disorders. The other three Cluster B personality disorders—histrionic, borderline, and antisocial—all share these common aspects of NPD.

Most of the people identified with any of the Cluster B disorders are insistent and demanding. They demand to be treated as if they are special and privileged. They often think they know better than their physicians or counselors, and often disregard treatment recommendations. Like narcissists, borderlines, histrionics, and antisocials often also think of themselves as unique, and display a large degree of grandiosity along with a diminished capacity for empathy. All four types of Cluster B disorders can be manipulative and exploitative.

It seems that all of the Cluster B personality disorders start out in childhood as trouble with personal development that peaks in adolescence. The negative behaviors that are characteristic of all four disorders affect all aspects of a person's life: work, interpersonal relationships, and social functioning.

Almost all patients with any of the four currently identified Cluster B personality disorders tend to blame the world for their problems and failures— a cornerstone of narcissism. In most cases, those with any of the Cluster B disorders do not believe there is anything wrong with them, or anything unacceptable about their behaviors. This is a very basic narcissistic trait.

ESSENTIAL

Some therapists have described those with borderline personality disorder as simply narcissists with an uncontrollable fear of abandonment. Those with BPD tend to be in relationships and try to maintain them by not abusing the people around them, but for an entirely selfish or narcissistic reason. They seem to care deeply about not hurting people, but only because of their deep fear of being alone.

Some behavioral scientists suggest that this interrelation is because each of the four disorders relies on its own kind of narcissistic supply. Those diagnosed with NPD get their narcissistic supply from gaining mostly positive attention, such as admiration and idolization.

Those with histrionic personality disorder often get their supply from flirtatiousness and strong sexuality. They may feed on many romantic and sexual encounters. They also get narcissistic supply from physical exercise and from showing off the shape and beauty of their bodies.

Those suffering from BPD get their narcissistic supply from the strong connections they form with others, as they suffer from severe separation anxiety and are terribly afraid of being abandoned. They may also engage in compulsive sexual behavior.

Those with ASPD get their narcissistic supply from power, money, and anything else that gives them control over others. They also get supply from the rush of living on the edge and having what they consider fun—even when that comes at the expense of others. They derive supply from mostly negative attention, such as fear and notoriety from others.

Treatment of Cluster B Personality Disorders

There has been a lot of research into personality disorders. With this greater understanding of how and why they develop, many effective treatments have been created. Treatments that have proven to be effective in dealing with Cluster B personality disorders may include individual, group, or family therapy.

Some medications, when properly prescribed by a physician, have been found to be helpful in relieving some of the symptoms of some of the Cluster B personality disorders, particularly in relieving problems with anxiety, depression, and perceptions of reality.

Talk therapy for patients with personality disorders is intended to help them see the often-subconscious conflicts that are contributing to or causing their symptoms. Therapy is also aimed at helping people with NPD and other Cluster B personality disorders to become less rigid in their thinking, and to help them to reduce the kinds of behaviors that are interfering with their everyday lives.

ESSENTIAL

One of the goals of psychotherapy in people with Cluster B personality disorders is to get them to better recognize the impact of the negative behaviors typical of the disorder on their loved ones and those around them.

The more that you can learn about personality disorders and the people in your life that may be dealing with them, the more you may be able to help yourself or someone you know live a healthier, more fulfilling life.

CHAPTER 4

Who Are the Narcissists?

Most people like to see themselves looking great in the mirror. Usually, that does not imply that they are queens with the "mirror, mirror on the wall" excesses. It is normal to take care and pride in your appearance. For sure, it feels good to have pride and to reward yourself for any great decisions you make and the good work you do. There is certainly nothing wrong with positive thinking about who you are and what you do. In fact, the array of self-help books talk about affirmations and pursuing dreams, even if those dreams seem difficult and far-fetched to achieve. So how is it that some of these behaviors might be viewed as narcissistic? Is the neighbor who always has to tell you about her life but never listens to you and anything about your day or your problems a narcissist, or just having a hard time?

Spotting Narcissistic Behaviors

The question that many people pop up with is, "How do I know I am not a narcissist?" Therapists might respond to that question with something like, "If you have to ask the question, then it is highly unlikely that you are a narcissist because narcissistic personalities don't think there is any problem with them."

Everyone has a personal scenario—the personal story of your own life, what you are about, and what you like. It's a growing scenario, taking in your daily history, experiences, likes and dislikes, successes and failures. As a small child your scenario in its normal stage of development can be saving the world on Mars or fighting a dragon. But as children mature they leave behind what is unreasonable and take in what is realistic—most of the time. But some people are not just occasionally unrealistic and a little self-centered, but highly unrealistic in their expectations and possess an exaggerated sense of self-importance and of their achievements, talents, and experiences.

ESSENTIAL

Behavior and culture theorists believe that each culture has norms for beauty, power, and wealth. How can you decide whether you are just working on these goals or suffering from NPD? You can look at the degree of your involvement or preoccupation with fantasies of unlimited success, power, brilliance, beauty, or ideal love that seem to be above the acceptable norm.

There are generally nine areas that narcissistic behavior can cover. And as you read over the list, probably everyone you know, including yourself, demonstrates one or more of these behaviors at one time or another. They are:

1. A grandiose exaggerating manner, capable of no flaws or failures, and grandiose self-importance
2. Preoccupation with fantasies of unlimited success, power, brilliance, beauty, or perfect love
3. Convinced of being special and unique

4. Always requiring special admiration
5. Feeling entitled to special treatment and compliance with all of one's expectations
6. Taking advantage of others for one's own purposes
7. Feeling jealous of others and believing others are envious of him
8. Arrogant and haughty
9. No capacity for empathy, or feeling for the needs of others

Even with these categories, there is a wide range of what can be considered narcissistic behavior, from mild to the severe personality disorder. The level depends on how many of these behaviors the person *consistently* demonstrates and to what degree. Five or more of these consistent traits may indicate a narcissistic personality disorder.

ALERT

The most recent edition of the *Diagnostic and Statistical Manual of Mental Disorders*, the DSM-IV-TR, of the American Psychiatric Association specifies nine diagnostic criteria. For NPD to be diagnosed, five or more must be met. But new research and information is always being reviewed, and the next DSM update, the DSM-V, is due to be released in May 2013.

Narcissists Are All Around Us

A narcissist can be any person in any capacity. One therapist recounted a patient, a mother who continually sighed about not being a perfect mother due to the fault of never receiving any help from her husband or family. She maintained this story despite the fact that the therapist knew she had divorced two devoted husbands, that her parents always supported her financially, and that upon their death she squandered her inheritance.

A narcissist may be a person working alongside you at your workplace. There are reported cases of business people who always claim spectacular results and benefits—more valuable than anyone else's, with little true effort or time of their own invested.

ESSENTIAL

You may not be aware of a narcissist, or person with NPD, in the workplace because they often present a face, or a front of likableness, patience, or even confident reasonableness.

Important Common Risk Factors

Still today, the cause of narcissistic personality disorder is not confirmed. Research from both the past and present by psychology experts and social learning experts has suggested various theories about what might lead to this disorder. The risk factors fall into three areas: parenting and caregiving, genetics, and social and environmental influences.

Parenting Is Never Perfect

Theories about how parenting may lead to the emotional coping styles of NPD range from child neglect to child overindulgence. These theories for the risk factors in parenting include:

- Lack of affection and praise during childhood
- Excessive praise, admiration, and indulgence from parents
- Parental lack of understanding and comforting
- Neglect and emotional abuse in childhood
- Unpredictable or unreliable parenting and caregiving—either purposefully or through illnesses or disability
- Learning manipulative behaviors from parents
- Having parents who themselves have NPD

The Role of Our Culture

Social learning theorists have argued that trends in our society are contributing to the risks of developing narcissistic disorders. These cultural trends include: media centered on celebrities rather than on average people; importance placed on status and achievements; acceptance and choice of leaders with emphasis on personality and appearance; and weakening of religious and social institutions as part of traditional family life that encouraged community rather than individuality.

Social researchers also describe "acquired situational narcissism," which they believe can affect adults as a result of social successes. This may especially be the case for film, music, and sports stars, or for politicians—individuals who are always in the limelight and always receiving special attention and treatment.

Genetics

New scientific evidence shows the possibility of a genetic basis for personality disorders like NPD. One type of evidence has been with identical twins who have been separated at birth, but who maintain similar personality traits even though their childhood family and social situations were different.

With newly developed technology in brain scanning, clinicians and other researchers have documented abnormal brain function or problems in individuals having certain personality disorders. Research has found that about 68 percent of children of parents with personality disorders suffered the same disorders as their parents. Approximately two-thirds of the children of parents who were diagnosed with NPD, for example, have NPD themselves. However, with this particular research, two questions still remain: If there is a genetic predisposition, does a personality disorder only develop if there is a trigger in childhood, some type of trauma? Or, could the disorder simply be genetic, needing no triggering experiences?

Are Some People More Likely to Suffer from NPD?

The data from clinicians, hospitals, and researchers on the percentage of the general population with NPD varies from less than 1 percent to 6.2 percent. However, NPD seems to be more common among men than women: Statistics show that 50–75 percent of people diagnosed with NPD are men.

Behavior experts have described a difference in the way boys and girls deal with criticism. Girls may tend to internalize criticism, while boys may tend to "act out" in response to it. One explanation for this is that there is a difference in brain functioning between boys and girls. This difference has also been used to explain part of the difference in traditional behavior roles of females and males. If the female role is nurturing, women may be more inclined to give up their narcissism to tend to another person's needs. Therefore, the more nurturing female may be less likely to suffer from NPD than a man. However, learned behavior, reinforced by societal expectations, is another means that determines differences in gender-role behavior.

Famous Narcissists

Narcissism and narcissistic tendencies are often compounded by the media and by society's obsession with celebrities, politicians, and socialites.

Narcissists in Professional and Leadership Positions

Psychology professionals note that NPD does not prevent people from being in professional and leadership positions. Many people with NPD have the talents and credentials to be successful in prestigious and powerful positions. Part of their disorder means they develop an attractive appearance, a persuasive social manner, and powerful charisma that encourages casual business acquaintances. These leaders do not necessarily have to develop close relationships with anyone, a core characteristic of narcissism.

Narcissism also works well in business situations where big changes are necessary for growth, according to several organizational psychologists. You may notice it in newsmakers who seem to work well in situations where growth requires large changes. They are able to make necessary tough decisions without being distracted by emotions that others would have, such as empathy, sadness, or guilt.

Organizational psychologists describe how people with this personality type are natural leaders because they have a freedom from internal constraints. You might imagine how much someone can accomplish with that go-ahead ability to see those great changes in the world without feeling they are too grandiose. Donald Trump has often been described as a productive narcissist. One example of his triumph includes the strategic intelligence he used to convince New York City officials to permanently close an exit ramp into Manhattan from the West Side Highway (NY 9A) to enable his own construction project.

A study of personality traits published in the journal *Current Psychology* found that politicians, clergy, and librarians scored highest on traits for leadership and authority, but also scored highest in total narcissism values.

Narcissistic Behaviors in Celebrities

A study at the Keck School of Medicine, University of Southern California, surveyed 200 celebrities using the respected Narcissistic Personality Inventory (NPI). The study revealed that celebrities ranked significantly higher in narcissistic traits than the general population. Celebrities in reality television shows ranked the highest in narcissistic ratings, followed by comedians, actors, and musicians. You may have already guessed the results with reality TV stars, but you may now be more aware of the behaviors you see in other celebrities.

Several doctors who have observed and treated narcissists who are also celebrities have found that these celebrities sometimes have severe problems, including narcissism and NPD, which motivate their actions, often coming from childhood trauma. This may be one reason that some chose to be a celebrity—as a way to make themselves feel better. But famous celebrities can become a type of role model even while they may be mentally ill. You probably know people who imitate a celebrity's unhealthy behaviors, just because the celebrity is so popular and is accepted as being cool.

QUESTION

Does the Commander-in-Chief have narcissistic behavior?
Perhaps. A published study of thirty-nine U.S. presidents from George Washington to Ronald Reagan used presidential profile data to conclude that narcissistic behavior is a trait that does predict charismatic leadership.

In the Keck School of Medicine study, published in the *Journal of Research in Personality*, researchers found that, on average, celebrities scored 17.84 on the NPI—about 17 percent higher than the general public—with females scoring significantly higher than males. That female celebrities scored higher than male celebrities is counter to results in the general public, in which males score significantly higher than females. Even more interesting is that the research also showed little or no relationship between NPI scores and the number of years a celebrity had been in show business. This probably means that it is not show business and fame that led to narcissism or NPD in celebrities, but that they probably had narcissistic tendencies before they became famous.

FACT

The Narcissistic Personality Inventory is a questionnaire that is used to measure narcissistic tendencies. The NPI ranks people on a scale of 1 to 40, with 40 being "extremely narcissistic."

Whether they like it or not, people are often fascinated by what can be seen as the narcissism and grandiosity of celebrities. And the media loves to paint top celebrities with the brush of narcissism, like Madonna, Michael Jackson, Tom Cruise, Suzanne Somers, Deepak Chopra, Oprah, and last but not least, Charlie Sheen. But it is not fair to just assume that anyone is a diagnosed narcissist on the basis of a statement. Celebrities such as Mr. Sheen may exhibit features of pathological narcissism in statements that everyone sees, but only his psychiatrist can classify him.

There are many outstanding celebrities and performers who are not always modest, and in fact are pompous and flamboyant, but often with real accomplishments to back them up. Such is the case with Muhammad Ali, famous for boasting, "I am the greatest! And the prettiest!"

FACT

Linda Martinez-Lewi, PhD, chose some famous people in the arts to feature in a book about narcissism titled *Freeing Yourself from the Narcissist in Your Life*. Author Ayn Rand, master-artist Pablo Picasso, and world-class architect Frank Lloyd Wright are described in the book as possible narcissists. Despite their accomplishments and fame, their behaviors created a great deal of pain and trauma in their personal and professional lives, likely due to their seeming narcissism.

Can a Narcissist Lead a Normal Life?

Therapists of all levels would agree that a person diagnosed with NPD would have an impaired capacity to be interested in or to love others. This diminished capacity can also be found in persons who have more mild narcissistic behaviors. However, therapists who are treating the disorder have encouragement to offer about living with narcissism and with a narcissist.

Therapist Barbara Leff describes her experiences with some of the narcissists she has counseled and the difficulties they have in leading normal lives. She explains that on the surface these individuals may appear to be leading functional lives. They can hold jobs and marry and/or have a family. But personally and professionally, narcissists have great problems in both areas. Often they use sex as a substitute for love and intimacy. They fear intimacy because it exposes them and because intimacy requires having empathy for another person's needs and feelings. Relationships often end because of the narcissist's grandiosity or because their partners feel alone due to the narcissist's emotional detachment.

In a profession, narcissists can hold good jobs and get along reasonably well as long as there is no contact with coworkers outside the workplace. This would endanger the facade that those with narcissism maintain. There could be battles with a boss because of grandiosity. These narcissistic individuals can go through a normal-seeming day of going to work, coming home, and taking care of their own needs, but they will feel emptiness inside, and have no true empathetic concern or energy for anyone else.

In these cases, it's suggested that therapy can help the narcissist get in touch with his real feelings. Therapist Leff works with strategies to engage the narcissist to use eye contact and to help him be able to verbalize empathetic feelings. This is a pathway to help a narcissist with interactions with other people in the world.

Psychotherapist Samuel Lopez De Victoria would agree; he too has counseled and seen extreme narcissists become healthier in their emotional and relational lives. His therapy helps the narcissist to get through two hurdles in order to find her feelings and be on the road to healing. The hurdles are dealing with early emotional wounds and with what the narcissist feels is the unsafe world of feelings.

ESSENTIAL

Even though most psychotherapists would agree that personality disorders, and especially NPD, are hard to treat, there is always the possibility of bringing some healing to their clients' suffering.

Putting NPD into Perspective

It is likely that each one of us is at some point arrogant, selfish, jealous, conceited, or out of touch with reality, or just seems to not be paying enough attention to another's feelings. Generally, if you can say to a person who is being insensitive, "Please have a heart," and you see a change or an apology, chances are that the person does not have a narcissistic disorder.

Narcissism can come in a wide range of seriousness, from very mild to an extremely severe disorder. Some people only have a few features of narcissism that may get in their way and can cause trouble for them and other people, while others, with their ways of manipulating and deceiving to get their goals met and totally lacking of empathy, will cause hurt and destruction to all those around them.

The greater you understand what are the narcissist's behaviors and motivations, the better you will be able to develop strategies for handling them. As you do so, you will find your hurt and frustrations replaced with the power to make the best decisions for yourself and any potential narcissists in your life.

CHAPTER 5

What Can Lead to Narcissism?

How did it happen that Harry met Sally? How did it happen that Sally had blond hair? And how did it happen that Harry exhibited narcissistic behaviors or even serious NPD? Some of these answers are traceable to fact, such as blond hair color—genetics determine factors about the transmission of genes. But some things are still about probabilities and possibilities. Today, there are still just the range of possibilities, probabilities with some evidence, and theories about what can lead to narcissism, and even at what age narcissism can occur. These theories cover genetics, psychobiology, parenting and caregiving, and social and cultural considerations. Much like the way we often consider physical illness today in a holistic way, NPD may very well be influenced by any or all of these factors.

Genetics or Psychobiology?

How is it that a person becomes who she is? Theories and research point to a combination of both genetics and psychobiology—the connection between the brain, behavior, and thinking. However, psychologists usually believe biology may be just one of many forces that shape an adult: culture, society, and parenting being more important.

ESSENTIAL

Well-known pioneering psychoanalyst Karen Horney (1885–1952) believed that insight and understanding of a problem could lead to healing or even elimination of the problem. If narcissism, then, is something that is learned, there is hope that it can also be unlearned with guided counseling to provide for the best understanding.

In one analogy people may be compared to the seeds and growing shoots of plants. The seeds begin to develop with the particular traits of their parents, and as they grow they require certain necessities. If they encounter some difficulties in getting what they need, they may twist and turn, or grow with deformity. However, it is true that even with the same obstacles to good growth, some trees will reach their normal height and others will not.

QUESTION

Are people with a particular genetic makeup destined to be narcissistic?
Not necessarily. Studies have suggested that narcissism and narcissistic responses to stress and trauma likely have a genetic basis. But additional factors are at play; otherwise, everyone with the same genetic trait would develop NPD. As in most genetic disorders, the potential for NPD may be in the genes, but it may need some environmental or other trigger to set the disorder in motion.

How Might Brains Be Like Plastic?

The good news is that research now shows that the brain has a lot of "plasticity." As with Silly Putty, brains and nerves are not rigid, and so personality traits are not carved in stone. Trauma and abuse can scar the brain emotionally. But there is a "window of plasticity." During that time the damage can be fixed with loving, caring, compassionate, and empathic experiences. The problem is, no one knows how long this "window" is open. But it is possible that it is open into adulthood.

But there are still many other reasonable possibilities of how narcissism develops in a personality or behavior:

1. According to some psychobiological theories, a person is born with a particular personality and meets the experiences of life in a particular way—all due to what he is born with.
2. Other theories propose that the roles and interactions of parenting and caregiving mark and influence a child's personality development. They note especially the role of the mother, who shapes the child's feelings of self, of self-importance, of value, and of "goodness."
3. Still other theories contend that the personality within a child causes the child to adapt to situations in the child's own way. While others propose that it is the flip side—the situations the child encounters—that cause the personality to become what it is.
4. Many theorists point to abuse or neglect that may be purposeful or beyond the parents' control.
5. More recently theorists have discussed the influence of culture, socializations, pressures, lifestyle, and the media as influences that overwhelmingly affect personality development—even into a person's twenties and beyond.

As you read through the range of these possibilities, you probably will begin to think about your own childhood development and that of the potential narcissist in your life. It is one way you can help to determine or understand what the needs and challenges may be for you and the person you suspect of exhibiting narcissistic behavior or NPD.

Child Abuse

The term "abuse" leads people to commonly think of physical abuse, striking or sexual perversions, or neglect of food, water, comfort, or sleep, and of caring for basic health. But psychobiological experts also consider certain lack of attention and catering to a child's emotional needs as abusive. Sometimes the abusive situations are purposeful, other times unintentional, as with accidents, financial or medical challenges, physical challenges, and disruptive family situations. To a child, any of these can be experienced as a horror story, or as violence.

ALERT

Child sexual abuse is a monumental problem. The alarming statistics are that one of every three girls and one of every six boys will be sexually abused before they reach the age of eighteen.

In response to any experienced abuse, the developing child may develop repressed emotions or denial of reality, may strike out in physical violence and anger, or escape into her own world of great fantasy where there is the love and security she needs, and where she is perfect and good.

Role of the Image

There is a theory that children's emotional development is based on the image they form of themselves inside their own head. They usually develop a positive, healthy image from loving and sensitively caring parents. But if a parent is cold or shows no empathy for the child's feelings, the child is hurt and looks for a safety inside his own head. What the child does is create a fantasy image based on anything that child can find that the parent *does* value, and hide away any weaknesses.

Role of Body Image

Studies have shown a relationship between narcissism and a female's body esteem. The American society still loves looking beautiful, and thinness is one measure of beauty. However, evidence shows that more males have also become concerned with their body image. To be sure, there has been a rise in eating disorders that includes both genders.

Excessive or distorted concerns with body image have been linked in medical studies not only with eating disorders, but also with narcissism. Research suggests that personality characteristics of bulimics match up closely with classic NPD traits.

Today our lives are bombarded with images of people with perfect bodies, most of them just to sell products and services. Seeing these bodies has a serious influence on children and young adults.

According to the Association for Body Image Disordered Eating (ABIDE), the average U.S. citizen is exposed to 5,000 advertising messages each and every day. Most if not all of these show beautiful people with perfect bodies enjoying the finer things in life. These kinds of images often provide a blueprint for the false images of perfection created by narcissists.

It is not just media and advertising, but parents too can be overly critical of their children's appearances in the way they talk, look, or act, which hurts the children's self-esteem.

Mirroring

Mirroring is basically how a child feels noticed or admired. Some describe it as the gleam in a parent's eye when looking at their children. Children want to see the smiles; they want the "great job" assurance that they please and do well.

There are theorists who believe that children's understanding of themselves comes from two areas:

- The right amount of mirroring or approval
- The understanding of a parent or parents' values

The mirroring develops a realistic sense of the self. Without the right amount of mirroring, the child may be stuck always needing to find and get approval from others in order to feel okay, and/or have an exaggerated need to be noticed and admired. Without the understanding of parental ideals and values, he will stay stuck with an underdeveloped fantasy about himself.

According to famed psychology researcher Heinz Kohut, the mother supports the child's future ambitions with her positive responses to what the child shares. The father who shows acceptance of the child helps the child's development of goals and ideals. On the other hand, however, recent theorists have described that over-the-top, excessive mirroring, where anything and everything about the child is awesome or better than anyone else, can cause the child to develop a narcissistic belief in false ideas about himself.

Denial of Feeling

Respected behavioral theorists discuss how important it is that a parent accept a child's vulnerability and any expressions of weak and hurt feelings by not responding with any type of reprimand to the child. Every child can and will be hurt, rejected, or humiliated. But it is important that the child does not fear possible humiliation, because this can cause a child to deny her feelings altogether and to show herself as cool, calm, and strong.

Is Narcissism the Result of Pampering or Neglect?

In recent years, many social learning theorists believe the development of NPD is a result of parents who overvalue their children, who are unrealistic, and who pamper. These parents make sure that their child has everything and anything, and is protected from feeling hurts or pains. Psychological behavior experts agree that children need to be allowed to fail, to feel frustrated, and to learn positive ways to deal with these normal stumbling blocks in life.

Too much love used to be called spoiling. Spoiling can cause children to feel that they are more special than anyone else. Too much love can also be a type of improper seduction. Some theories claim that too much love and spoiling may lead to the type of narcissistic behavior in which control and seduction of others is used to get needed admiration.

Parenting and Self-Esteem

Dan Williams, PsyD, has written about his experience with patients with NPD and has found commonalities. He believes there is a relationship to NPD with loss or absence of a strong father figure—a father who is either emotionally or physically absent. The father may also be critical and condescending, and fail to help his child feel empowered with a good sense of self-esteem. Dr. Williams feels this lack of self-esteem can lead to overcompensation or exaggeration of a false sense of self-worth, along with emotional distancing.

Interestingly enough, while at first glance it may seem like the narcissists in your life have very high self-esteem, in reality the false self they project is actually compensating for, or shielding them from, underlying low self-esteem.

Lifestyle

Therapists have described a theory called "acquired situational narcissism" that teens or adults may experience as a result of certain successes. Most therapists feel this is a temporary narcissistic experience. However, for people who continuously experience exceptional success, achievements, fame, fortune, and special treatments, this may lead to long-term unhealthy narcissism.

The term "millennials" refers to people born after 1980, and relates to their present lifestyle that is heavily media-oriented. Children start on computers with individualized avatars for each program. You might imagine already that this excessive focus on individualism could lead to an inflated view of the self that can lead to narcissism. Our culture as a whole is focused on gratification and social approval. So it almost seems that open narcissism and acceptability of narcissism is just about a way of life.

Everything kids watch, do, or play on computer screens has an enormous influence on their lives. You know the story: constant messages about families, friends, relationships, gender roles, sex, violence, and even the food they eat and the clothes they wear. So if there is an influence of narcissistic role models or a focus on overinflated "me," that is an influence you are probably already concerned about.

QUESTION

Is narcissism ever healthy?
Yes, sometimes. It's important to consider yourself throughout the day, and as long as you are being reasonably considerate of others, you shouldn't feel guilty about self-care. In fact, John F. Murray's Palm Beach Narcissism Diet™, for which he wrote a book with the same title, has been sweeping the nation. One of the main parts of the program instructs you to remind yourself several times a day what weight you want to be in four months. You might think this involves thinking about yourself more than you are accustomed to, but he feels it is a healthy kind of narcissism.

Parents Who Are Narcissists

Many studies have been performed confirming that narcissistic parents may influence the personality development of their children. A parent with NPD, often a father, may see the child as a threat to his needed narcissistic supply. Or the reverse is also true: A parent with NPD may see the children as their sources of narcissistic supply and encourage the children to idolize, adore, and obey them. Or children may invade the father's space, so he may belittle, hurt, or humiliate them.

There are many reported cases of mothers with NPD who reverse the role in child care. Instead of taking care of the child's needs, the mother requires the child to take care of her needs.

Research has shown that the media are among the most powerful forces in young people's lives today. Children and young adults in the United States ages eight to twenty spend more than fifty hours in front of a TV or computer screen each week. That is more time than most adults spend at their jobs each week!

Minimizing Narcissistic Behaviors

Experts from all sides agree that there are some measures to consider in parenting that may minimize development of narcissistic behaviors and NPD:

- Recognize and acknowledge real achievements.
- Encourage children to explore talents and skills they are good at while identifying those they can or need to work on.
- Help children to understand that for most people rewards and success are the result of hard work and discipline as opposed to what they may see on TV or in movies.
- Encourage children to be involved in the community and to identify and help others who need it.
- Tell a child "no" in an empathetic way that shows the child that she is still loved and important, but is not "bad" for asking or requesting something.
- Set boundaries with consistency in limits without criticizing a child for acting out, while still recognizing the child's feelings.
- Think about giving children their own "voice."
- Allow them to feel they are good, loved, and not at fault for wrongdoing or failures in efforts.

All children and teenagers are concerned with some aspect of their bodies. Concern is a normal part of their development and is not a medical problem, but an obsession with one's physical body and appearance is not normal. If your child is spending the majority of her time worrying about her appearance, it could be a larger and more serious issue.

According to the national Office on Women's Health Information Center, in order to help your children develop a positive body image, you should:

- Make certain that your children understand that gaining weight, especially during puberty, is a normal part of development.
- Do not make negative statements regarding food, weight, or body shape and size.
- Encourage your children to make their own decisions about food, but make sure that a variety of healthy and nutritious meals are in the mix of choices.
- Reward your children for their talents, efforts, accomplishments, and personal views.
- Limit television time, and when your children do watch it, watch with them and discuss the images you see.
- Encourage your school to not support any kind of size and sexual discrimination, harassment, teasing, or name-calling based on size or weight, and to support the elimination of public weigh-ins and fat measurements.
- Always keep communications open with your children.

CHAPTER 6

Treatments for NPD

It's very hard to get someone into treatment who doesn't even think they have a problem. Chances are the narcissist in your life will only seek treatment after they have had a major crisis or breakdown. Even then, most likely he will only be looking for an immediate fix to the problem at hand and not the underlying condition, which he does not believe exists. If that sounds challenging, know that it is, but take heart—the first steps can be very hard for narcissists, but once they see that there is a problem, help is available.

History of Treatment

For many years it was believed to be nearly impossible to treat narcissism. Admittedly, it is very difficult to get someone with NPD to change his behavior. But today, while recovery from narcissism can be tough, it's not impossible.

There is some evidence to support that genetics may set up a predisposition to NPD and other personality disorders. But it is generally accepted that narcissism develops early on as a defense mechanism to cope with difficult situations. In other words, it is *learned* behavior—and anything that can be learned may be unlearned. The bottom line is that if you suspect that you or someone you love may have NPD, there is hope.

People with NPD can be very stubborn. Do not ever expect them to admit that they are narcissists. However, in their quiet times, even the most egotistical among them can come face-to-face with the impact of their condition on their lives. People with NPD can be lonely and depressed; their social relationships tend to be superficial, and their working lives problematic. Many narcissists have an extreme fear of failure and suffer from anxiety.

Deep down, narcissists need to be the best they can be. Sometimes, when forced to confront the mess that his life has become, the narcissist may find the incentive to change it. It is kind of a double-edged sword with NPD: The image of perfection that often prevents narcissists from seeking treatment may also be the motivation that brings them to it.

ALERT

For full-blown narcissists looking for healing or for change, recovery can be a long, hard road for themselves and those around them. Realistically, it may take a person with NPD several years of various types of intensive therapy to recover—but it all starts with the first step.

How long is the treatment process for NPD? The process of changing deep-rooted personality traits and learned behaviors (some of which may have lasted the narcissist's entire life), such as those related to NPD, can be a very long one. This is true no matter what type of therapy or therapist is chosen. However, the short- and long-term goals of any kind of psychotherapy for narcissistic personality disorder are similar. In the short term, the therapist will try to tackle the immediate issues that likely brought the narcissist in, such as difficulty maintaining relationships, obsession with success, paranoid thoughts, or abusive situations with loved ones. Then, the therapist usually begins to work on a long-term treatment strategy. The long-term strategy can involve an attempt to reshape the distorted image the client has of himself and the world around him, or to give him skills he needs to function better.

Psychotherapy in some form is generally the most accepted treatment for NPD. There can be different approaches, based on varying schools of thought, and therapy can be individual, group, or a combination of both.

But no matter what the approach or type of therapy used, the ultimate goal is the same: to help the narcissist become more empathetic to the rights, feelings, and emotions of others.

ESSENTIAL

Psychoanalyst Heinz Kohut, renowned for his theories in identifying and treating narcissism, has suggested that children have a need to idolize and identify with their parents. They also have an equally strong need to see such worthiness reflected, or mirrored, back by their parents or other caregivers. When children do not receive this mirroring, they don't form strong attachments early on, and narcissism can be the result.

The Kohutian approach to therapy, or working through childhood issues, can be an effective strategy. To the patient with NPD, the therapist becomes the idealized parent. Through transference, the patient gets the things he missed out on at a young age. Part of mirroring therapy also involves getting the patient to reflect on how troubling relationships early in his life led to current personality problems.

Individual Therapy

The ultimate goal of individual therapy for people with NPD is to help them to unlearn negative patterns of behavior, and to learn better ways to relate to others, so that all of the relationships in their lives can be more intimate, enjoyable, and rewarding.

Individual therapy sessions are designed to turn the mirror inward, and allow the person with NPD to better understand what it is that drives her to be competitive, distrustful, and disrespectful to others. And then, with the light shining upon her inner demons, help her to find ways to better cope with them.

QUESTION

What is the best kind of therapy for a person with NPD?
The success or failure of therapy for people with NPD depends less on the type of therapy used than on the relationship between the therapist and client. In any therapy patients can learn, maybe for the first time, that they can safely express anger, or any emotion, with their therapists without the risk of rejection or fear that the therapist will stop treating them. Secure and comfortable in the relationship, these clients are then able to continue to discuss intimate secrets and painful issues that were locked away and previously not shared with anyone else.

Individual therapy for people with NPD usually has three stages:

- It begins with the client and therapist going over specific thoughts or feelings in detail.
- The therapist and client work on identifying distorted views.
- The therapist works with the client to entertain new nondistorted ways of thinking.

Each week the therapist will likely give the client some specific home-work assignments. These assignments are designed to identify verbal cues and keep track of the kinds of words and phases the narcissist uses when talking and thinking about herself and others. The purpose is to get her, through analysis, to recognize what such phrases reveal about herself. For example, a therapist may ask an NPD patient to keep track of the "I" or "me" statements he uses in a twenty-four-hour period. How often does he talk about himself? Does he continuously interrupt someone else's story with his own tale? Seeing the sheer number of times a narcissist references his own life or experiences each day can be a huge wake-up call.

In individual therapy for NPD, the role of the therapist is to teach and to help with recognition in a nonthreatening way. The therapist's subtlety helps to bend the person with NPD into new ways of thinking and behaving. Developing a positive and trusting relationship between therapist and client is key to successful individual therapy for a person with NPD.

ALERT

It is not often that hospitalization is suggested, or required, for people with NPD. However, there are some circumstances where inpatient therapy may be recommended.

If the person suffers from a form of narcissism that involves self-mutilation, suicide attempts, or other forms of self-destructive behaviors, hospitalization may be necessary. Inpatient treatment or detoxification may be required to deal with substance abuse. Such hospitalizations are usually brief, and the treatments deal with the specific symptom involved.

Psychotherapy

Another approach to individual therapy for treatment of NPD uses the more classic method originated by Freud: psychoanalytical therapy. Classical Freudian, or psychoanalytic, therapy is not used with NPD today as much as other styles.

Psychoanalysis based on the psychodynamic model has changed somewhat since the time of Freud. But basically, the Freudian model states that emotional disorders are based on inner unresolved conflicts between different aspects of one's psyche—the id, the ego, and the superego—or, more simply, between the conscious and unconscious mind. The goal of individual psychodynamic therapy is to reduce these conflicts, and in doing so, modify the personality of the individual for the better.

The therapist takes a less active role in this form of therapy. He remains fairly quiet and relies on the patient to reveal increasing amounts of distress buried in her subconscious.

Dreams are an important part of psychodynamic therapy. Freud believed that much of the subconscious conflicts are revealed in dreams. In this type of therapy, therapist and client will discuss dreams to gain insights into their meaning and what they show about the patient's inner struggles. Psychodynamic therapy can run from one year to as long as fifteen years or more.

Group Therapy

Narcissists are extreme individualists. They often walk around believing that not only are they the most important person in the universe, but sometimes they are the *only* person in the universe. It is not surprising, then, that as a whole, narcissists have difficulties in group settings. Therefore, the effectiveness of group therapy for NPD sufferers is questionable. They often upset the group dynamic in work and social situations. Narcissists often resist collaborative efforts, which can include group therapy.

On the other hand, being forced to work with a group in an inpatient environment can be useful. The need for teamwork, to listen to the moderator, and to respect others in the group could break the cycle of narcissistic behaviors. However, caution is needed that the narcissist does not take over or manipulate the group to his own ends.

ESSENTIAL

Narcissists seem to do best in group therapy at an inpatient setting. In residential treatment, the person with NPD can go to small staff–patient groups at the hospital and to large community meetings. These group therapies, along with constructive work assignments and recreational activities offered in residential therapy, can help patients unlearn negative and impulsive behaviors, and can help them develop a less vulnerable self-concept.

The goals of group therapy for NPD are much the same as for individual therapy: for the narcissist to develop a healthy perspective, instead of the falsehoods of narcissism, and an ability to acknowledge, accept, and respect others as equals. Group therapy for NPD is also designed to help the person to stop depending on self-defeating ways to cope. There are deeply rooted personality traits of people with NPD that can and do make group therapy challenging. But one reason that it has been suggested that group therapy can be effective for people with NPD is because in a group setting, the therapist may seem less authoritative and therefore less threatening to the patient's image of grandiosity.

In a group setting the narcissist also may feel less put upon then he would in a one-on-one setting. The intensity of individual emotional experience is less in a group. This may create a better setting for safely confronting one's past.

Cognitive Behavioral Therapy

The basic idea of cognitive behavioral therapy (CBT) is to get the person with NPD to recognize and identify untrue beliefs and negative behaviors, and replace them with healthy, positive ones. The basis of CBT is that our feelings and ways of thinking play a major role in the way we behave and interact with people and the world around us.

The goal of cognitive behavioral therapy is to get patients to realize that while they cannot control every aspect of their lives and the world around them, they do have power over how they interpret and choose to deal with people, events, and objects in their environment. CBT has proven very effective in personality disorders such as NPD and borderline personality disorder.

With NPD, the thought patterns and feelings that cognitive behavioral therapy is trying to change are those of inflated self-importance and lack of empathy. In order to deal with these destructive thoughts and behaviors, CBT begins by helping the client to see her problematic beliefs.

This first stage of the process is called *functional analysis*. The goal in this stage is to get the person with NPD to understand how thoughts, feelings, and situations contribute to negative behaviors. This can be a tough process, especially for narcissists, who have difficulty looking inward. But when the CBT therapist can break through the narcissist's defenses and gain her trust, the self-discovery and insight that are essential to the treatment process can be achieved.

The second stage of CBT focuses on the actual behaviors that are making life miserable for the narcissist and those around her. For example, the narcissist's lack of affection for her significant other is taking a toll on their relationship, or the focus on perfection is creating a huge body image and appearance issue for her children. This stage can be especially difficult, as narcissists tend to believe there is nothing wrong with their behavior, and if those around them are taking offense, it's simply because they are too sensitive, or even jealous. However, through intense cognitive behavioral therapy, a narcissist can realize that not everyone shares her worldview and that her actions are self-serving and hurtful.

In the third and last part of the process, the client begins to learn and practice new skills that can be used to get different outcomes in real-world situations. For example, working on lack of empathy is a major focus of CBT treatment for narcissistic personality disorder. The CBT therapist can use several techniques to address this issue.

ESSENTIAL

The best predictors of success of cognitive behavioral therapy in a person with narcissistic personality disorder are the degree of narcissism and the ability of the therapist to not fall into the trap of supplying the patient's narcissistic demands for approval and special treatment. Also important is the narcissist's willingness to address the issue—does she really want help? When faced with losing a spouse, a job, or a family, the narcissist often opts to make changes.

Role-playing, including role reversal, has been shown to be an effective technique. In these role-plays the therapist can get the narcissist to see that there are other ways of relating to people and situations. Specific language will be used in the role-playing to bring about new belief statements and new thought patterns such as "other people's feelings count, too."

CBT can be a challenging method of treatment for a person with NPD. It can also be the most rewarding.

The therapist may stroke the ego of the narcissistic patient to some degree. But a working relationship is developed by setting limits and balancing how much the therapist will buy into the patient's illusions of grandiosity, hypersensitivity, and lack of empathy. This can be the key to successful treatment outcomes.

Alternative Therapies

An alternative approach to therapy that has been used successfully to treat some people with NPD is known as dialectical behavior therapy (DBT). DBT has its origins in the treatment of people with eating disorders. But because of the nature of the issues this therapy was designed to address, some behavioral therapists believe it can also be effective in treating NPD and other personality disorders.

There are four basic parts of the treatment plan in dialectical behavior therapy:

- **Mindfulness Training:** The DBT therapist teaches the person with NPD to become more aware of his own emotions.
- **Emotional Regulation:** When more aware of their own emotions, narcissists then work to reduce or eliminate negative emotions.
- **Distress Tolerance:** The DBT therapist helps the person with NPD to better tolerate and cope with painful emotions.
- **Interpersonal Effectiveness:** The patient learns the skills to better interact with those around him.

As part of their therapy, patients undergoing dialectical behavior therapy will use diary cards to record emotional experiences and behaviors, and to keep track of the DBT skills they have learned and put into practice.

Another aspect of the DBT processes is the use of behavioral chain analysis. Patients record sequences of events, how they felt, how they reacted to them, and what disruptive or negative behaviors the events triggered.

ESSENTIAL

The dictionary definition of the word "dialectic" is the "juxtaposition or interaction of conflicting ideas or forces." The techniques of DBT seem to conflict with one another. This is intentional, and where the name "dialectic" comes from in DBT.

There are seven goals of DBT:

1. Patients should learn to fully experience thoughts, emotions, and urges without feeling the need to suppress them or judge them for fear of feeling guilty, ashamed, or embarrassed.

2. Patients should learn what precedes negative emotions, and learn the consequences of those emotions.

3. Patients should become more aware of the physical changes or bodily responses that accompany negative emotions.

4. Patients should come to understand the relationship between thoughts and emotions, and learn to change thought patterns that tend to trigger negative emotions.

5. Patients should develop some practical skills to cope with negative emotions, such as relaxation and stress-reduction techniques.

6. Patients must develop regulated sleep patterns and reduce excessive use of drugs and alcohol.

7. Patients should learn to reduce or eliminate negative emotions by facing rather than avoiding trigger situations, and by not being afraid to reveal feelings of shame or embarrassment.

Medication to Control Symptoms

Narcissistic personality disorder is treated with any one, or a combination, of the long-term talk therapies described. There are not any drugs or medications specifically prescribed to treat NPD itself, but sometimes medications may be used to relieve some of the symptoms of depression, anxiety, or other emotional distress that can accompany the condition.

ALERT

Recent research suggests that some of the SSRI (selective serotonin reuptake inhibitor) class of antidepressants, such as Prozac, may actually have the effect of increasing narcissistic traits, due to creating serotonin overload. Serotonin is a neurotransmitter, or "brain chemical," that regulates mood and levels of positive emotions. Serotonin levels are regulated by the absorption of serotonin by neurons, or nerve cells, in the brain. Certain antidepressants are designed to keep brain cells swimming in serotonin, because serotonin stimulates normal positive emotions. But at the same time, increased levels of serotonin may also stimulate the false feelings of superiority typical of narcissists.

Since no definitive biochemical basis for NPD has yet been found, it is unlikely that any drugs to specifically treat it will be developed in the near future. Therapy still remains the most respected means and hopes for recovery. Mood-stabilizing medication may be used to enhance the effectiveness of therapy in certain people with NPD.

CHAPTER 7

Additional Methods for Dealing with NPD

It happens: A child, or even an adult, has a hacking cough, phlegm, sweating fever, and constant sneezing, for example, but insists he is fine because of his great desire to participate in some appealing event. So he proposes that it must be *you* who has the problem, with your worries and concern. Most of us may find ourselves denying something true every now and then because of an intense desire or need to do so. But for someone with NPD, that denial goes beyond the "I'm fine" attitude of the flu-ridden person. To someone with NPD, the idea that he needs help is nearly impossible to believe. But there are always possible ways to help support anyone's road to better health and life fulfillment, including for the narcissist. And when you are able to find great ways to take care of yourself, you will be a better help to the narcissist in your life.

Lifestyle Changes and Self-Management

Choices and decisions can be a dilemma for you or anyone normally. But when you care about a person who may be suffering from NPD, deciding what to do to help, other than traditional therapies, can present a quandary. There are various suggestions and methods, however, that can offer support. All have a reported range of successes. A lot depends on what you learn and understand about yourself and the person with NPD.

Self-Management for Both of You

Usually, when the potential sufferer of narcissism or NPD sees a medical professional, the doctor most likely will refer the patient to a psychotherapist for further professional help and guidance. This may happen when the person reaches a point where important relationships or work situations become damaged. Yet, even when agreeing to start therapy, the person with NPD may keep saying that therapy is a waste of time and he wants to quit. But potential sufferers of NPD, either themselves or with a family member's or friend's assistance, can find other means of support for treatment.

Even if the person with NPD stubbornly feels treatment is a waste of time, the Mayo Clinic offers recommendations on how individuals in treatment for NPD may cope with, or self-manage, their behaviors:

- Focus on recovery goals as the rewards of treatment and keeping an open mind.
- Work at sticking to the treatment plan.
- Focus on keeping scheduled sessions with a therapist and professionals, and on taking any medications and/or other prescriptive plans.
- Realize that the treatment work is difficult but be encouraged that the hard work is being done.
- Learn as much as possible about the disorder, its symptoms, theories of its risk factors, and treatments. If there is any substance abuse, get treatment for substance abuse or other mental health problems as well.

Keeping positive goals in the forefront is especially important for the narcissist—especially if those goals involve repairing damaged relationships and being happier in life. Finally, remember that things take time—Rome wasn't built in a day, as they say.

Therapist Barbara Leff has a working technique to help her clients with NPD outside of the therapy office. This is something that you might be supporting or sharing with the individual with NPD. At the point when the client can acknowledge and recognize his disorder and the problem, Leff gives them two lists of 100 words each, one of positive feelings such as joyful, happy, pleased, rewarded, calm, and relaxed, and one of painful feelings such as abandoned, empty, sad, hurt, and angry. The client charts feelings about five times a day, from the time he wakes up until before he goes to sleep. As he begins to note how many painful feelings there are, he may begin to acknowledge the need for treatment. The goal is for the patient to experience feelings more consistently without numbing or grandiose swings.

If you are helping the person with NPD use these pointers, you may also be feeling some additional anxiety and stress. Addictions, depression, anxiety, and stress can feed off each other, leading to a cycle of emotional pain and unhealthy behavior. Stress management and relaxation techniques are valuable to everyone for soothing and calm in daily life situations.

The New York Presbyterian Hospital has a list of self-management suggestions for people with NPD that also helps those around them deal with stress, anxiety, and depression:

- Get through the emotional distress from hurts by being tolerant and accepting, rather than reacting emotionally, and the pain will lessen.
- Practice doing something difficult every day and getting okay with failing. You can still survive even when you fail at something.
- Practice playing games and allowing yourself to lose at them to learn that losing is okay without too much stress.
- Make a daily note of any way in which you put other people down. You can ask somebody else to help you with this self-management skill. Looking at your behaviors will help you to deal with them.

Alternative Ways to Help Yourself and the Person with NPD

There are various alternative psychotherapy treatment approaches that you can practice. One method is mentalization-based therapy (MBT). This technique focuses on helping someone separate which thoughts and feelings are one's own and which are other people's. A person with NPD often has a hard time with this because he claims to know another person's mind better than that person does herself, when actually he is just thinking thoughts about himself. But mentalization-based therapy helps him to learn the difference.

Eye Movement Desensitization and Reprocessing (EMDR)

There have been reports of individuals who suffer from NPD as having some success with eye movement desensitization and reprocessing (EMDR). This practice is said to help someone to put the traumas of the past behind him. Unlike more conventional therapies, EMDR does not rely on talk therapy or medications. Instead, the process uses a patient's rhythmic eye movements. The originator of the technique noticed that while being fearful walking through the woods, her own anxiety and negative emotions seemed to lessen as her eyes darted from side to side, scanning the woods for potential dangers. She then realized she could use this same technique by using rapid eye movements with her patients to reduce the power of emotionally charged memories of the past.

Twelve Step Techniques

Some individuals who report suffering from NPD find some success with Twelve Step program techniques. Since people with NPD are "addicted" to narcissistic supply, the Twelve Step approach used to treat other addictions could be effective. The Twelve Step method is used to target the narcissist's psychological makeup—feelings of grandiosity, rigidity, and sense of entitlement, for example—rather than focusing on behavior modification, as do other types of therapy.

Barbara Leff and other therapists have found that a Twelve Step model adapted to the individual can be helpful with NPD, as long as there is a strong bond with the therapist. A Twelve Step program involves doing a self-inventory and sharing it with another. It involves recognizing one's weaknesses and flaws. Leff cautions that the person with NPD might reject the program if that client believes it is treatment for addictions.

Neuro-linguistic programming (NLP) can aid in the treatment of NPD by helping clients learn to deal with stress. NLP is a kind of mental organization programming therapy that can be used in a personal or professional setting. The goal is to change negative emotions to positive productive ones. It often involves connecting the mind to how one is feeling in order to look at feelings and to develop a way to understand how and what one can or should feel.

Stress Reduction

There are various techniques and programs that are great for reducing stress for people in general. For those with narcissism and NPD, many of these techniques have also shown some promise. For individuals with NPD, stress and anxiety can accompany the behaviors, and then these additional problems can feed off each other, perpetuating the emotional hurts and general unhealthy behavior. Often times learning any of the well-known and proven stress reduction techniques, such as yoga, tai chi, and meditation, can help to calm and soothe.

The traditions of Eastern practices often focus on finding the true self or heightening awareness of the self. Meditation, yoga, and elements of Buddhism and other Eastern philosophies that turn the mind inward could be helpful for narcissists. Meditative practices are believed to change regular patterns of perceiving and thinking.

Mindfulness-Based Stress Reduction® (MBSR) has been reported as sometimes helpful with emotional overreactions in NPD. MBSR brings together mindfulness meditation and yoga. Its goal is to bring better awareness of the unity of mind and body, and the ways that unconscious thinking or behavior can hurt health.

Other Healing Strategies

Individuals suffering from narcissism and NPD have been vocal online in chat rooms and forums led by professionals, sharing their experiences and offering some healing strategies of their own finding. Here are some of their suggestions:

- Find and identify some faulty assumptions that were made early in life that could be the basis for certain behaviors (particularly, any that came from parents).
- Find and identify situations where one feels entitled. List things done to impress.
- Find and identify examples of belittling someone.
- Learn to love and relax. Learn that another person is not bad or stupid, and can be loved for just being normal.
- Develop better social skills in how to make and keep friends and relationships, including being interested in what others say. Make healthy friends who like each other no matter what.
- Develop interests in the world by learning about it, reading the news, and watching people.
- Use goal-setting skills to achieve goals rather than to impress others.

Lifestyle Changes

If either you or your loved one is considering therapy, you should also be thinking about what questions are important to ask; even rehearsing them or making notes can be helpful. In thinking about these questions, consider these suggestions:

- Ask questions that can be *answered* rather than creating a trial, a drama, or something to prove, to take revenge on, or to win.
- Think about the kinds of painful truths about family or parents you may want to deal with or not be ready to confront.

- Don't feel you have to sound like you know it all or can use any special language. However you express yourself is *you*.
- Look at it not as though there is a problem to solve but as something to adjust to, just as you would with any physical ailment.

Other ways that both you and/or a person with NPD may be able to improve her outlook on life could be to:

- Think about life as a full show to be treasured and that everyone and everything has a place here.
- Think about your disorder as your advantage, and figure out what you can do with it and how you can be a blessing to others. It is true that the Chinese ideogram for both crisis and opportunity is the same.
- Think about helping others in discussion groups on the Internet, or in shelters, networks, and help centers. This service to others gives you genuine purpose, self-confidence, reassurance, and sense of self-worth.
- Don't let the word or label of narcissism be the cause and root of your life.

The Possibility of H.O.P.E.

The various nonprofit organizations of H.O.P.E. groups support hope, the key to the discovery of meaning, value, and purpose in life. Hope's promise of possibility replaces fear, and opens the heart to intention, truth, and love. H.O.P.E. helps to build successful lives and to heal. H.O.P.E. gives hope and strength through a process called Attitudinal Healing.

The idea behind Attitudinal Healing is that anger, frustration, and other negative emotions are not caused by external factors but almost always arise from inner conflicts and inner turmoil. Attitudinal Healing tries to get people to see that they are not victims of the world around them, but it is the way in which they see the world that causes unhappiness. It is a philosophy that says just as you generate your own thoughts, you are responsible for the feelings that you experience. By gaining insight into the source of your feelings, you can eventually heal them.

Taking an Attitudinal Healing approach can help you deal with the emotional upheavals caused by narcissistic partners, friends, or relatives in your life. And if you can also get them to explore the roots of their own anger using the same approach, it can be a positive experience for all of you.

Here are some healing attitudes that can improve the narcissist's or your own relationships and outlook on life:

1. The essence of being is love.
2. Health is inner peace. Healing is letting go of fear.
3. Giving and receiving are the same.
4. You can let go of the past and of worrying about the future.
5. Now is the only time there is and each instant is for giving.
6. You can learn to love yourself and others by forgiving rather than judging.
7. You can become a love-finder instead of a fault-finder.
8. You can choose and direct yourself to be peaceful inside no matter what is happening outside.
9. You are both a student of and a teacher to others.
10. You can focus on the whole of life rather than on the pieces.
11. You can see other people as being either in the process of giving love or giving a call for help.

Short-Term Goals for Both of You

For a clear focus on whatever type of goal *you* have in mind, it is always helpful to begin with a list. Your list can include questions to answer such as: What do I want? What do I care about? Where do I want my life to go? What are my dreams and hopes?

Then, as with any large task, look at it in very small parts, working your way through each question carefully. Depending on your own particular situation and needs, short-term goals can be very simple such as one small morning accomplishment, a commitment you can stick to, or keeping a therapy or other health-related appointment.

Short-term goals in people with NPD are aimed at helping people with this condition recognize its symptoms, understand its underlying features, and work on changing behaviors. If there are also serious issues of alcohol or substance abuse or depression, these are important to take care of, too.

Most of the therapies that are shorter in duration use the therapist as an educator. The therapist shapes new thinking and behaviors, keeping a positive relationship going. Often the therapist and client record thoughts, correct distortions, and plan out new ways of thinking. The client is given assignments to work on at home.

ESSENTIAL

Psychiatry professors Len Sperry and Jon Carlson describe that NPDs often come into treatment to have their narcissistic wounds soothed rather than seeking change. Therapists need to be alert to these inappropriate goals, as do you. Does the narcissist in your life really want to get better, or is he just seeking a new way to feed his narcissistic supply?

For the narcissist who might choose treatment, the short-term goals and procedures can differ depending on treatment styles and what brought the narcissist into treatment. In the short term, a therapist would be as empathic as possible, watching for any possible wounding of self-esteem or empathic misalignment between patient and therapist, and any inappropriate goals the patient has.

Long-Term Goals for Both of You

There is no known cure for NPD. The long-term goal through counseling is to help the person with NPD relate to the people in his life in a mutually rewarding and positive way. Behavioral therapy can help the narcissist with better insight into his problems, attitudes, and personality traits that can be harmful to others, in the hope that this will change those behaviors.

This can be a very long process. The ultimate goal of therapy, or any treatment strategy, is to help the person with NPD find and accept the true image of himself and to develop stronger self-esteem and more realistic expectations of others.

Since many health experts agree that it can be difficult for a narcissist to set long-term goals, setting short-term goals in a treatment plan can be very important to any kind of recovery process or ability to live with his condition. Some narcissists may set small goals, such as being an active listener for an hour a day or focusing a conversation around a loved one every morning for a week. As with anything, small achievements not only add up but also encourage the narcissist to keep the positive behavior going in the long tem.

FACT

Since getting people with NPD into therapy and keeping them there is very difficult, some professionals use a most untraditional approach of going along with the patient's tendency to drop out of treatment, rather than fight it. The therapist lets the client begin and leave therapy as he likes (which may allow the narcissist to feel proud of a little victory), and then return to therapy when difficulties again hurt his relationships.

Therapists would agree that in working with people with NPD, goals should not be to make those persons what they are not and can never be. For the greatest possibility of success, therapists and clients would keep in mind that everyone has strengths and some positive potential, and treatment would aim at the best expression of the individual's personality style—the personality style that has the most confidence. Setting big, unrealistic goals can result in discouraging failures that end all efforts to improve. If a narcissist sets a goal of never making an "I" or "me" statement again, he is setting himself up for a failure, since that action is oppositional to his nature and is nearly impossible to achieve. When he does not meet his goal, he may view the failure as an indication that changing is not an achievable option and cease trying altogether, since narcissists do not embrace the concept of failure.

ESSENTIAL

According to the third edition of the *Oxford Textbook of Psychiatry*, people can only change their situations, not their natures. Most help for those with NPD aims to find a way of life that doesn't conflict as much with their character. Aims are usually modest, and a long term is best for achieving the goals of treatment.

A more realistic and achievable goal (not to mention one that future goals can be built on) would be for the narcissist to compliment or say something positive about a spouse, loved one, or child every day. This is relatively simple, and this easy act of focusing on someone else for a certain amount of time can help a narcissist see all the good qualities of people outside himself.

In therapies that are longer term, the therapist and client often work on strategies in the areas of relationship problems and finding solutions. Patients need to learn to listen to others' needs and to act less on impulse. Therapists work with the client in establishing specific work schedules and tasks, as well as work on their interpersonal relationships that are casual and outside of work. The therapist maintains a positive relationship and offers information, including family, work, and social and business skills and training.

Strategies to encourage a busy work schedule that focuses on competence and achievement, and developing more secure positive relationships, can help the patient with his extreme individualism, self-concern, and reliance on attractiveness or power. Working with the family is also important for developing appropriate attachment needs.

ALERT

Many therapists would agree with setting modest goals for treatment with NPD patients. Many narcissists cannot form a sufficiently deep bond with a therapist to allow healing of early-childhood injuries. Also, patients with NPD tend to criticize and devalue their therapists, as these clients do with most other authority figures, making it difficult—but eventually quite possible—for therapists to work with them.

One of the therapist's long-term goals for people with NPD is to break through the grand illusion they have of themselves. Counselors say that the key is doing that without making the narcissist feel vulnerable. The process is accomplished by slowly and subtly presenting evidence that the client may be overrating himself, that his evaluation of his superiority may not be true all of the time, so that he can gain a better way to judge what is real and what is not.

Integrating Spirituality

There are many who would say that in order to repair any psychological impairments, it is important to be able to look inside and self-reflect. But for the narcissist, self-reflection is often too hurtful because of too much pain underneath. In spirituality and religion, the idea is that people are not the center of the universe, that there is something bigger than any one person. Religious and spiritual leaders usually welcome anyone to come into their centers. This welcoming nature, and the help to look inward and find a path to the true self, can offer a path to wellness for anyone, including those with narcissism and NPD.

FACT

The definition of spirituality is the structure of significance that gives meaning and direction to a person's life and helps her deal with the variations of existence. This external focus can be very beneficial to narcissists, who rarely place significance on anything but their own lives.

Spiritual leaders would describe spirituality as recognizing the self as part of the whole life of the earth, the universe. Spirituality introduces the largest dimension and the importance of purpose, meaning, holiness, and love—of "a power greater than ourselves." Personal pains and fears can become less important and overwhelming within the context of the whole that embraces everyone as they are. There are a number of spiritual paths that one might take.

Buddhism

The essence of Buddhist philosophy is that the path to healing all suffering lies in the discovery of the "true self." Since narcissism, in its essence, can be viewed as a philosophy based on lies and falsehoods, narcissists in search of healing through spiritual enlightenment can learn a lot from Buddhist teachings. Buddhist teacher and psychologist Jack Kornfield teaches an important story about spirituality that speaks to those suffering from narcissism and NPD.

Could narcissism be a spiritual, rather than a psychological, disorder?
Dr. Maria Hsia Chang, professor emeritus of political science at the University of Nevada, has described her understandings that NPD may be a moral and spiritual disorder, rather than a psychological disorder. This is one reason why she believes it is one of the most difficult of conditions to treat.

In the story shared by Kornfield, in ancient Thailand's Sukotai, a large clay Buddha had been cared for, for hundreds of years. It endured everything and was revered despite not being a handsome or refined work of art. But one day a large crack in the statue opened up, and a monk looked inside and discovered inside the plain old statue the largest and most luminous gold Buddha in the continent. Now that it has been uncovered, the golden Buddha draws pilgrims from all over the world.

Kornfield explains that everyone must endure threats that may lead to covering up one's inner nobility and live from an outer protective layer. But sometimes a person can forget one's own essential goodness. It is the first principle of Buddhism to help a person see underneath the outer armor, to see the inner nobility, goodness, and beauty of all human beings.

Cultural observers and behavioral researchers have proposed a link between the growing number of Americans who express no religious affiliation and the rise of narcissism and narcissistic tendencies in American society.

Social psychologist, author, and personal advisor Dr. Matt Moody is one of many psychological professionals who believes there can be a cure for narcissism by taking in the spiritual or religious characteristics of humility and charity, and through choosing a supreme being or power or source of all creation. This might instill feelings of peace and love for one another.

Using the Twelve Step Program

Step three of the Alcoholics Anonymous Twelve Step program may be a helpful major turning point for a narcissist because it involves the individual turning her will over to a power greater than oneself, and being willing to do whatever it takes to recover. These measures can include daily behavior inventories and making amends for wrongdoings.

From a healing standpoint, the other steps of Twelve Step programs may also have value in helping someone manage NPD. Maybe this is because NPD resembles an addiction in so many ways, only in this case the addict is addicted to being adored and idolized by others. Originated by Alcoholics Anonymous and adapted many times over for many different addiction recovery programs, the Twelve Steps are as follows. Be sure to replace "alcohol" with "narcissistic behaviors":

1. We admitted we were powerless over [alcohol]—that our lives had become unmanageable.
2. Came to believe that a Power greater than ourselves could restore us to sanity.
3. Made a decision to turn our will and our lives over to the care of God *as we understood Him.*
4. Made a searching and fearless moral inventory of ourselves.
5. Admitted to God, to ourselves, and to another human being the exact nature of our wrongs.
6. Were entirely ready to have God remove all these defects of character.
7. Humbly asked Him to remove our shortcomings.
8. Made a list of all persons we had harmed, and became willing to make amends to them all.
9. Made direct amends to such people wherever possible, except when to do so would injure them or others.
10. Continued to take personal inventory and, when we were wrong, promptly admitted it.
11. Sought through prayer and meditation to improve our conscious contact with God as we understood Him, praying only for knowledge of His will for us and the power to carry that out.

12. Having had a spiritual awakening as the result of these Steps, we tried to carry this message to alcoholics, and to practice these principles in all our affairs.

(Source: Alcholics Anonymous, *www.aa.org*)

One self-identified person in recovery from narcissism described online his positive experience with a Twelve Step program, in which he believes spirituality is critical. He achieved a spiritual awakening and a level of humility that has allowed him to connect with others and to feel love.

Getting Help for Complications

What are the complications of narcissistic personality disorder? People with NPD tend to use drugs and alcohol as a way to deal with their symptoms. It is very difficult for people with NPD to develop any kind of healthy relationships with others.

Drug and alcohol abuse, depression, anorexia nervosa, and thoughts of suicide are all potential complications of narcissism, according to the Mayo Clinic. Treatment plans for NPD need to address any of these complications as well. These issues are often dealt with apart from and in addition to treatment for the NPD disorder itself.

People with NPD may use drugs and alcohol for various reasons:

- As an immediate relief from any personal pain
- To relieve the anxiety and tensions between unrealistic expectations and inflated self-image and failures and rejections
- To get a heightened sense of power and self-importance
- To throw a partner off balance or to shock

Often, addictive and reckless behaviors, such as alcoholism, drug abuse, compulsory sex or shopping, or addictive gambling, can all be a part of a narcissist's behaviors. These behaviors can work to enhance his fantasies of being entitled, superior, or above the law. For example, with inflated self-importance, those with NPD can feel sorry for others who can't handle substances as well as they can. Those with NPD may also believe that because they are special, they can control what they use and will not have consequences.

There are several individuals self-described as having narcissism or being diagnosed with NPD who use their self-knowledge to write intimate descriptions of the nature and internal workings of NPD. One of these explanations described how pursuing various substance abuses or reckless behaviors can give the narcissist a false front with its own agenda, goals, and achievements that he believes he is in control over. Narcissists may describe their reasons for these pursuits as doing research, or helping productivity or creativity.

For some narcissists, a dependency can become a way of life for those in certain positions or professions such as high-echelon executives, race-car drivers, or professional gamblers.

ESSENTIAL

When treating people with NPD who also appear to be substance abusers, psychological professionals believe that abstinence from drugs or alcohol is a prerequisite of treatment, and insist that consequences for using do apply and need to be enforced. Once a client has been clearly warned, continued using of drugs and alcohol should be confronted and may result in termination from treatment as a consequence.

There are varying results of the effectiveness of Twelve Step programs for alcohol or drug problems for those suffering from NPD. Because a person with NPD has difficulty being honest with himself or being patient, he may have difficulty accepting the Twelve Step premise that points to himself as being at fault or lacking responsibility. Other studies have indicated that people with NPD have a great difficulty with Step Three, the "God Step," of Twelve Step programs. Lack of humility might be a strong emotional barrier to those with NPD from being able to engage fully in faith-based, self-help addiction recovery groups.

It has been said that adult narcissists can hardly ever be considered "cured," but most behavioral scientists agree that narcissists can at least be helped, and can learn to live with their disorder. There is also agreement that the earlier the person with NPD gets help, the better the outcome. It has been found that proper diagnosis and early intervention with a mix of proven treatments has a good success rate in modifying antisocial behaviors.

CHAPTER 8

What Happens Without Treatment?

Sometimes when you don't feel well, you reach for the medicine cabinet and think, "Should I take a pill, or should I not?" You can be in a quandary in deciding what to do. "Do I really have to take this pill? Should I see a doctor for treatment?" If there is a potential narcissist in your life, you may have been through a similar dilemma of what is the best course of action for the person, or if getting professional help is the right thing to do. If you think you can fix these problems on your own or that they will just go away, you may be deluding yourself as much as the narcissist!

Splitting as a Defense Mechanism

Without treatment, in order to function on a day-to-day basis, a person with NPD will have to fall back on one or more defense mechanisms. There is nothing wrong with defense mechanisms themselves. In fact, people need them for emotional health. They begin as normal ways to help deal with anxiety, grief, fear, anger, and other hurtful emotions. Defense mechanisms exist so people can defend themselves against feelings that can threaten to overwhelm, or feelings that people simply are not prepared to deal with yet. Healthy defense mechanisms can help maintain self-esteem and a positive self-image.

People have different defenses that become ways of coping with the stresses of life. There are basically two types of defense mechanisms: primitive defenses that started in infancy, and more mature, advanced defense systems, which develop over time, and allow change in thoughts and feelings with changing situations.

Primitive Defense Mechanisms

Primitive defense mechanisms develop in the preverbal stages of infancy. At that time there is limited grasp of reality and no real sense of self. It is when a person gets stuck in a primitive defense mode that it can lead to emotional problems such as narcissism.

The primitive defenses that people use as very young children include withdrawal, where the child emotionally removes herself from the moment. As the infant withdraws, she can disconnect from the real world and live for a time in a different place, away from thoughts, feelings, or memories that are painful. *Denial* is the refusal of the child to accept reality or fact, acting as if a painful event, thought, or feeling did not exist or never happened at all. *Primitive idealization* is the way children idealize their parents as superhuman beings—ones who can protect them from all evils and pain, and fix everything.

Another primitive defense mechanism—the one most often used by narcissists—is splitting. *Splitting* is sometimes referred to as "all-or-nothing" thinking, in which the person sees things in black and white, with no shades of gray and no room for ambiguity. In splitting, people and things are either all good or all bad. It is a primitive defense mode that comes from a baby's lack of object consistency. When a baby's needs are met and it is happy and satisfied, the baby sees Mother as all good. When it is frustrated, it sees Mother as all bad. At this stage of development, the baby cannot understand the reality that Mother is the same person who can make Baby feel either all good and or all bad in different situations.

In some ways splitting is related to broad stereotyping, such as the statement "All the members of (a particular group) are dumb and lazy." Narcissists not only will use those kinds of statements often to describe how *all* people are inferior to themselves, but they also use splitting as the main way to create their false self-image. The false image paints the narcissist as an expert in all things, superior in every way, and absolutely right all of the time.

FACT

Extreme fundamentalist causes or cults often use splitting to indoctrinate and encourage compliance of their followers. Such skewed, zealous views see sharp and absolute lines between us and them, good and evil, the righteous and the sinners, the saints and the damned. In such organizations, doctrine is rigid and absolute. Eternal rewards are for the righteous, eternal damnation is for the sinners; there is no in-between.

People with NPD use splitting to preserve their self-esteem. By seeing themselves as entirely good and everybody else as entirely bad, they can't help but be superior to them. Splitting is often at the core of the instability in relationships with narcissists. Because the narcissist may see a spouse or other significant other as either all good or all bad, depending on whether his needs are being met or denied at any given moment, unstable and often violent mood swings can result.

How Loved Ones Are Affected

Everyone has some kind of family, immediate or extended; we all have loved ones in our lives. And all families, even seemingly happy ones, usually include some disagreements, ups and downs, and the need sometimes to work things out.

But when a family member or a significant other is a potential narcissist or has NPD, whether he is a parent or sibling, the family members and loved ones that surround him will be affected in negative and hurtful ways. Every family has its share of areas that are dysfunctional. The difference is that with a narcissist in the picture, there is continual damaging and hurtful behaviors. They can't easily be fixed or worked out by the family members alone, and will probably continue to happen if the individual does not take part in some type of treatment plan.

The Effects of a Parent with NPD

There are plenty of personal accounts, therapists' accounts, and clinical descriptions that offer consensus in describing a cycle of damage that a parent with NPD can inflict on his children. The arrival of a child may bring an initial threat to a parent's place in the house, in the family, or even in the world.

On the other hand, the narcissist may cultivate, nurture, and develop the admiration of the child as a form of narcissistic supply. He may encourage the child to idolize, adore, trust, obey, and surrender. He may use threats, shock, or oppressive and manipulative means to get the attention he craves from the child. The narcissist is in danger of comprising the healthy development of the child, often laying the foundation for his own child to develop NPD later in life. At this early stage the narcissist may overvalue and idealize the child. He may monopolize the child in order to receive attention for himself, such as "What a great father I am!"

A narcissistic parent may not be capable of seeing the child as separate from himself. This can leave the child stunted in self-development, since the child must always be prepared for what the narcissistic parent needs from him.

As the children of narcissistic parents grow older, they start to recognize some of the narcissistic parent's actions and moves, and can become critical of them. The narcissist may then see the child as a threat, and devalue and belittle the child. The narcissist may feel trapped, suffocated, burdened, or jealous, and want to abandon his commitments to the child as a stupid waste of time. He may become remote, cold, and uncommunicative, and respond with excuses of pressure and lack of time for his availability. During this stage of detachment, the narcissist may daydream with plans and delusions of grandeur. The family as a whole is at risk and often disintegrates.

ALERT

The relationship between a daughter and a narcissistic mother can be a unique and particularly damaging one. Most mothers with NPD see a daughter not as a separate entity but as an extension of herself. This kind of maternal narcissism makes any genuine mother–daughter bond difficult, if not impossible. It also can get in the way of the daughter's ability to grow into a strong, independent, and capable woman. Narcissistic mothers often set impossibly high standards for their daughters, and the daughters' struggles to meet such high expectations go unrewarded at best and punished at worst. In addition, narcissistic mothers can be envious of their daughters' youth and beauty, and this jealousy can take the form of aggression and cruelty.

It may be possible for an adult child to have a compassionate relationship with a narcissistic parent. But such a situation usually requires that the damage done by the parent is not too severe, and that the child understands the reality of the situation, accepts the loss of the parent he never had, and develops positive relationships with other people in his life. Unfortunately, any healing to be accomplished for children of narcissistic parents is usually achieved long after the damage is done, in adulthood. Children of narcissistic parents could probably benefit from therapy as children. But just as the narcissistic parent could never admit he has a problem that requires therapy, he certainly would not recognize the damage being done to the child, and would not bring the child to a counselor. It is usually only when people seek help for some emotional difficulties in their own lives as adults that they even come to realize they were the victims of narcissistic parents.

The Effects of a Spouse or Significant Other with NPD

On the Internet, you can find many heart- and gut-wrenching stories of spouses and significant others who have been traumatized by, or who are enduring the behaviors of, a narcissist who has not yet gone into treatment.

There is generally a pattern with the narcissist of idealizing, devaluing, abusing, and ultimately discarding a spouse or significant other.

The abuse or devaluation by the narcissist can be verbal, physical, and/or emotional. Sometimes the abuse can be open verbal threats, lying, berating, humiliating, ignoring (the silent treatment), controlling, or physical and sexual abuse.

Sometimes a narcissist can act in reckless and unpredictable ways that are meant to rock the world of the spouse or significant other, in order to keep control and be the master. A narcissist may come home and announce to his wife that, without consulting her, he purchased a new car. Or that she refurnished the house or gave away her husband's golf clubs. Any way to rock the boat and take sole control of a situation is a power move by a narcissist.

For the narcissist, the spouse or significant other may be a symbol rather than a person. A narcissist may expect adoration, submission, and availability, and any threat or slight to this can lead to tantrums; name calling; foul language; insults; or verbal, physical, psychological, or sexual abuse.

Sometimes the significant other, rather than break up a family or continue to believe in the goodness of a significant other, will attempt to find ways to live with the situation. However, continuing in a narcissistic relationship often requires a sacrifice of the self. In order to live with the narcissist's fantasies and try to avoid conflict, it often means giving up one's own opinions, wishes, hopes, aspirations, needs, and preferences. Any of these can bring on the wrath of the narcissist.

Spouses and significant others living with narcissists often have reported feeling a state of general confusion. If partners have to continually put off their own judgment, thoughts, and opinions on anything and everything, they can reach a predicament of not being able to know anymore what is right or wrong, true or false.

The Effects of a Sibling with NPD

Generally, the difficulties in siblings develop as they mature from childhood. With growing up they recognize the narcissist's actions and moves, and can refuse to be a part of his game playing. Siblings may hold grudges against the narcissist, because if they say anything even slightly critical of the narcissist, he may rage against them. Siblings often become threats to the narcissist, and he may begin to sabotage relationships with them. He may feel that the siblings are conspiring against him to humiliate or belittle him. The narcissist may feel that his siblings don't understand his significance and thus are holding him back.

When Patients Resist Diagnosis and Treatment

The consensus of professionals is that narcissistic personality disorder is difficult to treat due in part to clients' strong resistance to treatment. However, there are a number of techniques and methods that have had some proven success in dealing with this resistance.

Many therapists first begin to overcome client resistance by complimenting the narcissist, stroking her grandiose attitudes, and challenging her to prove perceived omnipotence by overcoming her problems. It is an appeal to her quest for perfection, brilliance, and never-ending love. This method can open up a line of communication and bonding, as the narcissist thinks the therapist "gets it."

Other therapists begin by putting a clinical spin on the narcissist's problem, attributing it to genetic or biochemical causes. In this way, the narcissist initially does not have to feel the direct responsibility for his disorder. While narcissists believe there is no problem with them, they may be intrigued with the prospect of having a genetic problem—perhaps another method of getting attention.

Continuing progress in therapy can become rough going, however, if the narcissist feels that she can't get the therapist to uphold her grandiose self-image. It takes a very soft touch from the therapist to maneuver into gradually decreasing the stroking of the narcissist's ego in a subtle way. If the narcissist notices that the therapist has begun to treat her like any normal person, whatever bond was being built may be lost.

Family, loved ones, and good friends can sometimes be helpful to the narcissist's agreement to continue therapy, by helping to shed light on things that are wrong with her life that, without help, will only get worse. At this stage in therapy, when the narcissist begins to look at her real self, some therapists suggest it is also a good time for spouses, friends, and relatives to break free of the cycle of codependency.

This can be the time for others to stand up to the narcissist without fear and without accepting her demands for special treatment. It is time, instead, to find a suitable way to disagree with the narcissist, to show her why she may be mistaken, rather than just offering the usual narcissistic supply.

Initially giving in to the needs of the narcissist may help to build the relationship between therapist and client. But it needs to be balanced with setting specific goals and giving specific assignments to the client. Just feeding the narcissist's needs alone will often lead to the patient giving up on therapy, or using it as another form of narcissistic supply.

Therapies for the Resistant Patient

Cognitive therapy has been successful in helping patients who resist treatment. Cognitive therapy helps to develop a curiosity, and sharing curiosity with a patient allows resistance to become a dynamic and meaningful part of the therapy. This works best when therapists do not personalize resistance. Instead, therapists should use the resistance in the therapy, which can help the NPD patients escape from the barriers of their resistant self-protection. *Schema therapy* is a specific form of cognitive therapy that uses many of these ideas.

Schema therapy recognizes that there can be many obstacles to successful treatment of NPD, including resistance and dropout, which can often be overcome by the use of *leverage*. Sources of leverage are:

1. Discussing some negative results of the patient's narcissism in which he sees that unless he changes, he will continue to pay a price in love and work. But at the same time the therapist avoids shaming the client.
2. The therapist's ability to keep the patient feeling as if he is still a needy or lonely child, so the therapist can serve as a surrogate parent. Then when the patient forms an attachment to the therapist, the patient has a reason to stay in treatment.

It is also very useful to keep patients motivated by getting them to identify, understand, and contradict self-defeating beliefs, and to let them accomplish and really see their small improvements made along the way.

ESSENTIAL

Dr. Jeffrey Young has developed a type of cognitive behavior therapy that he calls "schema therapy," which he believes is not only effective in treating narcissists but also helps them stay in treatment. Schema therapy is based on the idea that we all have different parts of the self, known as "modes"—such as focused, easygoing, angry, or carefree. Most of us move between these modes as the situation requires, seamlessly and easily. But people with NPD may become stuck in their particular modes. If they are stuck, they are extremely rigid and have difficulty going from one mode to another.

Therapists agree that keeping narcissists in therapy is often a difficult process. One of the best ways for a counselor to help keep a narcissist from leaving therapy is for that counselor to tolerate his own fears and avoid power struggles, maintain compassion through curiosity, and help the client begin to understand and change her patterns.

Asking for Help When Dealing with a Narcissist

"Help" is a word that is often put out of mind. Taking care of ourselves, knowing what we need to do and how to do it for ourselves, is what feels good. And having to ask for help can sometimes touch on that pride in self-sufficiency. One may rationalize and question whether it is a sign of weakness or inability to ask for help. However, when it comes to a potential or actual narcissist in your life, asking for help is the right thing to do. But then, who do you reach out to for that lifeline? And just what kind of help is out there for you and the potential or diagnosed narcissist?

When Should You Ask for Help?

Life is certainly rosier when looking at the plus side; the half-full side feels fulfilling. But there are times when only looking on the sunny side is no longer practical, like when there's a problem with a spouse, parent, sibling, or good friend. It's hard to admit that someone you love and cherish can also be a narcissist who is causing you too much confusion and emotional or physical pain. How much is too much? When is it time to admit you've done all you can and now need some assistance?

Don't berate yourself if you didn't notice anything "off" in the beginning, or even years into a relationship, because narcissists do have great charismatic and charming qualities—and great ways for turning the tables on any responsibilities for difficulties or problems.

With family members, you may have endured a lifetime of behaviors that were demeaning and cruel. You may have just accepted it as "family stuff." The following is a little list to look through. If you find that some of these apply to you, it is time to ask for help.

- If you start to doubt your own sanity and think you are crazy because a loved one continues to tell you that it is *you* who is crazy.
- If you are continually subjected to a loved one's disrespectful outbursts and comments toward you, comments that are demeaning and abusive in emotional and psychological content.
- If you are subject to physical abuse or feel a potential threat of physical abuse.
- If you feel lost and alone because of a loved one's continuing patterns of abandonment or not recognizing or caring to understand your feelings, of not having compassion or empathy for you.
- If you feel you have been enduring pain because of a loved one's ongoing behaviors.

Taking the First Steps

There are many women and men who share a similar experience. Someone you know—a spouse, partner, lover, sibling, parent, good friend, teenage child—seems to have a real problem. Narcissism—it is in the celebrity news, people talk about it, and they wonder, Is he a narcissist? Is it mild or severe? Am I being quick to judge? How can I help and fix things between us? Why didn't he love me, and why did it turn out like this? Whose fault is it? How can I make this okay for him and me? These are all excellent questions to be asking yourself, and to start with in looking for real answers. There will be no changes for the better until you put in your positive efforts. This book, through its easy-to-understand descriptions and information, is a wonderful start for you. The resource section in Appendix B also offers additional sources for you. The more you know, the more you can help yourself make the best decisions and choices about when to ask for help, where to go, and what kind of help might be needed.

But it is not always easy to think about getting help, to feel it is okay to need help. Many people who find themselves in relationships with a narcissist feel ashamed of asking for help. They may erroneously think they lack enough smarts or self-reliance, that they are being needy or too dependent on others, or even selfish for asking others for help. Just know that it is not a weakness to have needs or be lonely. In any kind of crisis people are needy; people need help from others. It is not a failure to need to ask for help.

Case Study: The Demoralized Woman

One young woman, typical of many others of both genders, has written online about how she came to ask for help in order to help both herself and others who may be in similar situations. After a five-year "exclusive" relationship with a man that she initially felt was a dream come true, a soul mate, her world collapsed with a crash, and she could not cope. It had really been an escalating nightmare for all those years. She talked about feeling so lost and alone, not understanding how things happened or why. Because of his constant berating and demoralizing ways, she believed that all the things wrong in the relationship were her fault. Yet, she still wanted this man in her life, even though he had found another girlfriend. She revealed the situation to a friend. The friend advised her to see her own therapist.

The therapist completed her psychological examination and told the woman she believed the boyfriend was a narcissist. The woman then had to accept the truth: This man, probably a narcissist, could not feel love, empathy, or compassion for her. The woman reached a point where she finally realized that this man had depleted all of her physical, emotional, and mental energy, and then had just discarded her. It was certainly time for this woman to ask for help; in fact, it was a long overdue.

Whom Should You Ask?

Sometimes people feel embarrassed about confiding to friends or anyone they know about what is really going on with them. Partners or family members may feel that it is important they cover up for a narcissist, whether it is a teenage child or an adult. But health professionals all agree that everyone needs a support system.

If there is a narcissist or potential narcissist in your life, health professionals agree that it is important for you to have two types of people as support: a trustworthy friend or family member who can and will listen to your feelings, your fears, your pain, and the help of a professional who can offer answers and objectively deal with you and your situation. It is often the case, though, that friends or family members are either unreachable or have too many problems themselves to deal with. Because of this, there are some online groups led by professionals where individuals can share their experiences and also receive some written help from a professional moderator.

You may wonder if it is a good idea to try to encourage the narcissist to go into therapy. Or, if it is the case of a child, you are right to want to address your concerns as soon as possible. For this, you may want to consider having a consultation with a counseling service or therapist. Talking to a professional will offer you objective insights about how to address this question. Most likely, the professional has dealt with this issue many times before. There is nothing to be ashamed of; if you feel you are at the end of your rope, make the wise choice to ask for help.

Who Has the Right to Know (and Judge)?

If you believe a partner, loved one, or family member is a narcissist, or if a professional has told you he believes this to be the case, you may be tempted to inform the narcissist about her condition. However, because of their denial system, narcissists believe they are not to blame for anything.

They usually don't believe they have the problem. You would want to try to explain the condition to her without accusation or blame.

QUESTION

Should I tell someone I am in a relationship with that she is probably a narcissist?
Psychologists generally do not like to tell people what to do, and feel it is better that people decide on their own what to do about problems in their lives and be comfortable with those decisions. But what therapists usually will do when confronted with this question is to point out the pros and cons of telling a person she may be suffering from narcissistic personality disorder and what effects that revelation may have on her.

Sometimes in the course of therapy an adult child discovers that the terrible behaviors he had to endure from his parents during childhood may have been due to a parent with NPD, and may have also caused his own struggles with narcissism. He may then have an overwhelming desire to confront the parent who caused him so much pain. The adult may feel justified in telling his parents that there is something psychologically wrong with them. But therapists advise caution before taking such action. They say to examine your reasons as to why you feel the need to confront a narcissistic mother or father. If you think that this parent will suddenly be filled with remorse for the pain caused and beg your forgiveness, this is unlikely.

Dealing with Varied Reactions

We all know people who rush to judge others—usually negatively rather than positively. And that can happen when speaking about a narcissist in your life to some of your friends or relatives. They may not understand how complex your situation is. They may not understand your decisions about yourself and/or your children. Sometimes the narcissist has made such an outwardly wonderful impression on friends that if you decide to tell them about his narcissism, they can find it difficult to believe. And this can reinforce your own feelings that everything is really your fault and you are just being overly sensitive.

In some cultures and social circles, a woman attempting to confide to friends about a potential narcissistic partner or boyfriend may receive responses such as "All men are dogs," "Just let him grow up," "Just give him time," or, "You have to be joking, no way, he's so charming and special." It often happens that with a circle of friends there is disbelief about a spouse, or boyfriend or girlfriend, with severe problems because the narcissist on the outside has done a great job of fooling everybody. Narcissists are masters of deception and illusion.

Assumptions and unfair judgments that people may make are just that—unfair. Set your boundaries about what you feel comfortable sharing or disclosing. It is your personal and private life.

Sharing with Friends and Family

Generally, when it comes to relatives and narcissism, only your partner, your spouse, and household or immediate family members need share in your experiences and explanations. For others—friends, business associates, acquaintances—you can choose to say as little as you want to without lying. You do not need to divulge personal information to anyone who may be nosy or prying. If you use a friendly tone of voice and tactfully change the subject, you would never be considered rude.

ESSENTIAL

A disorder or addiction that is kept a household family secret usually makes for uncomfortable family gatherings. Sometimes opening up with other family members or close friends can be a more peaceful relief of some of the tensions. Sharing painful secrets with an honest openness can often touch on others' compassion and bring on their support and sharing of their own challenges.

Coping with Abuse

If your significant other or spouse has been abusive and you have decided to leave, you might consider telling your family first, then your close friends, and then your employer. If you feel your safety is at risk, you may want your family and close friends to know so that they might come to your aid, should it be needed. If you feel the narcissist may cause you problems at work, you may want to tell your employer that you have ended an abusive relationship. However, do realize that it may not be possible to keep the narcissist away without a legal document like a restraining order, particularly if you work in an industry that is open to the public, such as a restaurant or a retail store. If you feel that your safety is in danger, investigate getting a legal restraining order with your local police department or courthouse.

Any therapist will have your strict confidence in whatever it is you tell them. You might consider right away looking into either individual or group therapy where you can begin to get things out of your system. This is the objective and helpful place to talk things out and express how it all was and is; to get the right kind of professional advice and help to gain strengths; and to make decisions about how to handle your relationship with the narcissist. In a group setting, you can be face to face with others who share similar situations and hear how they deal with their situations.

Narcissists are abusive emotionally, mentally, and socially. If there is physical abuse, call an abuse hotline and get advice on how to proceed and learn your options. One such number is 1-800-799-SAFE. If you have been battered, there are always women's support groups and shelters where women of every background and age share similar painful stories. At the first sign of abuse, ask for help. You are not helping your narcissist by staying silent, and your life could be at risk.

How Can You Best Help Someone with NPD?

Caring about wanting to help someone with NPD means that you are already approaching the situation with goodness and concern, rather than hatred. As for narcissists, what can be done for them is always at the forefront of their complete self-centeredness. So one important step is to take a step back, detach, and use your own wonderful empathetic abilities—abilities the narcissist doesn't have—to understand and be helpful.

Most therapists who deal with narcissists would agree that significant change for such persons is possible, but it does take work. You can start the ball rolling. You yourself can begin working with a therapist or mental health professional on communication issues, role definitions, and expectations. But therapists caution that you cannot be the one to help your loved one or friend figure it all out. It will be important for you to be supportive and hold your boundaries. By working with a therapist to learn how you can hold your boundaries, you can then model healthy relationship skills for the narcissist. Your therapist may work with you on how to relate to the narcissist, on what you can and should not accept. The therapist may want to work with both of you as well.

ALERT

It's hard to find a "right way" to speak to a narcissist. Even constructive criticism is taken as an insult and is met with anger and feelings that they have been betrayed. Agreeing with them so that they will calm them down often results in their making more demands. In fact, if you always excuse their egotistical behaviors and rationalize their constant demands, you are actually reinforcing and feeding their hunger for narcissistic supply.

If it is your partner or spouse that is suffering with a personality disorder, here are some suggestions on how you can help:

- Ask the partner with the disorder to define in writing what she expects from you and where she thinks that you are falling short. Consider anything reasonable and ignore the rest. Inform her about what you think is unreasonable and why. Be clear that this is not up for discussion or argument.
- To help her choose to go to partner or marriage counseling, you can tell her that you need her help to bring your relationship back to the kind of warmth, love, and intimacy it once had.
- Admit to some faults of your own that you would like "fixed" so that you can be a better partner or spouse. However, do not let your narcissist use this admission as an excuse to rattle off a laundry list of your shortcomings. Be firm, and tell her that if she continues this behavior, the conversation is over. And mean it!
- You can appeal to her narcissism by humoring her until you are able to get further professional advice on how best to continue and proceed.

Another positive suggestion is to not go home and proclaim to your partner, "You are a narcissist!" That can cause more trouble than benefit. Instead, when she exhibits a narcissistic behavior, such as interrupting your story with a story of her own, say something like, "I was finishing my story. Please let me continue. It hurts my feelings when you interrupt, because it makes me feel like you don't value what I have to say." This calls out a specific behavior, a small goal that the narcissist can understand and work on. It also concentrates on *your* feelings, something your partner should be doing!

ALERT

If you are in a relationship with a destructive narcissist, an outright initial confrontation with her about behavior and attitudes may be seen as threats to her inner self-concept. This action can cause her protection defenses to come out in hostility, aggression, and strong attacks.

How Can You Best Help Yourself?

Narcissistic behavior works to tear down other people's self-esteem. If you need some self-esteem bolstering, here are some suggested ways:

- Spend time with people who do think highly of you.
- Spend time in some enjoyable activities that make you feel great.
- Do some things to be good to yourself.
- Join service or community groups; sign up for classes or school.
- Develop new hobbies.
- Expand your friendship circle in healthy relationships with people who are not narcissistic.
- Develop a healthy support group made up of at least three or more healthy adults—people who are able to see the difference between manipulative behaviors and healthy ones. Share viewpoints with them often in a confidential and respectful way.

Develop your own healthy self-reliance. Teach yourself not to feel responsible for what the narcissist is feeling, but be responsible for your own emotional well-being. It is important to be compassionate and kind to yourself.

Don't let the narcissist be the center of your life—control the main parts of your thoughts and conversations with friends.

When Safety Is an Issue

Sometimes the best thing you can do for yourself is get out of a relationship. If you feel you must leave, Maxine Marz, columnist, safety and security consultant, and criminologist, suggests how to do it safely. If you sense that your partner's hostility is growing to the point where you are in danger of being physically attacked, simply get away from the house. Do not wait for things to get better, because the odds are they will not.

If possible, leave at night or when your partner is not at home in order to avoid confrontation. Go to a trusted friend's, neighbor's, or relative's home and tell them what happened. Telling others will help calm your nerves and fears, give you the emotional support you need, and make the abuse public. Consult your local police department and make them aware of your situation, and if necessary, look into getting a restraining order on your partner. If you fear for your safety, do not tell your partner where you have gone, but only that you have left.

One survivor described her experience after taking some time away from a three-year relationship with a narcissist boyfriend. She found that after only a few days on her own, all of her physical symptoms began to clear up and her mood elevated. She began to feel like her old self again. She finally began to see the connection between her relationship and how she was feeling. So after she returned home, she moved out in order to focus on her own well-being.

A Little Narcissism Is Healthy . . . Right?

CHAPTER 10

Exploring Myths and Lifestyles

After a childhood of play-acting as a superhero, most people find reality, accept who they are, and deal with the ups and downs of life by being the best they can. But are the real superheroes of our lives today—celebrities, business people who are larger than life—worthy influences on our own realities and lifestyles? What distinguishes people who seem to do grandiose things from plain great achievers?

A Little Narcissism Is Healthy . . . Right?

The way people today use the word "narcissism" can go either way: It has its good side and its bad side. Healthy narcissism is usually thought of as a confident attitude, with evidence to back it up. It's in people who know themselves, accept their strengths and weaknesses, and have a sense of self-pride, good traits, and bad traits so they can achieve their maximum potential. Healthy narcissism is also the self-appreciation or self-love that makes people want to look and do their best, with a balance of loving, caring for, and appreciating others. Everybody has some narcissistic traits; it's a part of both early development and adulthood. We all have wants and needs, and it is still normal to sometimes want and need more than at other times.

Basically, health is about balance. In the body system, much like a chemistry lab, all the ingredients need to have the right balance to avoid an explosion. When one ingredient is off, then another must step in to fix it, or sometimes there is sickness that results. It is similar with narcissism.

ALERT

A recent study showed that 65 percent of modern college students scored higher in narcissism than in generations past.

When psychotherapists or writers talk about healthy narcissism, they mean a person who demonstrates a balance of certain behaviors: a balance between taking from others and giving to them with compassion, and a good balance between caring for oneself and caring for others. Another way of looking at it is balancing your expectations of others with what you believe is expected of you. For example, most people want to feel liked by others, cared about, and even seen as special and worthwhile by some. Most people, however, do not purposefully look for special attention or consistently do or say things to people just to make themselves feel better. But truly narcissistic people do this.

Narcissism is often described as an extraordinary fascination with one-self, or as having excessive vanity. This is very different from healthy self-esteem. Healthy self-esteem is a kind of realistic self-approval and self-respect, which also is part of the sense of mutual cooperation and respect in interactions with others.

You Can't Love Without Self-Love

Love is a many splendored thing, as the old song goes, and whether it's self-love or love for others, we continue to try to explain it. But when it comes to self-love, you shouldn't confuse loving yourself with unhealthy narcissism. In fact, most therapists would describe those suffering from narcissism or NPD as having little self-love. That's because what they see in themselves is an *image* of themselves, something that's not true. Self-love is healthy; it is not selfish.

Although some believe it came from Gandhi or Buddha, the actual quote that "To truly love another person, one must first learn to love oneself" came from 1950s social philosopher Erich Fromm. There is a real difference between loving oneself and being arrogant, conceited, and egocentric, which gets in the way of being able to feel for another person.

How Can Loving Oneself Be Helpful to Loving Others?

In Zen philosophies, loving oneself is about total dedication toward becoming a better person, ensuring physical, mental, and emotional health, and not needing to put yourself as the top priority all the time. Thus, a person is available to put others' needs first, to empathize with others. Some theorists have proposed that self-love is a peaceful state of mind, a state where challenges don't bother you because you feel balanced and safe. This helps a person's inner strengths and abilities to shine outwardly.

A well-known Buddhist teacher described his self-love as follows: "Because of love for myself, it is easier to see the light in people. Because I love myself, I know I have flaws, but I can appreciate myself for what I have going, and so I know everyone has his or her own flaws—and they are lovable."

NPD and the Workplace

From the boardrooms of Donald Trump to anyone's place of business, there may be narcissists or those with NPD either in charge, in senior management, or in the ranks. How might this affect you?

Recent research statistics have shown that narcissists have what it takes for leadership: motivation, energy, assertiveness, and competitiveness. However, they may or may not be successful, and they may or may not cause problems for the business itself and for others in the workplace. Narcissists don't like failure, compromise, or admitting they made errors and are learning from them—all natural parts of working or doing business that need to be accepted in order to be successful.

Some researchers have described "productive narcissists." These accepted great leaders are gifted and creative; they can see a big picture, they take risks in changing the world and leaving a legacy, and they have charm and usually have great speaking abilities.

Social researchers have written books pointing out and supporting the amazing abilities of CEOs and business superstars, who are presumed narcissists, and their ability to transform today's industries. Narcissists are often major makers and shapers of our lives. Their advice on topics ranging from education to finances, to e-commerce and even lifestyles, is the stuff featured on magazine covers. The business world seems to be a major part of our lives, and society loves to hear about its leaders. Many researchers and theorists describe these larger-than-life leaders as narcissistic, just as they have described personalities in history who as narcissistic leaders have inspired and shaped the future.

The truth is that the world is changing faster than ever, and has more questions and needs for people than ever before. Because of this, narcissists may be just what the world needs now.

But there is the downside. What is known about a narcissistic personality is that if he causes a problem, it is difficult to get him to see the damage. He usually will either deny or distort it. Narcissists tend to justify themselves or to make rationalizations that only serve to inflate their own self-worth. Narcissists can make a business unproductive if their unrealistic dreams and grandiosity are not backed up with appropriate knowledge and trust. Businesses and organizations today are challenged to make sure narcissistic leaders do not lead the company into disaster.

ALERT

Narcissists have trouble facing reality, and have a hyperinflated belief in their own skills and abilities, which could spell disaster in a leader. Think about the captain of the *Titanic* or General Custer.

Narcissists generally don't like to learn from others. They prefer to make speeches or to dominate, and don't really listen to others. Some social researchers describe narcissistic leaders as not wanting teamwork, but to be surrounded by a group of yes men and women.

If you suspect your boss is a narcissist, keep the following tips in mind so as to avoid potential problems:

- Try to keep records of all of your work to prevent any narcissistic coworkers or managers from misinterpreting your intentions or efforts or from taking credit for your work and accomplishments.
- Try to keep your communications professional. A narcissist can sometimes seem easy to confide in, but can then use things you say to his own advantage, not yours.
- It may be difficult to endure a narcissistic boss, but know that insults, superiority, and charm are part of his narcissistic problem and have nothing to do with you.

- If you do feel the boss is making a bad decision, couch it to him by offering your alternative and showing how he will personally benefit from it.
- Make sure personal boundaries are respected.

Narcissism and Workaholics

If it is more likely now than ever to find narcissism in the workplace, it also seems that there is a link between the personality traits of narcissists and of people typically described as workaholics. Hard work is a good thing, just as self-confidence is a good thing. But self-confidence blown out of proportion to the point of grandiosity is narcissism, which always winds up hurting others. And work carried to the point of the exclusion of all else is workaholism, which can also be very harmful to the workaholic and to those people involved with him. And that is not all that the two conditions, narcissism and workaholism, have in common.

There is no denying that America is a hard-working culture. And many people are working harder than ever, sometimes at multiple jobs, merely to make ends meet. But there is a difference between hard work and truly loving and enjoying your job, and workaholism. For the workaholic, everything comes behind the work, even family. Vacation and social engagements are not part of the workaholic's life. The workaholic in a very real sense *becomes* her job, and that is why workaholism is so similar to and often goes hand in hand with narcissism—because the workaholic defines her sense of self with the job. To workaholics, the job is a false image of "who they are," which allows them to escape from reality, just as the narcissist's false self does.

Just as the Internet and other digital devices, smart phones, and portable computers have become enabling technologies for narcissists, they also do the same for workaholics, who can take the office with them everywhere they go.

With so many similarities between the personalities of narcissists and workaholics, it is no wonder that a recent study published in *Psychology Today* found that those who are admitted workaholics also scored very high on personality scales for narcissism and obsessive perfectionism.

A Wayne State University study examined more than 300 working students and assessed them using standard measures for personality traits. The research concluded that the overblown sense of self-importance and grandiosity that seems almost epidemic among college-aged adults in America is closely tied to the worst characteristics of workaholism and perfectionism.

Here are some typical traits of a workaholic; notice how similar they are to the signs of narcissism:

- Workaholics pursue power and value self-importance to support grandiose images of self-worth, and to produce admiration in coworkers.
- Workaholics overproduce to set themselves above or appear superior to coworkers.
- Work becomes an obsession to workaholics (much like the pursuit of narcissistic supply) and they only find value in themselves through their work.
- Workaholics set unrealistic expectations of perfection for their own performance.
- Workaholics are impatient.
- Workaholics are compulsive.
- Workaholics use excessive busyness as a defense to escape from emotional commitments or negative emotions.

At their roots, both narcissism and workaholism are conditions that result from a false or poorly defined sense of self. Developing a healthy sense of self requires a feeling of identity and of being worthwhile that exists separately from one's accomplishments or failures. This is something that neither narcissists nor workaholics have.

Some might believe that under certain circumstances, such as on the job, that perfectionism, workaholism, and maybe even a little narcissism can have a positive side. But the truth is that all three are harmful. Perfectionists, workaholics, and narcissists all have one more thing in common. Maybe these traits can help them climb a little higher up the corporate ladder, but they also all result in terribly hurting the people in their lives outside of work, and damaging their own emotional and physical health in ways they often are not even aware of.

Ways to Reduce Workaholism

Just as a true narcissist may not find any relief from the most damaging effects of NPD without counseling, a true workaholic may also need professional help to deal with what is, in effect, an addiction. However, here are some things you or someone you know who is showing signs of workaholism can do to help get life back in balance:

- Make time, even if you have to actually schedule it, for family and nonwork friends.
- When traveling for business, call home or use your computer to stay connected to family.
- Stop trying to do everything yourself—learn how to delegate work, and be willing to say no to new assignments without thinking it makes you less of an employee.
- Take some real time off. That means leaving the work behind. Maybe just for a weekend at first, and then gradually move up to taking an actual vacation.
- Try to substitute some work time for an exercise routine or some other physical pursuit; join a gym, or take a yoga or tai chi class.
- Try funneling some of that "must work" energy into volunteering instead.
- Realize that it's okay to just relax and do nothing sometimes.
- Reject perfectionism; stop holding yourself to ridiculously high standards.
- Get some real sleep.

Regaining Perspective

"Narcissism" is so popular a word now that it is often used with a grain of admiration, as many people in the limelight are termed narcissistic. But whether or not a person has "healthy" narcissism or has been diagnosed with more serious NPD, you will develop your own understanding and sensitivities to it from the knowledge and research in this book.

Daniel Ames, a social and personality psychologist at Columbia Business School, Columbia University, says that interest in narcissism is growing. He administers a narcissistic personality test to his students, which he finds is a useful tool for understanding and explaining behavior. For the students, as for many people today, narcissism just seems to be a lot of fun to talk about.

One price that is often discussed as resulting in the narcissism we face today is a focus on the need to have high self-esteem for our happiness and health. There is a push everywhere to be proud, special—entitled to enough gold stars. It's almost as though it's an insult to be just average and a must to be superior. People can be too critical of themselves if they don't meet their own expectations or if they are not better than others. These types of feelings are similar to the feelings of a narcissist.

Researchers believe that when people live day to day, looking to overly inflate their sense of self-esteem and worthiness, they can also come crashing down with a deflated sense of self, and this makes for an emotional roller coaster that ends up causing insecurity, anxiety, and depression.

Some researchers have even called the situation of society's pressures causing people to need to keep feeling better than others a "narcissism trap."

Social comparisons seem essential to a narcissist. In studies it has been found that narcissists, relative to those with healthy high self-esteem, made more frequent social comparisons, were more likely to think they were better off than those around them whether that was true or not, and saw themselves superior to others based on comparisons of physical and other traits.

It seems that comparison does play a crucial role in a narcissist's endless pursuit of status and admiration.

Developing Self-Compassion and Mindfulness

One beneficial skill has been described as developing self-compassion. Self-compassion is about being kind to the self when there are things you don't like about yourself, or things don't go so well. Instead of being self-critical and cold, just recognize that you, like everyone else, are imperfect, and know that other people are in the same boat.

Studies have shown that many people feel they are more popular, friendlier, funnier, wiser, nicer, more trustworthy, and more intelligent than those around them. Ironically, the same studies found that most people think they also have a superior ability to view themselves objectively!

Other theorists have encouraged the use of mindfulness. This means you can recognize and accept without judgment painful emotions as they come up. Instead of trying to avoid pain, disregard it, or make it a loud soap opera, face your pain and see it clearly with positive compassion. At times when self-esteem falls down or expectations fail, that's when you come to your own rescue with some positive kindness for yourself. Then you are clear and thus able to make the changes you need to improve or accept your suffering.

Replacing Lack of Empathy with Compassion

Nobody enjoys hearing about someone else's hurts and pains, but the ability to care about others is a human trait. Many religions feel that empathy is a high spiritual value. In fact, in Hinduism, compassion is known as the godlike quality inside a person. In Buddhism it is to act in ways for the welfare of all. In Judeo-Christian traditions, compassion is about God's love and mercy. Certainly it is about the heart—love in action, as Mother Teresa called it, or being able to walk in someone's painful shoes without judging or moving away.

A recent study at the University of Michigan Institute for Social Research found that college students today are 40 percent less empathic than they were decades ago. Why this disturbing trend is true is not clear, but some speculate that media exposure, the economy, and our fast-paced and extremely competitive modern world all play a role.

A person with NPD may not be able to feel or show empathy or compassion to others. Therapists often work with these patients in a similar way that parents speak to their hurt and angry children.

How can you raise a compassionate child?
Child specialists would agree that today, children need experiences that give them challenges and the opportunities to put in real efforts to care about other people. Team sports, community activities, and responsibilities in the family all have a healthy place in learning to relate to others with compassion.

Therapist Frank Cannavo described his approach to helping an individual with NPD in this way: The therapist recognizes the narcissist's hurt and neglect, understanding that the narcissist doesn't want to be hurt again. With the therapist listening carefully and getting to the client's painful injury, a relationship builds. The immature part of the narcissist's need to feel he is heard and validated can revive empathy and compassion. When the narcissist develops a stronger ability to soothe himself from hurts, he will be less defensive. Then he can function on a more mature, reciprocal, intimate, and empathic way toward others.

CHAPTER 11

Tools and Coping Techniques

"How did this happen to me? What did I do to deserve this? Am I crazy?" People might easily think something like this when the toilet overflowed and ruined the rugs, or when the babysitter you chose ate your gourmet tart for tomorrow night's dinner party. But when there's a narcissist or someone with NPD in the family or among close friends, these can become the questions asked every time you look in the mirror. No doubt you've endured a lot, tried your best, and used different methods to try to fix things and make them better. The narcissists keep on doing what they do, however, like a relentless thunderstorm. But take heart; there are many ways for you to open doors and make some changes in those cruel and energy-depleting situations.

It's Not Your Fault

We are always encouraged in everything to do our best, to try again and again until we succeed. You probably have done so with the narcissist or person with NPD in your life. Maybe you have tried to tell him how you feel or describe the way things play out. But this person may be responding as if he couldn't care less; he may put the problem back on you, even make fun of you or call you names. If you do not feel healthy in relationship to this person, then this is the right time for you to do something; the painful situations with the narcissist *are not your fault*. You, of course, did not cause this person's condition. You can't change the things he says and does, but you can change how you respond to them. You have the power to decide what you want from this relationship and how much you will tolerate.

Living with a narcissist can drive you crazy. But remember, it was Albert Einstein who first said, "Insanity is doing the same thing over and over again and expecting different results." Nothing will change unless the narcissist is fully engaged and is trying to get help. Otherwise, you're stuck in an unhealthy cycle.

Everyone deserves to be treated with love, kindness, and respect. If you find yourself with a partner who constantly makes you feel bad, sad, or angry by being mean, nasty, and disrespectful, it's time to consider making a change.

You can create more sanity in your day-to-day life and bring yourself more joy and physical and emotional well-being. One way to do this is to become more centered. Break the cycle of negative thoughts that keep telling you how awful your life is because of the situation; instead, find a more positive center.

- Make up a positive mantra to say to yourself any time you feel low. You can use something like: *I didn't cause it, I can't control it, I can't cure it.*
- Try beginning to center yourself with meditation. If you have never done it before, it will probably feel strange and uncomfortable at first.

But research shows it takes around twenty-one days to establish a new habit, and meditation is a positive one.

- Find ways to do things you like to do yourself, and do them. Join a yoga class or take painting lessons.
- Recognize the narcissist's shortcomings because of his disorder, and then take care of yourself.
- Stop buying into the abusive things a narcissist says to you. Having someone say awful things about you is hard to deal with, even if the insults are untrue. But take heart that this cruelty is stemming from his issues, and even though it feels deeply personal, it has absolutely nothing to do with you.

Redefining Your Family

Families make for great comedies and real tragedies. All families have both positive and negative attributes. But many families do have one or more members with dysfunctional behaviors and then become dysfunctional as a whole, which can include mild narcissism to severe NPD. A family is always affected as a whole by the health or sicknesses of each member and by the family interactions.

ESSENTIAL

Sometimes in a family dealing with narcissism, other members of the family may think that problems are only simple sibling rivalry and laugh them off, even well into adulthood. But they need to realize this is not a replay of childhood antics but serious emotional abuse, usually started by the narcissist.

Parents or siblings who suffer from narcissism or NPD have their issues. But it is not your job to feel responsible for the narcissist's feelings, even if she is a family member or partner. If she is always upset, it is likely that even if you gave her everything she says she wants from you, she probably will still find things to be unhappy about and ways to blame or belittle you, to make you feel you are not good enough.

Planning for family events and holidays is hard enough without a narcissist in the picture; add one to the mix and it can be nearly impossible. You can usually count on the narcissist in the family to want to manipulate or take control of anything that is planned, or show up and take center stage away from the host and hostess. It might be wise and might protect your sanity to make your plans before telling the narcissist about them, and then to let her know that this is the plan—if she doesn't like it, tell her not to come.

It is not easy for children or adults to accept the idea that they likely will never have the loving parent or sibling they deserve. But now they themselves also must revise their expectations, and not the narcissistic parent or sibling who has refused to. If you look at your family patterns in an effort to understand them, rather than to blame, you can help yourself to make some changes to better your life.

If you have suffered from growing up in a narcissistic family, or now find yourself part of such a family, there are five steps that may help you to work through your situation:

- It is helpful to first become aware of your childhood and the effects it has on you today. It is not to blame, but to understand why a person functions in the world in the way she does.
- It is helpful to have the courage to accept the hurts and sense of loss you feel when you recognize that things were not ideal, that they were not what you would have wished for. That ideal or perfect family of childhood will never happen.
- Recognize the behaviors that have resulted from the childhood experience, especially the ones that probably helped you to deal with your current situation.
- It is helpful to do a self-assessment, to see which behaviors are good to keep and which are causing difficulties.
- It is helpful to take charge of yourself to replace behaviors that are not helpful with better ones.

As part of this plan, therapists often recommend making a written list of both the positive and negative realities and actions of your parent's, sibling's, or partner's behaviors. These could include their behaviors, beliefs, personality quirks, unrealistic expectations, abuse, favoritism, absence, family myths, job stability, and illnesses.

ALERT

Setting strong boundaries is the best recommendation many therapists can give for dealing with a parent who is a narcissist or has NPD. But setting boundaries is relatively easy; it's sticking to them that is tough. Don't be afraid to explain and enforce consequences with your parent. For example, "I've asked you to stop discussing my weight, as it makes me uncomfortable. Since you have continued to push the issue, I think it's best that we stop speaking for a while, until you can respect my feelings."

Venting, Sharing, and Getting Unstuck

Getting things off your chest by expressing your feelings is a way to good health. And everyone needs someone to share experiences with—someone who can understand and relate. Too often, victims of a narcissist have trouble getting away, mentally or physically, to a safe place where they can talk about all of the things affecting them.

One goal of coping—to get yourself unstuck and not be so affected by your situation that it is damaging your life—is to move yourself beyond it. You may need to vent, share, and then move beyond. You do need to be able to talk about your experiences and share them with someone who can listen and understand. That is a first step toward healing and feeling good about yourself, to taking care of yourself. It is important for you to free yourself from the negative energy and then feel self-empowered.

Online Support Groups and Forums

Online support groups and online counseling are possible choices for some people. It is convenient in that you don't have to leave home. It may be easier to fit in counseling sessions around jobs, families, locations, transportation, physical challenges, and financial issues. In reputable and professional online counseling, your privacy and anonymity are protected. You can take charge of how often you have sessions, and you have a record online of the dialogue between you and the counselor to look back to for reinforcement. It is also a way for you to see your progress. Some people find it easier to begin to be more open and honest with online counseling. The goal is always to help you get your life onto the best track for you.

Online groups can always be tried out. Some groups may have a lot of angry and intense participants, while others may be better for a gentler approach to confusion and distress.

Many times even good friends can't understand or be helpful enough in your situations. A therapist or an online counselor can help right away to give you steps to get out of the fog and pain you may be experiencing. What you are feeling can be validated by an understanding therapist. Usually with online therapists, you can send them an inquiry e-mail and see if you feel their answer is a good match for you.

Face-to-Face Therapy

Face-to-face therapy provides a direct approach to recovery. Therapist Barbara Leff and many others believe that for people with potential narcissism or NPD, a face-to-face therapist is most important for learning how to form healthy relationships with limits and boundaries. The face-to-face therapeutic relationship becomes a model for relationships in the outside world. It is a safe place that allows for positive or negative transference at different times during the process. The therapist at some point can take the role to act like the narcissist herself, allowing the narcissist to work through feelings. Similarly, the therapist can symbolize someone positive and help the client work through feelings that the client can use outside the therapy room. In both situations, narcissists learn about themselves and how to relate to others.

Setting the Ground Rules

Many individuals from narcissistic families are uncomfortable setting any ground rules or boundaries for fear of disappointing others. But therapists often suggest learning how to set ground rules with family members to gain more personal control and to help you with your own needs.

If your lover or partner has NPD, professionals recommend making a list of the pros and cons of the relationship. Circle the areas that are most troubling. Then decide on some ground rules for what is acceptable to you or not, and decide how much more energy you want to, or are emotionally able to, put into the situation to try to make it work for you.

Write your ground rules out officially and check your list every day to make sure you and the person are sticking to the rules. Most therapists agree that ground rules are important for dealing with a partner or spouse with NPD. Here are some of their suggested ground rules:

- **Personal Limits:** Know your own needs, desires, hopes, and the things that bother you. These things need to be stated clearly by yourself and to the narcissist. Remember to take care of yourself in your dealings with the narcissist by only doing things you feel comfortable doing. If there is an uncomfortable or unacceptable behavior, only return to interacting with him when it stops. If he is disappointed, that is for the narcissist to deal with.

- **Rules and Toleration List:** Create an agreed-upon list of behaviors that won't be accepted by either of you. When a rule is broken, the partner can point it out calmly, privately, with words that are respectful, and with an apology and a plan for dealing with it in the future. These rules need to be reasonable; don't let the narcissist use this as a chance to make outlandish and selfish demands. If your partner pushes this issue, get up and walk away, and only return when this behavior has stopped.

- **Disrespectful Words, Tones, and Body Language:** Feelings of occasional anger or frustration are normal for everyone. But there is a responsible way to vent these feelings. Nobody should disrespect another with blame for making him have those feelings of anger. If there is disrespect, take a time-out until the behavior ends. Use grace when accepting an apology and then move on without rehashing.

- **If there is physical abuse, do hold the person accountable for that unacceptable behavior.** Set clear limits and boundaries about such behavior, don't isolate yourself, and make sure you have some type of good support. While no abuse is acceptable, physical abuse is a clear and present sign to protect yourself and get out of the relationship.

Understanding the Narcissist's Past

The saying goes that knowledge is power. How did the narcissist get to be the way she is? It didn't just happen overnight. You can get a clearer understanding of what is going on when you can see how the patterns of her narcissistic personality were learned and reinforced over many years. You can imagine that even if the individual narcissist chooses a therapy to try to better her life, it can be a painful and long process to undo the lifetime of learned behavior.

ESSENTIAL

Relationships with siblings may have caused some real emotional destruction in the history of a person with NPD. This can be very hard for even the most supportive of partners to understand.

When you do understand a little about how a narcissist's problems may have developed and the behaviors she has been demonstrating, you can begin to help yourself and perhaps the narcissist in many ways. It may be difficult but helpful if you can keep in mind that a narcissist's behaviors are not usually about spite but come from fear. When she may be lashing out at you, it is not about you; it's her shame, fear, or inadequacy that triggers her reactions. This tactic may make it easier to not take things too personally, but to be able to understand the narcissist's problems and difficulties, and then find the best way to work with them.

FACT

One patient finally realized at age fifty-three that it was his sister's narcissism that made him feel he was the most useless and unworthy member of the family. These types of issues can follow a person way into adulthood.

For example, a narcissist's history most likely will indicate she has an excessive need for positive attention, to be heard and acknowledged. This means that going head to head with her in any discussion or controversy will likely inflame the situation. The best strategy is to acknowledge her point of view first to show you are really listening. Take a step back while listening. You can acknowledge her point, but you don't have to agree with it.

By understanding the narcissist's history and then centering yourself, you can look at what she is trying to do in a calm way so that you don't fall into a trap of believing what she says. Use your understanding while you are in a centered place to find patience and sensitivity, rather than the temptation to fight back. That usually just fuels the fire.

If people with NPD or narcissism are open to gaining insight, a good therapist can help them find the path to wellness through awareness of how their history led them to their present coping styles.

Planning for Family Contact

If there are narcissists who are your relatives or part of your family, they may be adding too much negativity to your life for you to manage. If that is the case, the first thing to do is not to feel guilty about the situation, because narcissistic family members often use guilt for their purposes. It is probably not healthy for you to let a family member put a guilt trip on you in order to control and manipulate you to their own ends.

Whatever the situation that continues to go on with a narcissistic family member, you may need to evaluate how often you have contact with him and what might help you decide on frequency.

- Here are some pointers to consider: If your contact with the narcissistic family member is very often—every day, every other day, or more—you may try to decrease the amount of contact. You might consider that the only family members you must speak with every day are the ones you live with. Even then, try to keep the conversations civil and short, limited to pertinent issues.
- If you have tried to be more independent and cut ties and contact frequency, you probably were met with even more drama than before. There may be extra things the narcissist needs from you, extra emergencies, and extra tears. But it will help you and him to be firm by creating rules and boundaries.

- Decide on some rules for calling and visiting. Be sure to have rules about calling first, so he won't drop by unannounced. Absolutely do not hesitate to ignore phone calls or deny him entry into your home! Here are a couple of examples you can use: "Now is not a good time. I've asked that you call before coming over. Please do that in the future." "Yes, I saw that you called three times. I was unable to take your call, and unless it is a real emergency, please do not call multiple times. As I've told you, I'll call you back when I am available."
- Discuss your plans with your immediate household family members so you are all in agreement with your plans. They should understand that you need to gently but firmly distance yourself from the narcissistic family member's contact.
- Be prepared for the narcissist to try to reach you by speaking to other family members, possibly even instigating problems to make you respond to him. Don't be lured into that trap by thinking you have to call to give him a piece of your anger. Warn your other family members that the narcissist may try to involve them.
- If he shows up and tries to begin an argument, try to control your anger; stay calm and don't let him see you are affected. Again, do not hesitate to deny him entry into your home, or to ask him to leave. Calmly explain that you will not be having this discussion, and that you will contact the necessary authorities if he does not go.
- It will be a good idea to find some counseling about how you are dealing with the situation.
- Know that if you would like the narcissist in your life to see a therapist, he has to agree to it. A counselor or therapist as a professional can advise you on your needs but cannot make recommendations for the family member. It is not legal for the therapist or counselor to contact the family member without his written consent.
- When you are planning for family events or holidays, decide on your plans first and then tell the narcissist your plans and stick to them.

Always remember that the narcissistic family member is the one with the personality disorder, which means he is not behaving as he should. The best way to protect your health is to stay strong, and to keep rule of your own life.

Developing Realistic Expectations

With a narcissistic partner, you need to be realistic and honest with yourself about what kinds of change might or might not be possible. Of course, the situation is complex with love and commitments or with children; these factors affect making a decision about how long to stay, or whether to leave. It can happen that the narcissist may agree to some changes in the relationship for a short time and then go back to the behaviors she thinks are normal.

Most important is for the person with narcissism to agree to go for counseling or therapy, but this is often difficult. If she does, it is usually because of major life crises, mid-life crises, threat of divorce, depression, job loss, or illness. These situations may allow her to be open to looking at how her behavior hurts herself and others. Still, the motivation to stick with it is delicate.

Changes are possible, but it does take work from both parties. The therapist or counselor will need to work with the narcissist on communication issues, role definitions, and expectations.

Understand that narcissists themselves need to figure things out and take responsibility. But if you can hold boundaries and be supportive, you can model a healthy relationship. When you can show that you care but will not accept nastiness, and that you will not accept that her needs are always more important than your own, you will be showing a new way of relating. Since she probably does not know how to take care of you, you need to take care of yourself. Hopefully, with a therapist guiding her, she can learn better ways of relating. This process usually takes a long time and requires some personal changes.

Facing a Challenging Road

In order to be realistic about your expectations, you need to look to yourself and see how strong you can be in the relationship, whether you are too overwhelmed by the constant turmoil, or if there are children involved who may be suffering in the environment. Even if the narcissist in your life is willing to change, it can be a challenging and long road. For a person with severe NPD, it can take years of intensive therapy, and several years of hard work on your part to help him. Any change he makes probably will not be because of his feelings for you, since that is one of the difficulties of the disorder. It is always hopeful, however, that if the person with narcissism or NPD can try something new, he can lead a better-functioning life and create deeper relationships.

Anchoring as a Coping Tool

Have you ever heard a particular song on the radio or smelled a particular perfume and suddenly felt happy, because you were transported to a wonderful time in your life when you heard that song or smelled that scent? This is a very common and very real human emotional response, because that song or scent is attached, or "anchored," to the positive emotions you were feeling at that time. You can use this phenomenon to create your own anchors. So, instead of coming at random like that song or scent, something good can be triggered any time you feel angry or distressed. Use this to overcome those negative emotions, even when they are caused by interactions with a narcissistic partner, friend, or relative.

When done properly, anchoring is very powerful. Unlike other methods, such as deep breathing or other techniques to get ahold of yourself, anchoring can help you not only deal with but also overcome anger, fear, or anxiety. If you have experienced that gut-wrenching, overwhelming fear and anxiety during a confrontation with the narcissist in your life, then you might try this technique to quench that terror. The reason you feel sick to your stomach is because your nervous system has triggered an automatic fear response. It is reacting just as if your life has been threatened. The reason that proper anchoring can work to overcome that response is that it is tapping into parts of your brain and nervous system to replace that fear response with a pleasant one.

How Anchoring Works

The idea behind anchoring goes like this: Whenever you experience something good or bad, your automatic nervous system links what you are physically sensing in the environment at that very moment—what you are seeing, smelling, or hearing—to what you are feeling, good or bad. This probably has evolved as a survival technique to avoid bad or dangerous experiences and recall pleasant ones. This is why people may experience feeling mushy when hearing a song that reminds them of a first love.

Another example is walking by a bakery and feeling instantly comforted because it smells like Grandma's kitchen. In both of these examples the same thing is happening: Your brain created a link—the anchor—between a powerful emotion and a specific sensory experience.

ALERT

All emotions are created by two things: what you are thinking about, and what you are doing physically at the time you're feeling that emotion. If you are feeling down, you probably are thinking about what is troubling you. And you are also accompanying your troubling thoughts with some physical response, like dropping your head down, slumping your shoulders, breathing shallow, or even crying. If you then switch your focus to something positive in your life, and begin to move your feet into a dance or sing out some lyrics, you'd feel an uplift in emotions and feel better. That might not be so practical in public places, but you can accomplish the same thing with other forms of anchoring.

Utilizing Anchoring

You can use anchoring to overpower fear, anxiety, or any other negative emotion that is being triggered by exchanges with your narcissist. Make the same kind of links between positive feelings and a unique physical anchoring sensation, and use this to bring on a feeling of calm and relaxation whenever you need it!

ESSENTIAL

Some advocates of anchoring therapy think it is so powerful that it can be used not only to help those living with narcissists better cope, but in overcoming the narcissist's behaviors as well.

Then every time you trigger your physical sensation—squeezing your fist is a good one, for example—your nervous system will create new mind-body connections that replace the old negative emotions with new positive ones. The key is to find such powerful positive feelings and emotions when you first create your anchor sensation so they can overpower any bad thoughts or emotions whenever you call on your anchor technique.

How to Create Your Anchor

First, choose the way you want to feel, or the state of emotion you want to be in, when you trigger your anchor. It can be any positive state of being, and that differs for different people. It can be serene, happy, mellow, calm, euphoric, ecstatic, strong, powerful—the choice is yours. The only rule is that it should be something that is entirely positive for you, a feeling or experience that you know well and can re-create for yourself.

Other anchor feelings are:

- **Excitement and anticipation**—like that feeling you got as a kid coming downstairs on Christmas morning or before a big birthday party.
- **First love**—remember your first kiss by your first true love and how it made you forget everything else?
- **Uncontrollable laughter**—find a time when you just laughed out loud continually and uncontrollably.

Then once you have figured out your anchor state, find a part of your body to which you will attach your anchor. Anchoring works by linking those strong emotions to a certain physical stimulus. It has to be something physical, something you can do with your body or a body part, so it locks your nervous system in step with what you are feeling. And it must be something that you can control, something you can make yourself do, that doesn't ordinarily happen during your everyday life. One way that is most often suggested is to clench the fist of the hand you do not write with, or make fists with your toes. Some people tug on their ear or press hard on a particular knuckle. Whatever it is, choose something that you can comfortably and discretely do even when others are around.

Visiting the Anchored Emotion

Now here is the most important part: Drift back in time to when you most deeply and profoundly experienced your anchor emotion. Really feel yourself floating back to that time. This requires some deep visualization, and you may need the help of a professional anchoring therapist, but try your best. See through the eyes you had at that time, and see the things you saw, smell the smells, hear the sounds, and breathe that same air into your lungs. Keep doing this over and over, trying to increase the sensation each time. The key is that you must allow the positive feelings to flow through your whole body.

Another option, if you cannot reach back to such a place, is to create your anchor the next time you naturally feel great in your present daily life. This can be an even more powerful anchor, since this is how your mind and body normally work to create natural anchors.

Either way, whether a clearly visualized memory or a present-day good feeling, as the most positive feelings reach their peak, press on your anchor for five to ten seconds. Make sure that the anchoring sensation is something special and something you can repeat easily and discreetly whenever you need to. This is the part where you are connecting your nervous system to the anchoring stimulus and the good feelings.

Now relax, and let your feelings return to normal. Repeat this a few times to make the link even more powerful. You can build up your anchor or reinforce it by pressing on it any time an extremely positive feeling comes to you.

How to Trigger Your Anchor

To use your anchor, do your anchor trigger for as long as you need to in order to conquer a stressful situation. Your anchor is like a bank account; if you use it, you will have to replenish it. So after you have used your anchor to resolve a stressful situation, go back and do the steps to rebuild your anchor.

Anchoring is really just a physical way of realizing that you and you alone are responsible for your emotions. Anchoring lets you take command and control your emotions, instead of letting them control you.

The Role of Low Self-Esteem

CHAPTER 12

Understanding Megalomania

Sometimes living with a narcissist can feel like you are living with a maniac. And that makes sense, because narcissism was once called "megalomania." *Megalomania* literally means "power mad." Megalomania is NPD in one of its most extreme and destructive forms. The megalomaniac has a need for total power and absolute control over others. That means control over the way others talk, walk, dress—even the way they think. If that sounds like what you are subjected to, you are not alone. In fact, narcissism is probably one of the few pathological conditions that causes more pain and duress not to its sufferers but to those closest to them.

The Role of Low Self-Esteem

The word "megalomania" can bring up an image of someone who is conceited, egotistical, and pretentious, and that typically describes a narcissist. But underneath all the arrogance and self-importance often lies very fragile self-esteem. This is why, despite their bravado, narcissists often have trouble handling even the most minor criticisms. They may easily feel ashamed or humiliated on the inside. In order to make themselves feel better, they may react with rage. They may feel a need to belittle others to make up for what is really lacking in themselves.

Psychologists generally agree that while narcissists may believe in the false image they project, they do not feel that what makes up this image is enough to really make them superior. If they did, they would not feel the constant need for praise to make them feel superior in every relationship in their lives.

Therapists generally agree that as a whole, narcissists are emotionally immature and are often filled with fears and a feeling of being empty inside. This definitely does not match up with the outer confidence they seem to have.

Sometimes people with NPD may reveal their low self-image. But when they do, it is usually in an attempt to fish for compliments to feed their egos. In an online forum, one husband talks about this kind of situation with his wife who was diagnosed with NPD. He described how his wife would be self-deprecating, saying negative things about herself, but he finally recognized it was just an act. He noticed that what she wanted was for him to tell her how wonderful she was. When he realized that, he stopped doing it.

Whether narcissists have high self-esteem or low self-esteem has been very controversial. There are social scientists who believe that the push for high self-esteem by motivational speakers and self-help gurus, and the praise heaped on young people to encourage self-esteem, may have contributed to the recent rise in narcissism.

Harvard University psychologist Seth Rosenthal designed a test to find out how narcissists feel about themselves. The test first asks subjects to check "that's me" next to what they think of as their positive qualities, and "that's not me" for any negative qualities. This part of the test measures how quickly the subjects press computer keys to indicate those feelings. Then the instructions are reversed: Bad qualities are to be marked "me" and good qualities "not me," and response times are measured again. Those quicker to give positive qualities to themselves have high self-esteem; those who are quicker to give themselves negative qualities have low self-esteem. The test was run with individuals who already scored high on other tests for narcissism. Those high scorers for narcissism who project high self-regard actually showed low self-esteem, according to the test.

ALERT

One conclusion that can be drawn from Rosenthal's study is that parents should not worry that instilling healthy self-confidence in their children will turn them into arrogant, aggressive narcissists.

In fact, the researchers in this study believed that it is because narcissists didn't get enough positive reinforcement as children that they need to prop up their egos with a false self-image and the idolization of others. The tests show that underneath the narcissists' overinflated self-image is self-loathing. As in the Greek myth of Narcissus, the narcissist's self-image is fragile, like the reflection that disappears when the pond is disturbed.

NPD and Shame Issues

Many researchers believe that narcissism is related to a defense against shame. The narcissist may use shame to protect his image of the true self. It is a defense that causes a fight-or-flight response from people with NPD, when they feel shamed or embarrassed. This fight-or-flight response results in lashing out or running away. Guilt usually will trigger more personal responses, such as coming clean or asking for forgiveness. Shame may come easily to a narcissist, but often not guilt. Narcissists may feel ashamed, but they usually cannot admit that they have done something wrong.

Shame is an emotional response to being flawed or imperfect. Many believe it is tied into underlying low self-esteem, found in many people with NPD. While shame has a lot to do with how people feel about themselves, it is also tied to what others think and judge. If a person believes he is seen as inferior, lacking, or making a lot of mistakes, it can lead to feelings of shame.

QUESTION

What is the difference between shame and guilt?
Shame is thought to be a more basic emotion than guilt. It develops earlier in life than guilt. Guilt is a more mature emotion. Since narcissists often get stuck in an early stage of development, shame is more closely linked to NPD than guilt.

In narcissism this is what has been described as the grandiosity gap. For the person with NPD, the grandiosity gap is the difference between his over-inflated false self-image and the information he gets from the real world. The greater the contrast between the narcissist's sense of grandiosity and the evidence he receives from the world around him, the greater the gap and the greater the feelings of shame.

FACT

Many of the major thought leaders in the treatment of narcissistic personality disorder see shame as an important factor in contributing to NPD. Coming to grips with shame is an important part of almost all therapies for treating NPD.

Narcissists like to be considered separate from others by being above or better than them, but at the same time they fear being perceived as different from other people. This has been described as a feeling of "otherness," which is also linked to shame. Narcissists are ashamed of the flaws and imperfections that make them different than other people. They're terribly afraid that without the shield of the false self, others will see that they really do not fit in.

Real Strength Versus Covering for Weakness

Outwardly, narcissists, especially those described as megalomaniacs, can appear very strong, powerful, and confident. But in reality, it is more likely that the opposite is true. What appears to be strength on the outside is really only covering for weaknesses on the inside.

In fact, one aspect of "healthy narcissism" is the ability to recognize one's strengths and at the same time accept weakness. But people with NPD usually do not have the ability to realize that they are made up of both good and bad traits. They see anything negative or bad about themselves as a weakness, and therefore must cover up or overcompensate so that it doesn't exist in their false self. Narcissists, and especially those that could be described as megalomaniacs, usually see the world in absolutes. They, like everything else in their worlds, are usually either all good or all bad. In their minds, they wonder, how could they possibly be all-powerful if they have any weaknesses?

QUESTION

What is "healthy narcissism"?
Healthy narcissism has been described as the way people can use a healthy sense of self-worth to achieve what they feel they deserve out of life, to survive, thrive, and be happy without the need to consistently harm, belittle, or disrespect others.

Unlike narcissists, people who accept that they can have real strength alongside weaknesses understand that they do not have to be all-powerful or the best at everything in order to be a success.

Kohut's Model

One of the leading theorists in narcissism is Heinz Kohut. His masterwork *The Analysis of the Self* is one of the foundations in the understanding and treatment of narcissism.

All humans share the early childhood experience of a grandiose self-image, and idealize parents as caregivers who cater to the child's whims. Kohut first suggested that narcissism is a kind of stunted development.

Kohut wrote that as a child develops, these grand illusions are replaced with realistic expectations that become part of a mature personality. In healthy development, illusions of grandiosity slowly give way to self-esteem. But if some emotional trauma occurs, the most primitive image of the self stays intact and unchanged. He was the first to call this "narcissistic personality disorder."

ESSENTIAL

Many believe Kohut's work was responsible for the recognition of personality disorders. Kohut called these "self-disorders," different from the psychoses and neuroses of Freud's classic conflicts between the id, ego, and superego. Kohut also suggested more effective treatments than traditional Freudian psychoanalysis for them.

In his work, Kohut described the person with NPD as irritable, edgy, and quick to anger. He saw the frequent rage of narcissists as the result of narcissistic wounds to the idealized image of their false selves.

Kohut believed that the key to successfully overcoming narcissism was to get the person with NPD to develop empathy, and that any therapy for NPD needed that as its main goal. According to Kohut, who many believed was a narcissist himself, a narcissist could achieve the greatness she believes is her reality by learning to empathize with others.

Cultural Considerations

NPD is not just found in the United States. However, many people think the values and foundations of modern America promote narcissism. The main stressors of modern western society are alienation, loneliness, and isolation. Furthermore, our culture teaches us to withdraw when confronted with stressful situations. So it's no surprise really that pathological narcissism is common in a country like the United States that stresses individualism and self-gratification over community values.

Modern American society could very well be a culture that is causing an epidemic of narcissism. One reason may be overindulgent parenting that heaps huge rewards on even minor accomplishments in order to make every child feel special. But there are many psychologists who disagree with the overindulgent-parenting theory.

Another possible cause of the rise in narcissism could be that there is no longer the cultural idea, as in past generations, that pridefulness is one of the seven deadly sins. Today, there is a pridefulness that is encouraged and all around us. There are pastors who preach that God wants us to be rich. Sports celebrities call selfishness a virtue. Donald Trump names everything he owns after himself and calls anyone who disagrees with him a loser. Everyone can be a star on the Internet, and people compete not to be America's Best Singer but America's *Idol*.

Also, in this so-called culture of narcissism, a lot of people are living and working as separate individuals, apart from others because of technology. Of course, there can be many advantages to telecommuting, but interacting with an electronic device day in and day out could mean losing some humanity. People who work alone do not have to rely on others, make compromises, or show consideration to keep a peaceful working environment. This can reinforce self-centeredness.

ALERT

Digital dependence may be to blame for the recent rise in NPD and other personality disorders. Hyper-digital connections have led to a physically disconnected society. A generation or two ago, many people knew their neighbors and lived in the same neighborhoods with relatives. People could rely on teachers and other adult figures to model good behavior for children. But today, people interact with digital devices that don't respond with a human smile, a warm and gentle touch, or proper disapproval for inappropriate behaviors.

People with NPD can be driven by shame and by fears—fears of being made fun of, of being abandoned, and of appearing lacking in any way. The increased social isolation of the digital era can increase this state of anxiety for narcissists. It also can remove them from an environment in which they might see the impact of their negative behavior on others. Living in a state of high anxiety contributes to the often-negative defenses used by people with NPD that can be so hurtful to those around them.

Because the percentage of people with NPD or narcissistic traits is increasing, it is no wonder that you may have family, friends, partners, bosses, or fellow professionals who have the disorder.

The Depressive Narcissist

CHAPTER 13

Narcissism and Depression

It's hard to feel sorry for a narcissist, especially when you are bearing the brunt of his illness. Narcissists can come across as so proud, so boastful, and so full of themselves that it may be difficult to believe that often they can also be depressed. But just as it has been shown that under the external air of self-assurance projected by people with NPD, very low self-esteem lies within an insecure person; there are often tears hiding behind their confident smiles.

The Depressive Narcissist

Narcissists rarely enter treatment thinking they may have narcissism. It is usually some other side effect of the condition that gets them to seek help. That may be drug addiction, eating disorders, and for many narcissists, depression.

According to experts, although people with NPD tend not to show many of the typical signs associated with mental illness, they often seek help for symptoms of depression. Depression in narcissists is linked to what is often referred to as "narcissistic wounds."

Narcissists will get depressed over feelings of failure or of losing. Narcissists often complain of feeling empty, or become bored easily when they do not get high levels of stimulation. This also can cause depression in narcissists. Depression in narcissists is often the result of repeated failures, real or imagined. The midlife depression many people feel as they age is worse in individuals with NPD. They can become very depressed the older they get, as they are faced more often with the realities of their limitations or what they see as missed opportunities to have achieved greatness.

ALERT

NPD can be considered a depressive disorder. It is often grouped with other conditions that have depression as a major problem. Even without other diagnosed conditions present, narcissists often deal with feelings of sadness and hopelessness, and report a lack of ability to enjoy life. These are also typical signs of people diagnosed with clinical depression.

Authorities believe that shame and guilt seem to be very strong emotions in so-called depressive narcissists. Usually the depressive narcissists are extreme perfectionists. Then when life does not go their way, as it inevitably will not, unlike more-assertive narcissists, depressive narcissists will blame themselves and become racked with shame that can lead to even deeper bouts of depression.

If life with a narcissist is tough, life with a depressed narcissist can be impossible. Once a narcissist reaches a depressive state, he may turn everything and everyone around him into something negative. His sense of melancholy may become so strong that everything he experiences, from every song he hears to every image he sees, can bring him further down. Where he once walked around believing he could do anything, the depressed narcissist now walks around totally disenchanted, disillusioned, and in a constant state of "Why me?" This swing from one extreme to the other is very similar to the depressive state in persons with bipolar disorder, in which narcissistic personality disorder resembles bipolar disorder.

According to a recent study, more than 50 percent of those diagnosed with clinical depression also received a diagnosis of at least one personality disorder. And of those, about 4 percent were diagnosed with NPD.

When narcissists get depressed, they may cry, where before they refused to show any kind of emotion. But do not be fooled, because often these are crocodile tears, cried to attract attention and sympathy as substitutes for dwindling narcissistic supply. It is at this stage where other self-destructive behaviors not usually seen in people with NPD, such as self-mutilation and suicide attempts, may occur. But these will usually be half-hearted attempts. The depressive narcissist does not really want to harm himself, but only to gain attention and sympathy.

Many philosophies, particularly Eastern philosophies, say the path to happiness cannot be achieved until someone accepts the truth and gives up a life of lies and illusions. A narcissist's life is based on lies and a false self. This leads many others to believe that any happiness or satisfaction narcissists show is also an illusion, and that inwardly, all people with narcissism are depressed to some degree.

The problem is that most of the time, nothing you say or do is really going to help snap the depressive narcissist out of his depression. For the narcissist the depression just becomes another defense mechanism. The depressive narcissist becomes comfortable in his new persona, his negative false self. Anything you say or do is often turned around and reinterpreted to fit his depressed worldview.

Dealing with Unfulfilled Needs

"You can't always get what you want" as the Rolling Stones' classic song says. Whether Mick Jagger is or is not a narcissist is open to debate, but it is clear that true narcissists have a great deal of trouble taking his advice.

People with NPD do not always get what they want. Some might say that their expectations are so high that they can never really get what they want. And when they do not, those unfulfilled narcissistic needs can lead to trouble. For the people around the narcissist, there can be angry outbursts and potentially violent childlike temper tantrums. And trouble comes to the narcissists themselves in the form of depression.

Parents with narcissistic tendencies may create narcissism in their children by setting unrealistic goals for them, or by forcing them to accomplish things or participate in things like child beauty pageants. Narcissistic parents do this to try to make up for their own unfulfilled needs.

Sometimes being around a narcissist feels like being near a seething volcano about to explode. Depression is often a reaction to these pockets of aggression buried below the surface in people with NPD. In this case, depression is all that bottled-up aggression turned inward against themselves in addition to the people around them.

Depression as the Flipside of Adoration

Narcissists live to be adored and idolized—some would even say worshiped. But what happens when that is not the case? You may think of the image of the aging screen star who has lost her beauty, her fans, and her fame, and retreats into a bottle, crying over a scrapbook of old movie clippings. This may describe what it feels like for a person with NPD who stops getting the adoration she needs and thus depression is the result.

It is human nature to admire people and even to put someone on a pedestal sometimes. That can be a friend, a relative, a coworker, or even a celebrity, and there really isn't anything wrong with that. What often happens, though, is that someone put on a pedestal may not be able to hold up to the idealized expectations you have of her. And then, when you see that friend, that coworker, or whomever as they really are, maybe they no longer seem so admirable.

But this becomes a real problem if the person you put on a pedestal happens to be the narcissist you live with! When you first meet a narcissist, it may be easy to put her on a pedestal. She can be charming, charismatic, sexy, and successful, and on a pedestal is exactly where she wants to be. But when the truth comes out and you realize she does not belong there, there can be devastating effects for both of you.

In any relationship, when you think you have found the perfect mate, you can create this kind of idolized version of your partner. You see only what you want to see and ignore the rest. This is often the case in the early stages of a relationship with a narcissist, and just the kind of thing that the narcissist usually counts on.

ALERT

Psychologists say people with NPD crave adoration. But when they are so idolized by a partner, they are also put under pressure to live up to unrealistic expectations, both self-imposed and those put on them by the idolizing partner. That pressure can lead to symptoms of depression.

As soon as you come to realize that the partner you idolize has flaws just like you do, including the same insecurities and the same fears, it can actually improve an ordinary relationship. But for narcissists, it can be like ripping off their clothes in public and having them stand in their underwear for the entire world to see; shame, embarrassment, and depression are often the results.

Don't be surprised if just when you think you have had enough and want to leave a relationship, a narcissist beats you to the punch! It is true that people with NPD have a deep fear of abandonment. But they may be the ones to initiate a breakup in relationships in order to feel they are in control of the situation, only to then bask in the resulting depression and renewed attention of being a victim.

Depression and the Loss of Narcissistic Supply

Narcissists live off other people as a source of narcissistic supply, almost like a tapeworm lives off someone as a source of food. The emotional imbalances in people with NPD, such as mood swings and depression, are often linked to the conscious or unconscious fear of a loss of narcissistic supply. Fluctuations in narcissistic supply can seem life-threatening to the person with NPD, resulting in depression.

Once a narcissist becomes depressed, he may withdraw socially, and that means he will actually be cutting himself off from even more narcissistic supply. This means not only will he likely fall into even deeper depression but he will became even more reliant on his immediate partner, and thus likely become even more belligerent toward the partner. Depression in narcissists becomes a vicious downward spiral for themselves and those around them.

ESSENTIAL

Depression in narcissists can be the reaction to an inner conflict caused by their need for adoration from others. People with NPD know that they must rely on the positive feedback of others to support their inflated self-image. But they also resent the weakness of having to rely on others for anything.

Drug addicts and alcoholics are often filled with self-loathing. They know they need the drug or the drink they are hopelessly addicted to, but they also hate themselves for their dependency and the lack of strength to break away from it.

It is believed by many behavioral researchers that narcissists also hate themselves for their own addictions to narcissistic supply. Just as depression often accompanies alcoholism or drug addiction, the narcissists' addiction to narcissistic supply can be a source of depression. And who do you think they take this self-hatred out on? Themselves, in the form of depression, and everyone else around them, in the form of their belligerence and aggression.

Loss, or reduction of, or changes in, a trusted source of narcissistic supply, such as a life partner, can lead to depression in people with NPD in a number of ways. Narcissistic supply does not have to be removed altogether to result in depression for a person with NPD.

Depression can be the result of criticism from someone who usually gives only praise. People with NPD are very sensitive to criticism, not only because it upsets their worldview of perfection but also because they may see it as potentially becoming a total withdrawal of supply from that person. This anxiety can lead to depression.

At its most basic level, depression can be described as a feeling of desperate and complete loneliness. Because of their lack of empathy, narcissists have lost their ability to connect with anybody. Narcissists crave attention, but deep down they are likely the loneliest people on earth, wanting empathy from others but unable to give it to anyone.

CHAPTER 14

Changing Perspectives
of the Relationships

A perspective of where and how you are can change depending on how you are looking at the situation. When looking at a person in relationship to skyscrapers, trees, and the sky, a person is quite small, but in relationship to bugs and birds, a person is quite large. A change in perspective can give a person more insight. Sometimes, a change in perspective is even necessary in certain situations. Similarly, where you stand in relationship to a potential or diagnosed person with NPD can usually be viewed from different perspectives in order to gain insights that may help you both change for the better.

Recognizing Reality—Yours and Theirs

Advice on how to keep positive, creative, and exploratory in spirit in life often includes the idea of keeping in touch with your inner child. Many people do display childlike ways that are both useful and detrimental to their lives and to those around them. But some people carry some immature behaviors or developmental lags into adulthood, and often these behaviors prevent them from carrying out certain adult responsibilities. This is often the case with people with narcissism and NPD.

The different aspects of narcissism vary in people with the disorder. Some have behaviors that are grandiose and disregarding, while others act in rage, belittling and blaming rather than taking responsibility. Whatever the aspects of narcissistic behavior that you see, and whatever the possible causes—the result of a parenting situation in early childhood, genetics, or socialization issues—many therapists would agree NPD causes great pain and suffering inside the person.

QUESTION

Why might I feel sorry for a person with NPD?
People with NPD can cause hurt to their family and loved ones, but they too are most likely carrying great pain inside them. This pain or suffering may leave them powerless over their drive to focus on themselves. People with NPD may need others to understand that their hurt is internal although it surfaces in external ways.

Perspectives of the Narcissist

Therapists working with people with NPD have found that positive changes in their self-image may be made at the point where they are showing vulnerability. If narcissists can accept their vulnerability and learn to like their real selves, they may be able to give up some of the grandiosity and superiority they use to prove that they are not vulnerable, and their perspectives can change.

In one method of therapy, when the therapist sees vulnerability in a patient with NPD, the therapist will show the client an understanding of how painful that experience is, but that it is okay. In this way, the narcissists may begin to accept their true selves. They can begin to accept that they are special or unique just being who they are, rather than presenting a false front. At this stage they can more easily connect with others. They can begin to look at people not just for adoration but to see what is special about the other person. A new path of growth and development can then open up. Instead of needing to show off their greatness to others, they can begin to connect with other people.

Perspectives in Your Life

If you have a narcissist or person with NPD as a partner, you may find yourself in a state of loneliness, because your partner is not able to meet your emotional needs. It may be helpful for you to accept that this is where you are now, and that your focus may need to change from your partner to investing more time and energy in yourself. You may need to reconsider your expectations that your needs will be met by your partner and, instead, make sure that you provide for your needs yourself. Whether or not you had difficulties with your own self-esteem before your relationship with the narcissist, working on building your own self-esteem with challenging work, projects, and activities is always a healthy perspective to maintain.

If you are in a relationship with someone with NPD, you may tend to have trouble staying focused on your own life and goals. You may feel that your partner's anger with you is your own failure. You may feel that something is wrong and you must fix it yourself. Any or all of these ideas could change for the better if you take additional time to evaluate your perspectives. It may be helpful for you to change some of your own ways in life, such as by setting clearer and firmer boundaries and by holding your partner accountable for her actions. Making these changes may help not only you but both of you.

If you see that your relationship with a narcissist is really harmful to you, then you may need to change your lifestyle somewhat in order to protect yourself. Some therapists and programs refer to this as "detaching yourself emotionally" from the actions, words, or feelings of another person. You do this by focusing on what *you* need. Detaching means to distance yourself from the behavior and not necessarily from the person. However, you may find that what is needed for your own health is to make a break from the relationship.

Pitfalls and Problems with Love and Loving

Many songs describe the power of true love. It's true you can become addicted to it. Love addiction plays a major role in the dynamics of narcissistic relationships, because love addiction can be easily wrapped up with narcissism, as well as with codependency.

Narcissists are sometimes thought to have addictive aspects to their personalities. They may have a kind of addiction to narcissistic supply and can become addicted to other things—drugs, alcohol, sex, shopping, gambling, or work. So it should not be surprising that one of the types of love addiction identified by Love Addicts Anonymous (LAA) is narcissistic love addiction.

Narcissists can be seen as "love addicts" in that they may equate love to admiration, adulation, and narcissistic supply. True narcissists are typically believed to not be capable of true committed love. Narcissistic love addicts, as described by LAA, have many of the signs and symptoms of narcissism: They need to dominate and control their partners; they have the self-absorption and the grandiosity. Where narcissistic love addicts differ from the typical narcissist, however, and act on their addiction is when they feel that the object of their addiction is going to leave. Narcissistic love addicts often have a deep fear of abandonment, and can panic and do anything they can to hold on to a partner they believe may want to leave. Violence, self-harm, and suicide attempts are not out of the question. It is when a narcissistic love addict thinks he may find himself alone that he shows how truly "hooked" he really is.

FACT

Up until about twenty years ago, "love addiction" was not seen as a separate condition or disorder from "codependency." It is only through the efforts of organizations such as Love Addicts Anonymous, which have helped to provide a greater awareness and understanding of this condition, that the behavioral community now generally recognizes that love addiction stands on its own as a distinct disorder with several variables.

But narcissistic love addiction is not the only form this disorder takes. In fact, some of the other types of love addiction could be the very thing that drew you, or someone you know, into a relationship with a narcissist in the first place. That is why love addiction can be so closely interwoven with codependency and the world of narcissists.

According to LAA, besides narcissistic love addicts, there are these other types:

- **Obsessed Love Addicts (OLAs):** OLAs are obsessed with their partners and are unable to let them go, even if they are abusive. OLAs are commonly the partners of narcissists who stay with them despite their destructive behaviors.
- **Codependent Love Addicts (CLAs):** CLAs are the most common. A CLA is what is usually referred to as "codependent" in any kind of relationship with any kind of addict or person with any personality disorder. The CLA fits the classic profile of the "enabler."
- **Relationship Addicts (RAs):** RAs may have once loved their partners but no longer do. They are addicted to the need to be "in" a relationship, and therefore will not leave or end it. They are very unhappy in their relationships, but fear being alone or out of a relationship even more.
- **Ambivalent Love Addicts (ALAs):** ALAs obsessively need to be loved, but are terrified of any real emotional intimacy. Because they fear true intimacy, ALAs may be involved in multiple romantic relationships with multiple partners.

These categories are not cut and dry; there is considerable overlap. For example, while the partner of a narcissist is probably an OLA, the narcissist himself in that relationship could also be considered obsessive, because he is obsessively addicted to the need for the narcissistic supply he is getting from that partner.

There can be any number of other combinations; in fact, because of the nature of love addictions, it is very common for love addicts to attract one another and wind up in relationships with other love addicts in which they feed off each other. This is a very common situation in relationships with narcissists.

There is not only overlap among the types of love addicts, but the same love addict may even switch his type of love addiction: You may find yourself in a relationship with a person with one type, only to have him switch to another type. This is because the dynamics of any relationship change over time, but the needs of the addict do not. So he may "switch" between one type and another just to keep his partner "hooked."

According to Love Addicts Anonymous, the most frequently seen "love-addicted" partnership is between a codependent and a narcissist. Narcissists appear very charming, attractive, and even seductive in the beginning of relationships, just to "hook" their codependent partners.

Narcissists often do this kind of "switch hitting," especially as they may move from one relationship to another. For example, they could have spent years in one relationship as a dominant, harsh, and uncaring partner. But when it all falls apart, they can easily play the victim in the next relationship, and become the codependent love addict themselves.

By recognizing the different types of love addicts that you may be dealing with in your relations with narcissists, or certain love-addicted behaviors you yourself may be doing, you can find better ways to cope and heal.

Helping to Turn the Narcissist's Focus to Others

Some theorists believe that people with narcissism or NPD need to be able to feel compassion for themselves in order to feel compassion for others. The ability for people to feel compassion for themselves is believed to involve two areas: accepting one's strengths, weaknesses, accomplishments, and failures, and being able to look at one's own frailties or suffering. When people can do this, they can find it easier to have compassion for others and feel a commonality with others. For many people in general, this is a painful and fearful process, and therefore not easy to do. For narcissists and those with NPD, it is most difficult.

Some clinical theorists believe that narcissists have an unfulfilled need for understanding and empathy. And this may be one reason they have a problem with being able to experience compassion toward others. Developing a person's ability to imagine another's situation helps to see, feel, and know another person, and share in an experience that has greater depth and meaning than just talking.

Dr. Akhter Ahsen developed a field and method called Eidetic Image psychology, which is a tool for developing empathy using images in the brain. This method uses a system to store images in the mind, and these images affect emotions and can help to overcome obstructions and open up parts of the consciousness that may be locked away; then, solutions, powers, and abilities are made clearer.

An explanation of how Eidetic Imaging works includes three parts: seeing an image, the bodily sensations or feelings while seeing the image, and the meanings that come up with that image. This is an example of instructions for Eidetic Imagery:

- Create an image in your mind of the person you want to better understand.
- Visualize where that person is and what she is doing.
- Take special notice of her attitude, body language, and emotions. Open yourself up to this information as you strengthen the image.
- As you see the image take shape, you will gain a better understanding of the person.
- If you are not feeling empathy or gaining understanding, try the next step.
- Try to see through her eyes. What is it that she is seeing?
- Now, how does what she is seeing make her feel?
- Feel this understanding of her view deep inside of you. You should now feel more empathy toward her.

Accepting Limitations

If there is a person in your life who is a narcissist or suffers from NPD, it is important that you realize the limitations his issues or disorder may be causing in your relationship. There are some pointers to think about in ways to help you accept his limitations and continue to interact with him.

1. You may find the need to reduce your expectations so there is more of a balanced give and take in the relationship. Most likely you will find your role to be limited mainly to support, acknowledgement, and recognition.
2. You may find there is not an equal balance of listening to needs and interests between the two of you, that your role may be limited mainly to being the careful listener.
3. You may find there is not a balance of providing for positive recognition, that your role may be limited to frequently providing the positive recognition.
4. You may find there is not a balance of decision making and planning, that your role may be limited to avoidance of challenging his desires, decisions, or plans.

Enforcing Boundaries

People who are narcissists or who suffer from NPD are usually grandiose and largely disregard everyone else. This is one reason it is important and helpful for you to be able to establish and maintain strong personal boundaries with the narcissist. When you do attempt to set boundaries, the narcissist may try to rewrite the history of the circumstances or say that what had transpired didn't actually happen. But try not to back down.

Therapist Barbara Leff offers an example of a situation in which she clearly enforced boundaries in dealing with a narcissistic patient's disregard and respect for her rules. The patient said he would be coming in for his next visit on May 15. She reminded him that he had previously set other dates and had even requested that accommodations be made for switching dates to suit him, which they had both agreed on. However, he continued to insist that May 15 was the date he now wanted. She told him that in that case he would be expected to pay for the appointment spots they had previously arranged. The patient finally relented and said he would come in for the appointment times they had originally made and agreed on.

In order to know what boundaries you want to enforce, you need to be aware of what you will accept and what you won't. If a partner's spending is an issue for you and you feel you need to take steps to protect your mutual financial situation, set limits. If the narcissist in your life wants something and is forceful about it, that does not mean that he needs to get it. You can negotiate while still enforcing boundaries. Even with the most minor detail, remember that giving in is telling the narcissist that if he keeps pushing the envelope, eventually you'll give in. Don't mistake reasonable compromise for rewarding negative behavior.

Setting Mutual Goals for the Future

It might be tempting to think that all the madness in your life is the result of your partner's disorder. But in reality, you are experiencing the interplay of yourself and your partner's disorder. It is only by understanding how you both function, and how your narcissistic partner's disorder affects her behavior, that you can begin to really judge what is happening in the relationship.

Some therapists feel that marriage counseling can help your mutual goals by challenging the narcissist's controlling patterns in the relationship. It can be helpful to deal with issues of power, control, closeness, distance, and independence and dependence.

If the narcissist in your life is a partner or spouse, you may wish to set mutual goals to work together with a therapist. Therapist Barbara Leff describes one situation as an example of how mutual goals gradually can be worked on in therapy. One client is able to arrange for his narcissistic partner to go for a session. As is often the case, the partner explains that he gives so much to the family and feels so empty. The goal of the therapist is then to demonstrate how all the family members are involved. She counsels that perhaps if he allows the therapist, his partner, and himself to all do some work together that he wouldn't feel it was just him who was doing all of the giving. She suggests they contract for three months and then tell her whether or not they'd like to continue. Leff explains that the skilled therapist may challenge the individual with narcissism in an encouraging way, yet allow him to feel he is in control.

If the narcissist in your life is a partner or spouse who has agreed to seek therapy, marital counseling can sometimes be helpful in addition to individual counseling. You and your partner can then be helped to look at both of your contributions to what may be unhealthy in your relationship.

In marital therapy, you can learn together your own needs and the kinds of boundaries you need and how to establish them together.

Perfectionism Versus Authenticity

Narcissists are drawn to perfectionism in their lives. But perfection is an illusion; no one, or nothing, is or can ever be perfect. This is one of the realities that a person with narcissism often has difficulty accepting. On the other hand, you, the partner, friend, or relative of a narcissist, has the ability to not only accept but also embrace the imperfections in yourself, in your narcissist, and in your relationship with her.

This concept emphasizes authenticity as opposed to perfectionism. It stresses living authentically: having the strength and the courage to accept your own imperfections and vulnerabilities as being part of the "real you." In many ways it is a manner of living that also opposes everything narcissistic. When you are authentic in your own self-assessment, which includes flaws, fears, and things you may be ashamed of, you are able to be truly compassionate and empathetic toward others, including the narcissists in your life.

ESSENTIAL

Researcher and life coach Brené Brown, PhD, LMSW, has coined a way of living authentically as being "wholehearted." Wholehearted people, as Dr. Brown describes them, realize what makes them vulnerable is also what makes them beautiful, and allows them to connect to all of humanity that shares similar pains, struggles, and vulnerabilities.

Here are ten ways you can learn to live more authentically:

- **Understand your purpose.** Does it feel like your life lacks direction? Do you think that health and prosperity will just come to you? You need to identify your life purpose. Think of it like a major corporation's "mission statement." Knowing your purpose means you will always have a way to find your authenticity.

- **Recognize your true values.** Make a list of the five things you value most. Then think about your goals. If your goals do not match up with your values, you are not living as authentically as you can or should be.
- **Embrace your own needs.** It is not a selfish act to take care of yourself. Having unmet needs can keep you from living authentically.
- **Know what you love or feel passionate about.** Recognize and embrace the things that make you genuinely happy. Whatever it is, from writing poetry to karaoke singing, if it makes your heart soar, do more of it!
- **Try living from the inside out.** Use yoga, meditation, or any other relaxation technique that can work for you to increase your awareness of your innermost thoughts and wisdom.
- **Accept your vulnerabilities, but respect your own strengths.** Recognize yourself for your positive traits and special talents. Make a list of at least three things that you know you are really, really good at. Honor your true self by doing things that express the strengths on your list.
- **Take time to relax.** You cannot be true to yourself or anyone else if you are burned out. Give yourself time to recharge by doing things just for fun or by doing nothing at all.
- **Get rid of negative self-talk.** Listen to your internal dialogs. Are they supportive and encouraging, or negative and self-deprecating? Choose your mind's voice. Change negative messages into positive daily affirmations.
- **Inspire and encourage yourself.** Keep a journal of all your accomplishments, big and small, every day.
- **Do unto others as you would have them do unto you.** It is not just the Golden Rule; it is the way to live authentically. And once you are living authentically, giving to others becomes your natural state of being. Because if you are true to who you are, living purposefully and sharing the best of yourself with the world around you, you are giving back in every possible way.

Living more authentically will improve your own emotional health and will likely help you live better with the narcissists in your life in many ways. But beyond that, once you have embraced living authentically, you also will be a good role model for the narcissists in your life. And it may be easier for the narcissists in your life to also make some of the changes that you have made; perhaps they will trade in some of their narcissistic traits for some more authentic ones!

The problem with trying to achieve any kind of perfectionism, but particularly narcissistic perfectionism, is that it negatively affects and impacts every effort. Take even an Academy Award–winning film or performance that has achieved Best Picture or Best Actor. There is something in that film or that performance that could still be judged as less than perfect. Ultimately, perfectionism, as opposed to authenticity, can be just a way to feel bad inside, no matter how great a job you may have done.

Perfectionism can be the enemy of everything good, because to the perfectionist, even the very good is not good enough. To someone who is able to live authentically, on the other hand, doing something very well will likely feel great!

Negative and Positive Thoughts and Feelings and Narcissism

It may sometimes feel like your narcissistic partner, friend, or relative is heartless or lacks any emotions whatsoever. But the truth is, all of us have both negative and positive emotions, and that includes narcissists. It is just that most of us are better equipped to handle negative feelings or negative emotions than are people with NPD.

Take anger, for example. Anger is a very powerful emotion, and if you are living with a narcissist, then you know it is one that he expresses very often. Anger is, at its most basic level, a survival tool. The emotional state that is recognized as anger evolved to help people stay alive. Long ago, our ancestors faced the very real danger of being eaten alive by predators. Anger triggers the body's fight-or-flight response when a person feels threatened.

The narcissists in your life feel endangered not by lions or tigers but by anything that threatens their false self-image, and their usual response to that threat is anger. All that energy unleashed by a narcissist's anger is like a 1,000-watt charge of electricity: it can be used to run huge machines, or it can electrocute someone. Unfortunately, most narcissists lack the capacity to turn their anger into positive directions.

Narcissists not only have trouble dealing with their negative emotions, but they also may have trouble distinguishing negative from positive emotions. This may also be one reason that they often appear emotionless, with their positive and negative emotions canceling each other out. In their early years, rather than the unconditional love and affection she craved, the person with narcissism was likely subjected to different and inconsistent emotions from her parents or primary caregivers. Anger, aggression, jealousy, and rage were likely heaped upon her as much or more than any real affection. The result was that she suppressed emotions, locking positive and negative feelings way down within her true self, to be replaced with the falsely powerful self-image of narcissism. Then, having not learned how to express any emotions positively, those feelings, both good and bad, get mixed up together. Often, the narcissist cannot express a positive emotion without dredging up something negative along with it.

ESSENTIAL

Negative emotions can be used in positive ways, but narcissists seem to lack this kind of insight. For example, the fear of losing control can help most people take healthy steps to gain control of their lives. But in people with NPD, that same fear of losing control can drive them to be manipulative and aggressively controlling.

You have heard of the power of positive thinking, and how keeping good and uplifting thoughts can fight stress and improve everything about your life. Focusing on your positive emotions is a powerful coping technique for dealing with the narcissists in your life. However, this is something that your narcissistic friend, partner, or relative has a great deal of trouble doing.

Narcissists cannot accentuate the positive because any sense of "positiveness" they express is false. Confidence and an expectation of success could be considered positive emotions, but so too are feelings of compassion, love, tolerance, and understanding. But these are the kinds of feelings that narcissists have little capacity to show, as you may well know. But here are some ways you can try to live more positively in your own life, even if you are sharing it with a narcissist:

- Simply refuse to buy into negative thoughts and feelings.
- Start each day with a smile. Wake up and say to yourself—or better yet, shout it to the world—"Today I am going to have a wonderful day! I will be happy. I will be patient and positive no matter what in every situation."
- Take the time a few times a day to recall, visualize, and really feel some happy moments in your life.
- When something makes you angry, take a deep breath and wait a few seconds before reacting.
- Try to feel and express some positive feelings toward people you do not like very much. That does not mean you have to be their best friends, but just try to allow yourself to feel some warmth and understanding.

Are Narcissists Evil?

This is a question you have probably asked yourself on more then one occasion if you have been dealing with the emotional pain that comes with being involved with a narcissist. At times it may feel like the narcissists in your life are evil. Certainly, there have been many truly evil beings, like Hitler, Stalin, and Charles Manson, who could be described as narcissists. But the question of whether narcissists are inherently "evil" begs the greater question of what is evil? Or at least, how do you personally define evil?

It may seem like it is evil behavior to belittle, disrespect, bully, and make fun of someone until they are totally traumatized. It may seem evil behavior to need to totally control others and show no respect or empathy for their feelings. These are all the things that narcissists do. But are they evil? To answer that question you have to look at the intent of the narcissist. And in the skewed worldview of the person with NPD, narcissists are not doing these things to be evil, or even nasty or mean, but to serve their own self-centered need for narcissistic supply. To label narcissists as being evil when they do these things would be just as wrong as labeling them "good" when they do "nice" things in order to gain supply.

Narcissists can be callous and unfeeling, and care little about their fellow human beings. The results of their indifference, callousness, and carelessness are extremely destructive and damaging. But for the most part, they do not intend to do harm, and so in that respect they are not "evil."

It may very well be that evil, like beauty, is in the eye of the beholder. But to someone being victimized by a narcissist, it may make very little difference if the pain is caused by the narcissist's lack of capacity to be any other way, or if the pain is caused out of true malignant and maliciousness intent; the pain is still painful. But more to the point, as with all things with narcissism, "evil" is probably a matter of degree. There may be narcissists who truly are evil, but that evilness probably exists in their being in addition to their narcissism, and narcissism is just another means of expressing it. If you are living with someone who is truly psychopathically evil, then you, your friends, or relatives would likely know it, and there would be very little point of continuing the relationship with such a person. However, understanding that a person with narcissism is not "evil" but suffering from a condition from which they may be able to recover can be very helpful in making the relationship work, if that is your choice.

CHAPTER 15

The Digital Narcissist

A narcissist can be uncaring, unfeeling, empty, and emotionless, a person who reacts to things and situations the same way over and over again, as though she is programmed like a robot or a computer. So it is little wonder that narcissists feel very at home online!

Does Digital Technology Breed Narcissism?

Technology always seems to have an upside and a downside. Computers and mobile devices certainly have improved communications and productivity. Social networking has been a great way to reconnect with old friends, to meet people, and to advance careers. But there could be a hidden danger to this new online lifestyle, especially to young people, and it's not just possibly tripping into a fountain while walking and texting in the shopping mall. Many experts believe that the Internet and mobile computing may be breeding narcissists.

Early in life, everyone is basically narcissistic. But most people eventually learn to give up their juvenile self-centered attitudes and develop normally through social interactions with others. This is how most people learn consideration, compassion, and empathy for others.

QUESTION

How can cell phone use encourage narcissism in teens?
Cell phones allow teens to maintain contacts with select friends and block out communication with other people outside of their peer group, such as kids younger than them or older adults. This kind of social isolation can hamper the normal process of developing healthy empathy and a feeling of belonging and caring about the larger community as a whole. It also provides teens with instant access to their friends—a direct line to narcissistic supply.

There can be many reasons why a narcissist gets stuck in an infantile stage of development, but it seems like the Internet and digital technology may be adding to what some are calling an "epidemic of narcissism" in America. All of this nonhuman interaction via digital devices, especially among adolescents, may be getting in the way of the natural process of growing up, and growing *out* of narcissism.

Cell phones, for example, are a fixture among teens. Cell phones enable teens to create a very self-centered environment in which they are interacting only with peers who could be feeding narcissistic tendencies, and blocking out interaction with anyone else who could offer healthy criticism necessary for proper development.

The relationship between cell phones and narcissism is not limited to teens, however. In many ways cell phones are the ultimate narcissism machines. How often have you been in a public place and your peace and tranquility is shattered by a boorish person blathering away on a cell phone, prattling on with personal details about his ailments or social life, with no mind to you or the others around?

This is a daily part of life today, repeated over and over again—and it is the ultimate expression of narcissism: digital total self-absorption with complete disregard and disrespect for others.

ALERT

Narcissists crave instant gratification. The ad campaign for Apple's iPhone is "There's an app for that."™ The iPhone and similar smartphones are developed to give the user what he wants, immediately, no matter what it is, from thousands of apps instantly obtainable.

Before such mobile devices, people had to interact with others in public places, or at least show them some respect and consideration, whether that was in a doctor's waiting room or the local coffee house. But now, some say that cell phones and mobile devices enable narcissists. The decline of newspapers may also in some way be contributing to the digital "me-centric" generation. The news in newspapers was always about other people and other people's problems—just the kind of things narcissists couldn't care less about. People may be reading more news, but the ability to get the news online, as the vast majority of young people now do, means they can filter out the stories that do not concern them and focus only on the "news" that they consider relevant to themselves, news stories that can benefit them or their immediate peer groups in some way.

Statistically speaking, this generation of students entering college is far more narcissistic than any before. Early exposure to digital technology during their formative years may be part of the reason.

Narcissism and Social Networking

Did you hear about this book from a friend's post on your Facebook wall or via a tweet? If you did, that's a good thing. But a growing number of respected researchers are pointing to a possible link in the rise of narcissism in young people and the enormous popularity of social networking.

Social networking sites such as Facebook, Twitter, and YouTube really are not all that "social" if you stop and think about it. In fact, in many ways they are antisocial. Such sites do allow you to actually *socialize*, but are more like "me-centric" private clubs than any kind of true social environment. On a social networking site, you are completely in charge of whom you will and will not interact with. You can easily screen out those whose opinions differ from yours. Such sites are designed to build a network of growing fans and followers—a narcissist's dream!

FACT

Two-thirds of young people in a recent study said they felt that, as a whole, their generation was more narcissistic, more overconfident, and more in need of instant gratification and attention than that of their parents.

It is not just the researchers who are saying that the decrease in face-to-face interaction among young people could be the reason for their increased lack of empathy. A whopping almost 60 percent of college students admit they feel that social networking makes them more narcissistic. The same students also said that the reason they believe they all use social networking sites is mainly for self-promotion and getting attention.

No one is saying that if you or your kids or loved ones use Facebook they will automatically turn into narcissists like in some bad horror movie. After all, there are more than 500 million users of Facebook at this writing, and not all of them are narcissists. But for a teen prone to feeling she is a bit more entitled than others, who needs to draw attention to herself, or who has a deep-rooted need to show the world just how great she is, Facebook is a great place to do so.

The virtual persona is a powerful thing that can lure anyone in. Even famous and renowned celebrities and politicians have fallen under its spell. New York congressman Anthony Weiner resigned from his seat after sexual pictures he had sent to various women via text message and Twitter surfaced in the media. Weiner later admitted to having "virtual" affairs with several women while in office.

So how do you know if your loved one is using Facebook to feed narcissistic needs? Look for these signs:

- Is she primarily using the site as a place to be "all about me"? Budding narcissists use Facebook as a way to self-promote, rather than to listen to and commiserate with the problems and concerns of their peers. Look for the use of "me," "I," and "my" in every post.
- Try to monitor how often she is using the site, maybe by seeing how many new Status Updates she makes every day. Does she feel she needs to check back often just to see if her number of fans or friends has increased? Does she constantly feel the need to post such increases in connections as if it were a competition?
- Watch for the selection of her profile picture, and how often she feels the need to change it. Is it a simple snapshot, or does it always have to be the most glamorous picture, taken in an exotic locale? Is she wearing revealing clothes or dressed in a costume somehow?

If you ever see that a child under the age of eighteen has posted sexual, violent, or inappropriate messages or pictures of herself online, you must act. If you are the parent, remove the pictures, delete the messages and the profile, and deny Internet privileges until your child learns the dangers of posting such things. If you are not the parent, notify the child's parents immediately, and if necessary, notify the site's administrators, who will be more than happy to remove the inappropriate content from their network.

Narcissism at its most basic level is all about creating a falsified persona behind which the narcissist can hide her true feelings of self-loathing. There can be no better place to create a false identity, profile, or avatar than on the Internet.

Recognizing an Internet Narcissist

Social networking profiles and the like can tell you more than just people's birthdays, where they went to school, and what their favorite movie is; they can reveal a lot of quirky personalities, including NPD.

Not everyone who asks you to be a friend on Facebook is a narcissist, but there are some telltale signs that could reveal a narcissistic personality hiding behind an online facade. Just as in the real world, where narcissists tend to surround themselves with many shallow relationships, those with huge numbers of online friends can be digital narcissists. Basically narcissists use online relationships the same way they do every other relationship in their lives: to self-promote, emphasizing quantity over quality.

Interestingly enough, since online narcissists tend to have infinitely more contacts than other users of such sites, you are far more likely to encounter narcissists within your group of online friends than you would in the real world. So the more you use social networking sites, the more likely you are to become involved with a narcissist.

ALERT

Narcissists are very susceptible to what clinicians have described as Internet addiction. On social networking sites, the narcissist can be the center of his world, attracting an ever-growing throng of fans, friends, and followers. The digital narcissist can be treated to an almost unlimited source to feed his grandiose fantasies and inflated self-image, without any of the usual risks associated with his behaviors in the real world.

Narcissists, or people with narcissistic tendencies, can sometimes feel as if cyberspace, and in particular social networking sites, were created just for them. It is a world where false identities are not only acceptable but encouraged. The Internet world is bound by few rules or laws of societal norms—in other words, it's the perfect playground for narcissists.

If the bad news is that social media outlets on the Internet are crawling with narcissists, the good news is, you can train yourself how to spot them fairly easily, and just as easily unfriend them. The problem is, since you don't have tone of voice, eye contact, or body language to go by, how do you spot a digital narcissist?

In addition to large numbers of friends, and posts that are almost exclusively about self-promotion, if someone's profile and page gives you the feeling that he looks as if he is a celebrity but clearly is not, it may be a good sign that he is a digital narcissist.

Age does matter. Not all Gen Ys are narcissists, but they do trend toward more narcissistic tendencies, so look for birth dates after 1980.

Just as they would in real life, digital narcissists use all of their online accounts, blogs, social media, whatever, to build up themselves and the people they want to manipulate, and to slam the people they have no use for. But unlike when they do these things in real life, they are even less shy about it online. Attacks are more scathing and more vicious in cyberspace, where the digital narcissist can say whatever he wants to about whomever he chooses. Look for particularly cruel or critical posts on his pages.

Not every profile you run into that shows these signs means you may be getting involved with a dangerous narcissist online. But just as you would in any potential relationship, use these signs as red flags and proceed with caution before answering that friend request!

Narcissism and Cyberbullying

If the Internet and social media sites are the ideal playground for narcissists, then you know every playground has its bullies. The recent, sometimes dangerous rise in cyberbullying is also related to the link between the Internet and narcissism.

Like any kind of tool or technology, there are some very good uses of the Internet. But the positive aspects of cyberspace are usually of very little interest to narcissists. The people in your life with NPD or narcissistic tendencies are not trolling around the Net looking to expand their horizons, develop true new and positive relationships, or reconnect with old friends because they really care about what is going on in their lives. If they could just Google "narcissistic supply," they would, because that is the only thing they are searching for! And they will use any method to get it, including bullying and intimidation.

Teens and Cyberbullying

This is particularly a problem for teens, where narcissism is already on the rise, and cell phones and social media pages are taking the usual teenage taunts, teases, and ridicule of the "in crowd" hurled at the "out crowd" to an entirely new level.

It used to be that kids who were the subject of such teasing could leave it behind on the playground and escape to the safety and solitude of their own rooms. But not anymore; with every teen now having a cell phone and social network accounts, such taunts can be relentless and never-ending. So much so that cyberbullying has pushed harassed persons into deep depressions and even resulted in some suicides.

Teens need to forge real friendships through shared experiences and peer bonding. Most social networking friends among narcissistic teens are barely even acquaintances, without any real feelings, connections, or intimacy.

Cyberbullies can be so much more powerful, cunning, and hurtful online than they could ever be in real life. Since there is very little oversight or regulation of social media sites, a narcissistic cyberbully could easily set up a false profile using someone else's name and totally destroy another person's reputation and real-life relationships by posting lies about him. Social media sites have terms of service rules in place that allow other users to report spam and abuse, and fraudulent profiles are usually quickly deleted when reported. But there is no real way to stop the profiles from being created.

Under the surface of any bully there is usually a weak person with low self-esteem, basically a coward. The Internet provides a safe shield for cowardly bullies to hide behind. So what can you do, or how can you advise your child or other young friends or relations about how to deal with a cyberbully?

- First and foremost let a parent or teacher know about the situation.
- Do not reply to any hurtful messages or posts at all. By not responding back, you are not allowing the bully to get to you. You are disarming her power over you. Report any harassment to the site administrators immediately; do not even engage the bully directly as there is nothing to be gained. If possible, block the account so she can no longer contact you or even send you a message.
- If you know that the cyberbully is under the age of thirteen, sites like Facebook will delete the profile, as currently that is the minimum user age allowed.
- Do save any taunting or teasing e-mails, tweets, texts, or posts. While it may be your first gut reaction to just delete such hurtful messages, you might need evidence in order to take action against the bully. Building up a paper trail is a valuable tool, and sometimes it's the only proof you have.
- With the help of parents, teachers, police, or other authorities, try to discover the true identity of the cyberbully without the bullied person engaging with him online. Remember, the cyberbully may be hiding behind a false screen name. This is another reason why it is imperative to get a parent, teacher, or some other adult involved: Authorities have ways of tracking ISP addresses and finding out where hurtful messages are being sent from, no matter the e-mail address or screen name that is being used.
- Have a trusted teacher, school administrator, or peer mediation group approach the cyberbully in the real world. Assert that this behavior is not acceptable and will not continue. Attempt to reach a mutual agreement, and be very clear that any further bullying will be reported.
- Do be willing to press charges if the bullying is severe and does not stop. There is nothing more encouraging to a cyberbully than empty threats, because she knows she can keep behaving this way with no real results.

Cyberbullies All Grown Up

Unfortunately, cyberbullying does not always end when high school is over. Adults, swept into the unreal vortex of social networking sites, are usually captivated by the prospect of social media and can get carried away with narcissistic behaviors and bullying tactics. Adults discover old friends and reconnect with people, and make new friends through social media and dating sites. The same rules apply if you find yourself a victim of cyberbullying or harassment at an older age:

- Be wise as to who you engage in the social media sphere. Sites have protections and privacy settings in place for your use, but one thing they cannot control is how much information *you* choose to share with the world. (This goes *double* for your profile picture. Once it goes online, it never really goes away!)
- Keep both a virtual and paper record of all threatening, offensive, and unwanted messages, posts, and comments. Also be sure to keep any requests you have made to the cyberbully to stop.
- Don't give mixed messages to anyone! If it's not funny, don't laugh. If it's not appropriate, don't say it is. Be painstakingly clear about what is okay, and what is not. Tell the bully in no uncertain terms that this behavior is unacceptable, and that they will be defriended or blocked if it continues. And follow through! Don't continue to engage with the cyberbully.
- If you are being harassed online via social media sites, message boards, or online forums, do not hesitate to report this harassment to the site administrators, moderators, or anyone else in charge.
- If your harasser is a coworker or someone you deal with in a professional setting, block or defriend them just as you would anyone else. Discuss this matter with your human resources department or manager to determine what your possible options are. (And this is a great reminder to *always* keep your personal life private, and your professional life professional. If you can avoid being "friends" with coworkers online, you should!)
- If at any point, the cyberbullying gets to the point that you fear for your safety or the safety of your family, contact law enforcement officials.

- On the other hand, if someone with whom you are interacting online requests that you stop contacting them or restricts your messages somehow—please stop. You may have gotten carried away with your Internet persona.

Avoiding the Trap of Internet Narcissism

So if the Internet can be such an enabler of narcissistic tendencies, how can you or someone you know avoid being sucked into the trap of digital narcissism? The first thing you need to do is to take a step back and try to regain a little perspective. It may be nice to let your online friends know what you are thinking, but just how important is it to broadcast what you are thinking every hour of every day? Try limiting your social-networking time to once or twice a week, and then only to update people with really important or relevant information. Make it a competition with yourself: "Let me see if I can go without social media until Saturday!"

ALERT

One of the best ways to avoid being led into digital narcissism is to avoid posting nasty, demeaning, or negative statements by following the cardinal rule of *If you wouldn't say it to a person, don't say it online.* The Internet does not make you invincible, nor does it stop your words from hurting someone else. And worse, your words can last forever online.

When you are on social media sites, try limiting the time of your visits there to just a few minutes to catch a quick update or two. Don't spend hours and hours delving into other people's pages!

Try not to let your online identity dictate how you act, react, or participate in events in real life. For example, do not accept an invitation to a party just so you can put pictures of yourself being there on your online social-network "wall." Similarly, do not decline an invitation to a party you really want to attend because you are afraid pictures of you might get posted on other people's online walls!

And finally, if you really feel yourself being swept up into the temptation of digital narcissism, just quit doing social networking! Go cold turkey. With a few clicks of your mouse you can cancel or temporarily deactivate your Facebook or Twitter account; many who have done so said it was the best decision they ever made.

CHAPTER 16

If You Believe Someone Needs Help with NPD

Living with a person with NPD most often means you find yourself in a state of confusion—confusion about who you are, where you are in the relationship, how you got there, where the relationship is going. And you probably find yourself asking, "What, if anything, can I do to help?"

When to Intervene

Sometimes it is obvious when to step up and get some help for someone who is struggling with NPD. These times are when his narcissistic behaviors have led to a major life crisis, such as job loss, or when he has succumbed to serious depression or other form of mental breakdown. But what if you want to get him help before that point is reached? That can be very challenging for you as well as for your narcissistic partner.

It may be easy for you to know when you have reached your breaking point with your relationship, and either you have to do something to fix it or get your narcissistic partner some help. But before you start pulling your hair out, here are some other sure signs that it's time to intervene on your partner's behalf:

- If he is drinking more alcohol than usual.
- If he has started using street drugs.
- If he is abusing prescription medications, or is taking medicines that were not prescribed for him.

You should seek immediate help if you think your partner with NPD is a threat to himself, you, or others.

ALERT

More people are killed or seriously injured by domestic violence in the week or so immediately after ending a relationship than at any other time during the relationship. Intervention can be a far better and safer idea than leaving and angering a partner with NPD.

All couples have difficulties and argue. Very often those arguments are about money. But if you know you are living with a person with NPD, and you are arguing with him about money almost constantly, it is a good sign that he may be lying to you about paying bills, racking up credit card debt, or hiding the true state of your financial affairs. If your narcissistic partner is abusing the family finances, it is certainly well past time to take action.

Expressing Your Concerns

Either you feel it in your bones, or physical evidence demands that it is time you do something to help your partner with NPD. How do you approach her? Just how do you intervene and get your partner to realize she has a problem, while keeping yourself and the rest of your family safe?

This is not easy when dealing with NPD. Typical interventions for a friend, spouse, or relative dealing with a condition such as alcoholism or an emotional disorder usually involve a form of confrontation that gets the person with the problem to face reality and stop denying that there is a problem. But NPD is not exactly like alcoholism, or even other personality disorders for that matter, because the basis of the condition is self-denial and a false sense of reality.

If you are going to confront a partner with narcissism, and try to hold up a mirror to show him the damaging effects his behaviors are having on you, on him, and on everyone else around him, expect to be met with anger, rage, and aggression aimed at you. Expect to have everything you have said about him thrown back at you and then some! Only when you feel strong enough to take all that should you be prepared to express your concerns.

ALERT

What can you do when you're at the end of your rope? If you really want to intervene, then stand your ground, don't back down. Do not show the narcissistic partner you are afraid of her. Do not negotiate, but do not put yourself at risk. If things get too rough, disengage. For example, say: "Okay, I see I've chosen a bad time to discuss this. We can just talk later." And take a walk. Do not be afraid to involve law enforcement, friends, or other relatives if you feel threatened.

There really aren't any rules as to how to express your concerns to your partner, friend, or relative with NPD, as everybody's circumstances are different. But here are some suggestions:

- **Don't use generalities.** Be specific when addressing the narcissist. Don't say things like, "I can't stand that we can never go to family gatherings."

Instead, be sure to add specifics to this complaint such as, "I am so angry how last week at my mother's, you said to my sister that it's no wonder she can't hold a job with hair that looks like that, and you sent her from the table crying. It was very hurtful to her, and to me."

- **Choose your timing.** A narcissist will very rarely show any signs of hurt, pain, or weakness. But on occasion he may let his guard down and show some sign of vulnerability. If there is any indication that he wants to change something about his life, that is the ideal moment for you to suggest he seek help and offer your support.

- **Realize there is strength in numbers.** Nothing adds strength to your concerns like the team approach. Think about not confronting the narcissist in your life alone; involve the rest of the family, maybe her parent or parents. This may result in the narcissist feeling as if she is being "ganged up on," but as long as your intentions are pure and not an attack, she has no real reason to feel that way.

- **Use an either-or approach.** Be prepared to give her a type of either-or scenario. Tell your narcissistic mate exactly what will happen if she does not seek help with her behavioral problems. But *don't* make it a threat or an ultimatum. Instead say: "Either you stop saying hurtful things to my family, or I will attend Sunday dinner at my mother's alone from now on." Do not make the "either-or" something you can't or won't do. If you do say that the narcissist will not be welcome at family events, for example, be prepared to make good on that promise.

Formal Interventions

In psychological terms, an intervention is a combination of specific actions and strategies designed to produce behavioral changes or improve the health of troubled individuals. Interventions have proven most effective in dealing with close friends, partners, or relatives struggling with alcohol or substance abuse. However, such interventions have also proven to be effective in getting people with certain emotional disorders into treatment, including people suffering from NPD.

There are three goals to an intervention for a person with NPD. The main goal is to get the person to a therapist. This would involve getting the narcissist to recognize the need for therapy. The second priority is to help him get rid of behaviors that could get in the way of therapy. The third priority is to get him to see and eliminate behaviors that impact quality of life, both his and yours, such as criminal or high-risk behaviors.

Similar to a typical intervention staged for drug or alcohol abuse, friends and family of the person with NPD come together and tell that person they see he is in a bad place; they see the horrible effects that his disorder is having on himself and on each one of them. Members of this "intervention circle" tell the person that it hurts them to see how the problem is hurting a person they care deeply about.

Before confronting your partner with NPD, or staging any kind of formal intervention, it is recommended that you yourself see a counselor. Not only will she be able to help you with techniques and tips on how you can best confront your partner, but if your intervention is successful, you will have a business card to hand to the narcissist to set up his first appointment!

The key to staging such an intervention either by yourself or, better yet, with others, would *not* be for all of you to address the NPD itself, because the narcissist will have great difficulty accepting that he has a disorder. But far more effective is for members of the intervention circle to confront the damaging *effects* of the disorder on each of them, and more important, what the narcissistic behaviors are doing to the person with NPD. If you can get him to see how his behaviors are getting in the way of his false self-image of superiority, he may be convinced to seek help—not so much to be "cured" of NPD, but to regain his image of grandiosity!

Dealing with the Aftermath

You have taken the emotional and difficult first step of confronting your narcissistic partner with your concerns about her well-being and the well-being of your relationship. What happens now for you? How do you deal with the fallout from your intervention?

Every intervention, whether it is staged for substance abuse or to change negative behaviors such as narcissism, ends with that "either-or" choice— "either you get help to fix this, or . . ." Now that you have expressed your concerns and had your intervention, what happens next? Hopefully, you have reached your narcissistic partner at the right time and your intervention was successful, and she has asked you to help her find a therapist who can take her and your relationship onto the path of healing.

But if as may be, especially the first time you intervene, the narcissist does not see the light and refuses to get help, what then? In the event that your intervention fails, you must carry out your "or" condition. This is why it is so important that you do not make the "or" something you are unable or unwilling to carry out. But, if you did say that "either you come with me next week to see a counselor, or I am leaving," and she refuses, then you must pack your things and go. Maybe just for a night, or a week, to a friend's house or whatever, but you must show the narcissist that you mean business if you ever want to see her get the help she needs.

Choosing to leave under this set of circumstances may be the hardest thing you can ever do. But when your partner with NPD is causing severe hurt to you, your family, and herself, and she refuses to get help, your taking a break is a necessary step. Is it worse to leave or to stay in these conditions?

ESSENTIAL

There are a lot of misunderstandings about what an intervention is. Some people think it is an emotional ambush or a kind of attack— neither of which would be a good idea when dealing with a narcissist. But, in reality, a proper intervention is something that is founded on love and honesty, a carefully planned and executed process. That is why you should never consider staging an intervention without a counselor to help you do it, and to help you in the aftermath, no matter how the intervention turns out.

Dealing with the Aftermath

For sure, you will feel bad that the intervention failed, and you will feel bad for your partner whom you see as refusing to get the help she so desperately needs. But on the other hand you may also feel a sense of relief, like a great load has been lifted off you. That is because, in a way, it has.

By confronting a partner with narcissism, by trying to intervene, you have done the best you could to get her the help she needs. You no longer need to feel responsible. It's all back in your partner's court now.

You can stand strong in your determination that you are doing the right thing in leaving, if that is the ultimatum you made. You can find peace and strength in knowing that you are making the right choice for everyone, not only for you and your family, but for your partner as well. There is a good chance that your loved one with NPD will still make the right choice once you leave and get the help she needs. If that happens, it will be due in no small way to you and the strength you have shown by sticking to your guns.

Helping Yourself

Living with a narcissist, it is very easy to find yourself giving constantly to feed his narcissistic needs and forgetting about your own needs. In getting to the point of getting help for your narcissistic partner, don't forget about helping yourself as well.

ESSENTIAL

> Even if your partner has started therapy, you cannot expect a narcissistic person to stop behaving badly and selfishly overnight and start treating you with the respect, empathy, and compassion right away. It will likely take many months of therapy, with lots of ups and downs, before things get better. That is why it is so important that you also help yourself during this healing process. The effort and time you both make could ultimately lead to the relationship becoming equally satisfying for both partners.

Now that you have faced what was perhaps one of the biggest fears in your relationship—"What happens if I stop giving in to my narcissistic partner?"—take a few steps back and re-examine what you can do to make yourself and your life happier. No matter which direction your intervention may have gone—either your partner is getting help or you are in a new place emotionally, physically, or both—now is the time to spend more time on *you*.

Start spending more time worrying about your needs than you have been about your partner's. Stop depriving yourself in order to spoil your partner. Now that you have cleared the air by expressing your concerns, the most healing thing you can do for yourself, and probably the overall relationship, is to put at least as much time and energy into your own well-being as you did into getting your partner to face his problems.

Recognizing a Codependent of a Narcissist

When a family knows that a family member has a serious problem, such as drug addiction, alcoholism, or narcissism, someone in the family—whether one individual or even an entire family—may feel the responsibility or need to help this person. Of course, this is what families do to be supportive and loving. But sometimes the helpful person's defense and aid to survival of the narcissist becomes so involved that there is no clear line as to where the helpful person ends and the narcissist begins.

Clinicians define "codependency" as being in a relationship in which the relationship itself is more important than you are. This is one aspect of what is called "being codependent." Codependents do not have their ego boundaries defined clearly enough for themselves. So what happens is they can get lost in the narcissist. Sometimes other terms are used for codependent behavior with a narcissist, including enabler, covert narcissist, inverted narcissist, and conarcissist.

Feelings and Behaviors of a Codependent

A codependent is always looking for safety, self-worth, approval, and even identity from others. A codependent may feel responsible for the behaviors of another person and try to control that person in order to "make right" those behaviors. A codependent may find it difficult or impossible to express herself in an open manner.

Codependents feel a responsibility to be caretakers, but they are usually frustrated in that role. But they continue because they get their sense of self-worth from those around them who see them as self-sacrificing and giving.

Codependency usually starts in life as a means of self-protection. For example, as children, perhaps the only defense they had against anger, abuse, or other volatile family situations was to keep their eye out for signs of a blowup and then to either withdraw and become invisible, or become the "little helper" in an attempt to diffuse the situation.

Why Codependents May Be Drawn to Narcissists

People who not only admire confidence, self-importance, and grandiosity but are lacking it in themselves may be drawn to people who display these qualities. Narcissists *appear* to be confident, even overly confident, and display their airs of superiority and positiveness. They look for admiration from others for these qualities, and when codependents latch on to them with the very admiration the narcissist seeks, there is an almost parasitic type of relationship established where one feeds off the other.

Since the narcissists don't like to be challenged and don't like confrontations, codependents (who already have a hard time making choices and decisions, who look to avoid confrontation, who don't mind being subservient because they don't have the courage to push themselves forth) seem to make ideal partners for narcissists. Codependents will usually give narcissists the attention narcissists need by always checking with them before taking any steps, or making any choices and decisions. Generally, codependents look up to the narcissists and feeling a responsibility to defend and protect them.

ESSENTIAL

When a codependent feels the need to protect and defend the behaviors of a narcissistic spouse, partner, friend, or boss, she may resort to dishonesty and denial. Be cautious when questioning a codependent friend or family member about her partner's actions, as she may react intensely and protectively to preserve the relationship by getting aggressive, lying, or making excuses.

Codependents can sometimes be called "love addicts" when they feel they must take care of another person no matter what. A codependent love addict may do whatever it takes, even make great sacrifices, to protect the narcissist from anything negative, including anger, sadness, or disappointment. Some examples of this are situations where love-addict codependents give partners money to save them from any hurts, embarrassments, or anger.

Codependents feel anxiety when the narcissist is not happy, and will defer to the narcissist rather than disagree to avoid anger, even if the codependent feels right or justified. Often this is to protect the codependent's fear of being alone or being abandoned.

Usually, a narcissist will maintain the view that the codependent has no right to ever be different and to care about her own self and well-being, feeling the threat of the loss of narcissistic supply. An ending to this type of relationship needs to be handled delicately, with support and counseling to ease any separation anxiety.

ESSENTIAL

> A codependent female may continue to settle for an abusive and destructive life with a narcissist because she doesn't believe she is able or capable of leaving and making a life on her own.

Codependents tend to have the following behaviors:

- They feel they must be responsible for the narcissist's disposition. If the narcissist seems to have negative feelings, they will do what it takes to try to resolve the narcissist's situation.
- The codependent can feel that the narcissist's unhappiness or bad mood means she has failed, and she will not be able to focus on her own needs and situation.
- A codependent will usually look for reassurance, encouragement, validation, and happiness from the narcissist.
- A codependent usually has a need to be in a relationship and stay in that relationship, without looking at her own needs and goals.
- A codependent may not be taking the time to recognize her own emotions and what her emotions should be telling her about the reality of her life. If codependents see something is wrong in a relationship, they tend to blame themselves and work on fixing themselves.
- A codependent may feel insecure about leaving a narcissist for fear of being alone or lack of confidence in being able to manage.

If you believe you or someone you know is a codependent of a narcissist, you might consider the benefits of counseling—individual, group, family, or marriage counseling. A counselor or therapist will first diagnose the condition, then identify which of your behaviors are self-defeating, and finally, offer you tools to change self-defeating behaviors.

ALERT

Counseling can be beneficial to a codependent in several ways. Some of the main goals of therapy for codependency are for clients to recognize the differences between taking care of others and being needed, and between being a rescuer and being a victim.

Counseling for codependent behavior with a narcissist can focus on the following areas:

- Working on the development of personal boundaries: Codependents do not have healthy personal boundaries. As the expression goes, codependents tend to let others walk all over them.
- Learning to recognize how her catering behavior can sacrifice her own needs and wants, and how to set goals for these areas.
- Learning to identify and become aware of her own needs and wants in her everyday life.
- Working on a personal sense of identity, strengthening a fragile sense of self, and building up self-esteem.
- Creating a safe place where a person with codependent behaviors can talk about any deep feelings that may have been pushed aside.

ESSENTIAL

There is a Co-Dependents Anonymous (CoDA) group that offers tools for recovery from codependency. CoDA meetings are designed to teach individuals how to take care of themselves and build healthy relationships.

Many advocates of the codependency theory see codependency as a kind of addiction, much like narcissism itself can be. Just as some aspects of narcissistic behavior can be overcome by undertaking a Twelve Step process, codependents too can benefit from such programs. Such programs bring codependents together in group meetings to open up about their experiences and struggles. These kinds of meetings can provide hope and a real source of emotional and practical support to the attendees. A key factor of most traditional Twelve Step models usually involves embracing spirituality and acceptance of a higher power, but such programs are nondenominational. As in most Twelve Step programs, the first step in a program for codependency recovery involves admitting that your codependent relationship has made your own life unmanageable. Then you must be willing to express your feelings, let go of the things you can't control, and be willing to do whatever you can to get better.

Codependents and Narcissists in the Workplace

It happens fairly often today that a CEO is a narcissistic personality. Usually, narcissistic CEOs will select senior management support people who are codependent. Another name for the typical "yes man" could just as easily be "codependent"! The codependent personalities are looked to by the narcissistic boss to do his bidding, and to not be questioning their opinions. Narcissistic bosses also force a kind of codependency by insisting that their subordinates do nothing but offer accolades and praise, and strengthen their position of dominance. It does happen that narcissists will try to surround themselves with only codependent followers, and for those who do not accept this type of relationship, the office situation may become so difficult for them that they will have no alternative but to leave.

CHAPTER 17

Living Every Day with Someone Who Has NPD

The story of Dr. Jekyll and Mr. Hyde is well known as the ultimate example of a person who appears to be all kindness and good but is also destructive and mean. These people are even family members, relatives, partners, spouses, coworkers, and bosses. It sure would be great to be able to get along with a person wonderfully day in and day out, but even when you try your best, some people seem impossible to get along with, like a Mr. Hyde. Their behaviors can result in pain and damage to your health and your productive life. That's how it usually is with a person who has NPD. When a person you see every day has NPD, you probably experience it as more than being able to roll with the punches. But understanding what you are dealing with will help you handle the ups and down, and get your life on a better course.

Life with a Narcissistic Partner or Spouse

Nobody's family can be perfect. There are always differences, and working things out is par for the course. But when your partner or spouse suffers from NPD, it can seem to be nearly impossible to work things out.

As a partner or spouse, people with NPD often show the following types of behaviors:

- Demand to be the only important person, commanding constant respect and admiration, even demanding to be chosen above the children who may be seen as competitors for your attention
- Seem to have little or no regard for your boundaries, feelings, or needs, and does not appreciate your separateness in the relationship
- Experts in seduction and manipulation in order to get a partner to do what they wish

FACT

Narcissists may use sex as a substitute for intimacy or love. If you suspect that you are living with a narcissist, observe all the intimate moments you share and notice which—if any—are not sexual. If they are almost all sexual, your narcissist may be using the act to avoid real intimacy.

People with NPD may or may not be aware of exactly how their disorder is affecting their behaviors, although they may have an idea that something is wrong. They may know that they like to be respected, adored, and admired. But unless they have a background themselves in psychology, or have had some therapy, they may not really understand their feelings or behaviors.

They do not accept criticism in any sort of reasonable way. Pointing out bad habits or behaviors is a "no-no" with narcissists, even though this would be an important part of working out most other intimate relationships. Statements that don't confirm their perfection are viewed by them as an attack, and they may lash out violently.

Even if in the beginning they did things to impress you, when they begin to feel they are not getting the supply they need, their behaviors will change due to their frustrations and may include raging, abandoning, sulking, silent treatment, risky behaviors, humiliating, belittling, possibly becoming abusive, and otherwise devaluing you.

If their own abilities in their jobs, hobbies, or activities do not meet their standards—for example, losing at sports, receiving criticism at work, or not getting a promotion—their frustrations are often transferred to you, their closest relationship. Or, frustrations can be transferred into harmful activities including drugs, drinking gambling, and reckless spending. A narcissist that was passed over for a promotion or struck out at a baseball game may come home and berate you for no reason or go out drinking—anything to get back that sense of control.

Sometimes narcissists can do the opposite: They come home and lament that they're no good, they behave badly, and so on. They are looking for you to defend them and tell them how wonderful they really are. And if you are codependent or enamored with your narcissist, you probably will fill their narcissistic supply.

ESSENTIAL

"Transference" is the term psychologists use when the narcissist takes his experience of not being adequate, or feeling guilty or bad, and transfers that to you because they usually don't want to deal with things that may interfere with their good image. They believe they didn't get the promotion because you weren't supportive and were rooting against them all along, for example.

What You May Be Feeling and Finding

- You may feel you have to do whatever it takes to balance your relationship with your partner or spouse.
- You may find yourself questioning what you did wrong to cause a change in the person, and try all ways to fix the situation.
- There may be a moment of believing that behaviors have gone back to the way they were at the beginning of the relationship, renewing your hope and canceling out the realities of unhealthy, unproductive situations that have gone on for some time.

- You may feel lost and confused, not knowing what is the real truth or not.
- You may find that the narcissist has left you and found someone else, usually not feeling they have done anything wrong or caring to dwell on anything negative.

FACT

There is a "fusion delusion" that occurs often in relationships with narcissists. What happens is that one partner's autonomy is wiped out in order to service the other's narcissism.

Dealing with a Narcissistic Partner or Spouse

Here are some pointers to consider for yourself, whether or not you decide to stay in a relationship with a narcissist, and for how long:

- Because he probably has difficulty expressing needs and feelings to you, it can be helpful for you to model the communication skills of identifying feelings by starting your statements with "I feel," "I felt when you," "I'd like you to do . . ."
- You may wish to try what's called active listening. After he says something, repeat what he said with "Did I hear you right? You want me to do *xyz*?" This does not mean you are agreeing with what he said; you are just validating him and showing that you are listening to him.
- One technique that can better interaction is to take your own space or timeouts when you need them. Or if you sense the beginning of a conflict, simply say, "It doesn't look like we can talk about this right now, so I'm going to take a short break and continue later." Then go to another room, take a walk—take charge of your situation.
- You may try to detach from feeling responsible for what the narcissist is saying or doing, or not doing. Even if you gave him every single thing he wanted from you, he would probably still not be satisfied and content.
- You may try to learn to accept and let it go, and not feel that you must experience the ups and downs with him.

- You may try to avoid paying attention to his distorted view of you, such as "It's your fault, you're selfish, you do not understand, you do not love me."

NPD and Infidelity

Narcissists' lives are built on lies and falsehoods. They also walk around with a sense of entitlement and a feeling that the normal rules of society do not apply to them. It is no wonder, then, that people with NPD often cheat on their partners or spouses. Just look at the news headlines about this or that celebrity marriage ruined by infidelity, and you can see that this is true! Unfortunately, it is not only the partners of celebrity narcissists who have to come to grips with cheating.

ESSENTIAL

The film *Solitary Man* starring Michael Douglas is an excellent portrayal of the downward spiral and terrible destruction caused by narcissistic infidelity.

Once infidelity is discovered in any marriage or significant partnered relationship, it can be very difficult to recover and keep the relationship together. Given all the other complications of staying in a relationship with a narcissistic spouse, once cheating is added into the mix, you may very well consider that the last straw, making leaving or divorce an option. Whatever you are considering, it is best to make these decisions with the help of a counselor, good friends, and family. A counselor can help you with the best way to approach and think about your own unique situation.

Life with a Narcissistic Parent

All parents play favorites from time to time. A narcissistic parent has favorites at one time or another, but actually may see each child in a specific role that remains unchanged. In one role, the parent sees the child as perfect, golden. In this role the child is always seen as great, the parent is the total fan club, with no criticism, always complimenting and bolstering the child's ego. This role can continue even when the child becomes an adult. The parent still raves about her accomplishments, family, partner, and offspring. As an adult it may be difficult for her to recognize problems, difficulties, hardships, or imperfections.

For the other sibling or siblings, criticism is always "for the child's own good." There is often coldness and a distancing from the parent or parents. This shunned child becomes very jealous and frustrated because of the other sibling who gets the golden child type of attention. As the shunned child matures, she may turn her feelings inward and not show or express her inner feelings.

A narcissistic parent may ignore respectful boundaries of everyone including her children—at all ages and stages. With teenage children this may include actions such as walking into a child's room without knocking, expecting the child to be a buddy even with things that are inappropriate, taking as a personal affront any disinterest from the child in the parent's interests.

A narcissistic parent may have any or all of these characteristics:

- The needs of her children are secondary. She puts her emotional needs above her children's.
- She is always turning the conversation to herself.
- She pays no attention to the effects of the terrible things she says about you, her child; she responds to your feelings by saying you are overly sensitive or touchy, and tells you what you should feel or not feel.
- She constantly puts you down or belittles you, even in front of others, but can't handle you being critical of her in any way.
- She always thinks she knows what is best for you and wants to control everything you do or say.
- She makes you feel stupid or helpless when you try to do things on your own.
- She looks to blame rather than take credit, and refuses to take responsibility for her own actions.

194

- She's involved with her own interests or addictions and pays no attention to your needs.
- With excessive need for attention and admiration, she can brag, complain, sulk, tease; she is loud, flamboyant, vain, seductive, or overly charming.
- She never discusses her own mistakes.
- She only has her opinion and cannot listen to yours.
- When her needs are not met, she can be angry, even violent.
- She has an attitude of one-upsmanship, or "Anything you can do, I can do better."
- She must have the biggest or the best; she seeks status and may spend money to impress.
- She feels she is above the law and does not need to follow directions or guidelines.
- She keeps reminding you about what she has done for you, but never points out what you have done for her.

ESSENTIAL

The most basic needs of a child for trust and safety are usually not met by a narcissistic parent or parents. In fact the relationship can be topsy-turvy with the responsibility of satisfying needs falling to the child. This can leave the child believing his feelings are not important, and then feelings are either denied or detached.

What happens with children of a narcissistic parent when their emotional needs are not met, or when they become used to fulfilling a parent's needs? Often these children will feel an exaggeration of their power to fulfill the parental needs. But when they, as children, cannot help the parent because as a child they don't have the ability to do so, they can develop a sense of failure. Also, in their involvement with their parent or parents, they don't learn how to care for their own needs and feelings. As adults they may feel only frustrations, dissatisfactions, despair, and a general numbness of feelings.

On the other hand, there are children who do have a narcissistic parent or siblings who manage to find support with other relatives or friends, and are somehow motivated to find healthy role models for themselves and make their lives better. They may have elected to take themselves through a healing process that may involve therapy, education, and support or "survivor" groups.

FACT

NPD tends to get worse with age. If your parent's NPD is not under treatment, your adult relationship with that parent can be even more challenging than it was as a child.

What You Are Feeling

Growing up with one or two narcissistic parents may have left you now finding it hard to know who you really are, hard to find your inner self, especially if you were not allowed to tell your own story growing up. You may not have had the chance to grow enough yourself and find out things for yourself if you were always directed toward giving your love and attention to the parent or parents. You may still be programmed to only please others rather than pleasing yourself in a healthy way. You may also be feeling depression, anxiety, or another mood disorder if you grew up not feeling safe and your self-worth was not valued or was attacked. You may feel an overwhelming anger at one or both of your narcissistic parents because of their codependence or inability to deal with or fix their relationship for the better.

Dealing with a Narcissistic Parent

There is no set way to deal with a parent who suffers from NPD. You need to find the best way for you and your own unique situation. You need to consider your past history with your parent or parents, and your present lifestyle and family situations. And know that whatever your situation is, it is important that you have healthy support from friends, other family members, or counseling to help you move yourself along in coming to grips with your past and a better present and future.

Some children of a parent or parents with NPD choose to break off a relationship with the parents due to the disharmony in their own family life. Others learn to cope, usually and especially with the help of counseling.

Contact with your parent or parents will most likely be helped by working with a counselor or therapist to set strong boundaries in place, ground rules to be aware of and follow. You will want to make sure you are not compromising your own self-esteem in your relationship with a narcissistic parent.

ESSENTIAL

A narcissistic mother can often play one child against another in order to keep a power base. For the mature child, learning to be able to take a step back from this parent's controlling behavior can help in the relationship.

Life with a Narcissistic Sibling

Sibling rivalry is a common occurrence and even siblings who are best of friends have their differences. But having a sibling who is narcissistic is a painful family experience that no child could be prepared to deal with. And the difficulties probably don't get any better with age, unless the sibling decides to go for therapy for her problem.

Siblings often develop narcissism as the result of a narcissistic parent who selects one child to be the special one. This child may be gifted or superior in certain ways, and the parent focuses on this brilliance or superiority to develop, mold, and give her all the positive attention. The other child or children are basically invisible since all the attention and talk is about the chosen one. Excuses are made for this child; he does not have to listen to any rules that may apply to the other children. This chosen child comes to believe she is superior, and can develop NPD.

Growing up with a sibling with narcissistic personality disorder can be a gut-wrenching experience, especially if the narcissist is an older sibling. One self-disclosed sibling of a sister with NPD never understood why her older sister continuously belittled her, or the reasons behind her older sister's horrible treatment of her. When she realized that the sister was treating other people just the same way, she realized that it wasn't her fault, and it was the sister who had a problem.

A golden child, the favorite, may often cut corners, lie, steal, and cheat, finding they receive no punishments and still remain golden. The golden child grows up thinking he never does anything wrong, yet may blame the parents for everything. The "annointed one" will usually demean, criticize, and humiliate his siblings, and does whatever he wants to show his superiority and the sibling's inferiority. This pattern will likely continue into adulthood.

The parents offer no help with the situation, either being in denial or narcissists themselves who are encouraging and supporting the chosen child. Some parents actually join in with the narcissist sibling and also bully and tease their other children. These children may become very fearful, and feel hurt and alone. They may spend a lot of time in their rooms or staying over at friends' houses as often as possible, just to get away from the abuse. The child who bears the brunt of this behavior feels she has no one in her own home who is there to protect and nurture her.

Children who are subject to this kind of abuse from narcissistic siblings can respond to it in different ways. Some can become terrific survivors, who turn their pain in a positive direction. They can become creative, excelling in the arts, or become extraordinary friends and build some wonderful relationships outside of the family. Others may sink into deep depressions and feel they have nowhere to turn, being trapped in their own homes. Sometimes in multiple-sibling families, the other siblings may band together to defend themselves from the narcissistic sibling, becoming very close.

Dealing with the Narcissistic Sibling

If you have a narcissistic sibling or one with full-blown NPD, there are no set rules or means on how to deal with your situation. You need to evaluate to make a decision based on your own unique situation—your particular family's history and relationship with this sibling, and your present lifestyle, family situation, and needs.

You can learn how to detach yourself emotionally from this sibling to be able to manage your reactions to his projections. When you understand the nature of your sibling's disturbance, this can help you to see how that works in your relationship. You may decide to sever the relationship to protect yourself and your own family from continued disruptive behavior from your sibling.

With the help of some counseling, you may be able to set boundaries and deal better with your expectations. If your sibling tries to sabotage family interactions with other siblings or your parents, it may be necessary for you to strengthen your relationships with other family members or friends outside of the family. This way you can see that there really are people in the world who can appreciate and accept you, in ways that your sibling and your parents could not—and may never be able to do, because of their illness.

Because your parents may never have been helpful to you due to denial or narcissism, you need to be able to accept that you can't change your parents or take responsibility for them, even if your sibling may be hurting them with his behavior. You might be able to help a parent, however, by giving her information on your sibling's disorder from your reading and/or counseling.

If you have a sibling who is a narcissist, you may still be feeling an ongoing crisis in family situations. It might be helpful for you to vent to people who can understand what you are dealing with, others in similar situations who may understand the nature of your sibling's disorder. This can help you to then understand and determine what to do in relation to your sibling with NPD and to your parents. Your own education on the subject and/or counseling can help you set better boundaries and ground rules within your family, and make better decisions on the type or frequency of contact you may want to have with your sibling. You may be able to let go of some of your anger toward your sibling because of her self-absorption, selfishness, constant criticism, and even sadistic treatment.

Life with a Narcissistic Teen

Living with a teenager, any teenager, is tough! All teens are at a difficult age, struggling to establish their independence and "find themselves." It may be hard to tell if your teen's attitudes are typical teenage behaviors, which can include selfishness as he is trying to establish his own identity, or if there is a potential problem with NPD.

But one thing is for sure: If your teen is narcissistic or has developed NPD, besides the usual teenage angst you no doubt will be dealing with some very hurtful behaviors and damaging manipulations. Your teen may not even be consciously aware of what he is doing, or be able to express the emotional turmoil going on.

How Can You Tell If Your Teen Is Narcissistic?

Recognizing a narcissist is not easy to do, generally. And separating a narcissistic personality disorder from typical teenage behaviors can be even more difficult. Note how many of the list of narcissistic behaviors are regular and ongoing with your teen. As with an adult narcissist, if you feel your teen shows at least five of these symptoms, she may have a problem with narcissism or even NPD:

1. Grandiosity or overemphasis of achievements, exaggerating accomplishments and skills, and lying about them, to be seen as superior to others.
2. Fantasies about having exceptional beauty, fame, success, power, or physical strengths.
3. Believes that he is unique and special and should only associate with similarly fantastic individuals.
4. Needs constant praise, admiration, and attention, or the opposite; expects to be feared or held in awe, and any perceived slight results in anger or even violence.
5. Shows total expectation of being entitled to special treatment and expects obedience from others to demands.
6. Exploits other people to achieve his own goals.
7. Believes others envy him.
8. Does not consider feelings of others, and is either unable or unwilling to see others as people with unique thoughts and feelings.

As you observe your teen with these characteristics in mind, take heart that just by wanting to help your teen you are demonstrating positive steps in your love and concern.

If you do find that your teen is narcissistic, you do have a difficult parenting job, which becomes a double job: You need to deal with his present behavior, and you need to consciously be shaping his future behaviors and attitudes to help him grow into adulthood.

Here are some suggested pointers in dealing with your narcissistic teen:

- It is important to set limits that are age-appropriate and reasonable. Do enforce them with both gentleness and firmness, with specified consequences for violations. Consequences must be enforced consistently, and without worrying about tantrums.

- Do encourage with praise and admiration for real behaviors or accomplishments, but don't expect the narcissistic teen to be interested in adoring you.
- Do show love and concern, but don't expect the narcissistic teen to be able to demonstrate real love in return. They have trouble with emotional connections.
- Make sure that you know your personal boundaries, that your teen knows them, and that you hold firm to them.
- Hold the narcissistic teen responsible for unacceptable behaviors with consequences.
- Try to be patient, and believe that he is suffering from great hurts underneath.
- Consulting with a counselor or therapist can help you and the family work on the problems.

In therapy, treatment can be challenging, as it is with adult narcissistic behavior. The goal is usually to teach the teen to value herself on a more realistic level and to adjust thinking about others' value in relation to her own. Exercises to help the teen develop compassion and empathy for others are part of the treatment plan. Medication is usually not used unless depression and anxiety are determined to be interfering with coping skills.

Dealing with the Narcissistic Teen

As always, the best way to help anyone else is to first make sure that you are taking care of yourself. Treat yourself with love and respect, and this makes the best model for your teen. Otherwise, you may start to take your teen's behavior personally or resent her selfishness.

Try not to label your teen, which may just reinforce negative behaviors. Instead, you can comment on the negative behaviors by describing the way the behavior makes you feel. Set limits, and give choices. "It hurts your sister's feelings when you call her stupid. In this house, we don't do things that are hurtful. If you're angry at your sister, tell her why." "The rule is that you call me when you say you will. I need to feel comfortable to give you the freedom you want, and your calling me when you agree to is what makes me comfortable." "Do you want to commit to calling me when you leave where you told me you would be and head to another party, or do you want to stay in this weekend?" "The rule is everyone in this home cleans up their own messes. Do you want to clean up your clothes now or after breakfast?" Set boundaries, making it clear which behaviors are not allowed and rewarding positive behaviors. "Thank you for calling me when you arrived at the party. I feel better when I know where you are and that you're safe." "Your sister really appreciated that nice compliment you paid her about her haircut, and I did, too." "It was very nice of you to help your brother clean his room, too—thank you for being so considerate!"

Teens are still growing and changing, so there is always a path to healthy adulthood. You can never make a mistake by loving your teen.

Life with Narcissistic Relatives

Usually you are able to get along with your relatives because you can understand how other people think, or why they do the things they do. But people with NPD cannot properly interpret what other people do, or the importance of other people's experiences. So even though relatives are blood, it may be easy for narcissistic relatives to trample on your boundaries, to try to manipulate you to their own ends.

Since you are developing an understanding of where and how this disorder may have come about, and the kinds of behaviors you can expect with that disorder, you can find a compassion for relatives who are narcissistic or who suffer from NPD. At the same time, it is important that you maintain your own boundaries with an assertive attitude. This does not mean that you need to be hostile, or passively let them have their way. But you may need to distance yourself politely to maintain your own health and that of your family.

Problems with narcissistic relatives can be lifelong. You may have cousins or other relatives that you recall were so superior and smug, or critical of you as children, and now as adults are even more hurtful with verbal attacks and criticisms. In a family gathering, this relative may still care nothing of saying hurtful things to you in front of other family or strangers. You may still hear from him grandiose accounts of major achievements and success, awards, and honors. He may even sabotage you by pitting one or more family members against you.

How You Are Feeling

The charges, the sabotage, the hurtful barbs thrown at you by a narcissistic relative are emotionally damaging. Even more than that, what might be hoped for as a thankful or rewarding family gathering can become a nightmare to endure. Just remember that it is not about you. The comments, judgments, and accusations they make are about them and their perception of the world. If they are adults, this personality was probably developed as a child and was perhaps the way they needed to survive some of their upbringing.

Know that you probably cannot change this relative or expect changes, and your explanations will probably have no results in their behaviors. And if they feel confronted, their behavior will be worse. They will probably always confront you with the same barbs and issues they know rub you the wrong way and get a reaction from you, but try to stay strong and calm. This is probably most difficult because what they say and do probably infuriates you and gives rise to negative feelings and/or actions yourself. When you are hearing some verbal attack, you might picture that person talking to herself in the mirror. This way you might be able to see that person with the ideas she has about her *own* self.

With this kind of empathy for the relative, you might think that underneath this steely outer self, there is a person with deep fearful scars inside, well hidden.

Dealing with the Narcissistic Relative

You need to decide what kind of contact you will have with this relative. Think about what you need for your own peace of mind and family well-being, and balance that with what kind of relationship you must have with this relative in your life, whether you choose to limit the time you spend with them, remove yourself from the relative's presence, or use the coping tools in the situations where there is contact. Keep your sense of humor. The worst of families is always somehow made into jokes and comedies, even if it is in your own mind. Try talking to some other relatives about this narcissist. You may be surprised that everyone else feels the same way as you. Having this camaraderie and understanding can make dealing with this relative a lot easier, and you may even discover that there are other members in your family that bear the brunt of the narcissist's criticism and abuse. Don't let anyone tell you to "get over it," or that your feelings are not valid.

Sometimes if you see this relative on rare occasions only, you can easily ignore them or make very sparse, civil conversation for the time you are together. If you see them more often, you can develop coping mechanisms and defense strategies to deal with them. For example, if a narcissist cousin is always berating you for your weight and mocking you, you can choose to respond with cool civility, "Cousin, I'm not sure why my weight bothers you so much. There must be something else we can talk about?" This puts the focus back on your narcissist relative's fixation on you. If they persist, a curt "No, I do not wish to discuss that. Have you tried the salad?" is appropriate.

Of course, some people opt for the even cooler approach coupled with the "either-or" option discussed earlier, said in a firm voice: "Cousin, I have asked you several times to stop commenting on my weight. It's hurtful, cruel, and embarrassing. Either you stop bringing it up, or I stop coming to your cookouts." At this point, the narcissist may get defensive and employ the "I was only trying to help" argument or say, "I was just making a point, why are you so sensitive?" This is the narcissist's attempt to put the blame for your emotions on you solely, because you are just *so* sensitive! To which you can simply repeat: "As I said, your comments are hurtful, cruel, and embarrassing to me. Either you stop bringing it up, or I stop coming to your cookouts." And if the comments or defense continue, gather your belongings, make your exit, and remark, "I'm sorry we couldn't have a nice visit today. Maybe next time."

However, sometimes ignoring the relative doesn't work, or he seems oblivious to your cues, and your only option is to stop seeing him altogether. Cutting the relative off completely may be difficult, particularly if this act affects how other relatives of your family are viewed. For example, if you have a toxic narcissist of an aunt who is downright abusive to you and you wish to cut her out of your life, you may experience resistance from your other relatives, arguing that "she's family" and "you know how she is." (Often people will encourage others to overlook the faults of older relatives especially!) She may be your mother's only sister, and any familial discord will reflect badly on your mother. If you receive any pushback from relatives on your decision to no longer see your aunt, you can express to them: "Aunt Ethel treats me abusively, berates me, and mocks every choice I make. I have tried talking to her about how her behavior makes me feel, and she refuses to listen. For my mental and physical health, it is best that I avoid being in her company, at least for the time being."

Your aunt will undoubtedly get defensive, angry, and drag your name through the mud when she finds out you've cut her off. A long-held belief is that when someone is in your family, through blood or marriage, you *must* keep a relationship with them regardless of their behavior, and this concept is how many narcissistic parents, siblings, and relatives stay around. But consider this: Family is supposed to love and cherish one another and raise each other up, and if a narcissist is doing the opposite, there is no sense in exposing yourself to such bad treatment.

When you are dealing with a narcissistic relative, you may experience abuse and feel broken, unhealthy, and filled with hurt. The narcissist will blame everyone else for his problems. He will distort the truth and cause you to feel pain and confusion. Realize that he is in a dark place, and as a result is emotionally and verbally abusive toward others. Narcissistic relatives will manipulate you, so don't get locked in.

FACT

It probably happens too often: A caring family member allows a narcissistic relative who is having some hard times move into her house temporarily. Then, the narcissist takes over every room in the house, and it takes years to get this relative to move out!

"But We're Family!"

It happens that the "we're family" argument does overrule narcissistic behaviors. For example, a girl in her mid-twenties allowed a narcissistic cousin to move in with her after he fell on hard times, because he was family. He assured her that it would only be temporary, and she would barely notice that he was there. You can probably guess what happened: Soon the narcissistic cousin's clothes and belongings were everywhere; he was eating her food, having late-night guests over, using her products, making messes in the bathroom, and eventually his promised financial contributions dwindled to nothing—even after he got another job.

Nearly a year into the arrangement, the girl had finally had enough and asked her relative to find his own apartment within the next month. He exploded and abusively berated his kindly relative for her cruelty and callousness in kicking him out into the street (despite her willingness to open her home to him for almost a year nearly free of charge), even involving family members to try and convince her to let him stay, but she stood firm and he had no choice but to move out. She demanded his key and changed the locks after he left. He continued to use her address and receive mail at her home, and she forwarded it to him briefly before notifying him that she would leave the next week's mail on her porch for him to pick up (he was not to enter her home), and thereafter would be sending any mail with his name on it back, telling the sender there was no one at this address by that name. He was furious, but she did not budge, citing their relationship in regards to the home as that of a landlord and a tenant, and he violated that relationship by trashing her house, refusing to pay his rent, and neglecting to reroute his mail. This stance cost the girl her relationship with this cousin and other members of her family that took his side, but ultimately she did what was best for her.

Narcissistic relatives can abuse your boundaries. Let the relative know who is boss with firm rules, and without criticism. Remember that emotionally, the narcissist has can have immature behaviors.

Life with Narcissistic Friends

From childhood on, life revolves around friends. Friends are enjoyment, support, help, companions. From BFFs to drinking buddies, you love your friends. But sometimes, you find that someone you thought was a true friend, someone you may even have had a longtime relationship with, is really not capable of being a true friend.

You have probably realized that this friend does not support you when the time comes that you want or need support, even insults you in subtle ways or makes you feel bad. If this friend is narcissistic or suffers from NPD, if he is not getting therapy or help, your situation will probably not improve.

Think about the behavior of this person. What things does he say to get attention or to build himself up and feel important? You probably will see that the person does not naturally have self-esteem, so he shows off his career, busy life, status, parenting, and possessions in order to feel important. You will probably note that this friend talks about others only to point out their failures, their ineptness.

You will probably see that he punishes you with verbal attacks if you don't give him the support he needs. You will probably note that this person never asks you how things are going with you, or may ask in a way that is really a putdown.

Instead of asking how a job search was going, a person with narcissism or NPD would say to a friend between jobs, "So, are you sitting home doing nothing again, as always?" This shows how the narcissist offered no warm support but rather a subtle dig in order to feel superior and in control. This type of "friend" may also talk behind your back and say things that are untrue.

You have probably noiced that anytime you have tried to tell this person about something that bothers you, the person will turn it around, calling it your fault that you are never happy with what he does. Or he will say, "That could never happen to me," and turn the conversation back to himself. He will never look at anybody with admiration or credit.

If you decide that you need to limit or end your contacts with this person, plan your responses to him. If you continue to respond on online chats, limit it to just checking a "like" button rather than a written comment. He is probably already spreading tales about you, so take care of your needs and don't act out of fear about what he will say about you. Your character will speak for itself.

Because narcissists are so prone to anger and abandonment issues, explaining your reasons to one for ending your friendship typically is useless. But you still may wish to have a sit-down with your friend and try one more time to make him see your point. "I love you but our times together make me feel stressed, anxious, and drained of energy. I feel like you can never say anything positive about me even though I try to say positive things about you. It breaks my heart, but I feel like our friendship is not where it used to be and I cannot be the friend you need." And if excuses or abuses start (and they most likely will), the "either-or" argument is a perfect response: "Either this friendship starts being more equal, or I have to end it."

If you do want to continue some relationship with the person, when he turns anything into an attack, just quickly change the subject to something neutral, like the weather, TV shows, or celebrity news. This technique can get pretty old pretty fast, and soon your friendship will become little more than a discussion of current events. Also, the diversion tactic will work with a narcissist for only so long, as he needs to fill his narcissistic supply somehow. Don't feel the necessity to defend yourself to him, because a real friend would not require you to do that. You will probably then see that the narcissist is not a true friend, but one who only works to gain a value for himself from you.

Dealing with a Narcissistic Friend

There are four ways you can deal with a narcissistic friend.

1. Play the role they want you to. See that they are always at the center of attention, which actually means denying the ability to share your own thoughts and feelings. This can put a drain on your friendship really quickly; don't expect this option to last unless you're prepared to always keep their needs ahead of yours, which is not healthy. It may work if it is a friend you rarely see.

2. Don't play the role when you feel them bullying you, and just refuse to comply with their demands.

3. Go all out to praise, giving ego reinforcement. Don't lie about anything; there is always a way to find something good to say about anyone.

4. If you feel a conflict, quickly change the subject to something neutral to stop your own feeling of irritation, or walk away with giving a neutral excuse.

The bottom line is that a friend, unlike family, is someone whom you choose to be connected to. If you are friends with someone who exhibits symptoms of NPD, evaluate your relationship. Do you feel comfortable suggesting they may have narcissistic tendencies and offer the idea of therapy to them? If you do, you may be doing them a huge favor. If you don't, it may be in your best interest to withdraw from the friendship if it is beyond repair.

Life with a Narcissistic Coworker or Boss

Of course there are no visible identifying ways to tell who is or is not a narcissist in the workplace. Even in your own family, a partner, spouse, sibling, or relative might have narcissistic behaviors or even suffer from NPD and you may not have known what the problem is for a long time, even for years. So it goes with your workplace, and those with narcissistic behaviors or NPD who are coworkers, bosses, or new hires. Knowing how to handle yourself in dealing with them will be helped along by recognizing their symptoms and then looking to the best way for you in your situation.

The Coworker

Narcissists on the job tend to do well and advance, but do so with little concern for those they step on or climb over on the way up. They like to be in control of personnel and all aspects of a project. They can be very manipulative, and can fabricate things to always make themselves shine and let others take the heat for their foul-ups. Other ways to spot a narcissistic coworker include:

- They can be self-centered and bigheaded, expecting unique treatment and special privileges, while being charming, well-spoken, and funny.
- They are likely to show no concern for the physical or personal space of others, but yet will go ballistic if someone touches their stuff.
- They can be very belittling and critical of others but cannot take any such criticism themselves.
- They often are fearful or paranoid; they can be violent and quick to anger.
- They like to set up traps for coworkers to fall into, and like to pit one worker against another.

- They can be office bullies, often targeting one person with so much abuse until she quits.
- They may need to surround themselves with "yes men" as an ongoing narcissist supply.

Narcissistic people do not do anything nice for others out of the goodness of their hearts—that requires empathy, which is something they do not have. Instead, they put something out only so that they get more back from you in return. By getting positive feedback from you for gestures of seeming kindness, they verify that they are important or special.

Tips for Getting Along with a Narcissistic Coworker

- Do not engage in arguments with your coworker. Speak when necessary, and firmly make your point.
- Don't expect a feeling of loyalty or teamwork. A narcissist may step on anyone to get ahead or put the blame for anything on someone else.
- Keep communications with such coworkers respectful, polite, and professional without any criticism or gossip about them or others.
- Keep track and document all of your work, keeping records of communications, e-mails, texts, phone messages, and meetings. This will save you from any false accusations about your responsibilities.
- You will no doubt hear insults, belittling remarks, or false compliments from this coworker, but just don't allow yourself to take them personally. Know that these behaviors are covering over deep problems that the person with narcissism probably is not aware of, nor is he aware of his behaviors displayed to you. Do not be afraid to report any abusive behavior to a human resources manager or to your supervisor, especially if it is affecting your work or how you are viewed in the office.
- You may be angered, frustrated, or hurt by the narcissistic coworker. But you might also allow yourself to feel some compassion that this person has deep-set hurts, shame, and loneliness that have caused a

defensive behavior pattern that has carried this person through the years.

ALERT

You may want or need to check with your immediate supervisor or human resources department to see if you should file any type of official grievance against a narcissistic employee who may be harassing you. Since narcissism is not easily documented, you may need a long paper trail to file a proper report. Document any and all incidents and keep any correspondence.

If you are in charge of hiring personnel, it can be difficult to initially know that the coworker you hire has a narcissistic personality disorder. It can happen that a new member of a work team is hired who is initially charming, offering help with the agency or business's issues. Staff usually welcome good changes to keep the business or organization afloat. Then this person may begin to take over the whole agency or business, placing himself as the only voice, involving himself in aspects that don't concern him—essentially gaining and taking control of everything. Then, this person will probably not take any challenging opinions from anyone, may keep things at a safe distance from himself, or may pit work people against each other in order to benefit himself, selecting certain allies.

The Bosses

Narcissistic bosses are often highly regarded, respected, and recognized in the community, the organization, and even in wider circles. Many of the particular traits and behaviors of narcissism—such as individualism, unstoppable ambition, dedication to success, competitiveness, and the need to be the best—are usually highly valued in corporate America.

On the other hand, this kind of boss probably will not be able to truly care or have an interest in other people in the organization. He can be exploitive of others in the business, and is single-minded so that opinions or suggestions cannot be well taken.

If you have a narcissistic boss, there are things you need to consider. To protect yourself, you need to weigh your love for your job and how the situation is affecting you. Do you choose to stay and deal with your situation or walk away? If you wish to stay in your job, but are having a difficult time due to your boss's narcissism, weigh your options. Is your boss's behavior destructive, or just annoying? Are you able to do your job, or does his constant belittling and unreasonable expectations keep you from succeeding? If your boss's tendencies are offensive and prevent you from doing your job, you may attempt to speak to him about it. Present the case as "I am concerned I'm not doing this task the way you would like. Can you please clarify to me exactly what it is that you want?" rather than "When you constantly change your mind, you'll never get what you want!" Perhaps persuade your boss to relay his instructions in writing or in an e-mail; then if he accuses you of not following directions, you have his own written version of his instructions to back up your actions.

ESSENTIAL

There can be excellent benefits of working with a narcissistic boss, such as was portrayed in the movies *The Devil Wears Prada* or *Wall Street*. These types of bosses can help to launch or move your career along, and there is a great deal you can learn from them as long as you can deal with any emotional costs.

If this does not work, and your job continues to be difficult, it may be time to involve the human resources department. This may seem like a drastic, cowardly thing to do, but human resources personnel are there to help you. They can offer suggestions or even organize mediation between you and your boss to get you both on the right track. And regardless of anyone's position in the company, human resources departments are required to respond to and investigate all complaints.

If you choose to stay and tough it out with your boss, here are some pointers to consider:

- Remember that in the mind of narcissists, they are always right and you are always wrong. And they will turn things around and/or manipulate other people to make sure that this is the case.

- Keep a safe distance from such a boss; don't believe that you can ever be a confidante. If he tries to speak with you about anything personal, try to change the conversation to something more professional.
- Make sure that you are secure with your own performance evaluation and take pride in your self-worth, because you probably will not get that from these types of bosses.
- Expect that there may be belittling remarks and comments and even disrespectful treatment from a narcissistic boss.
- You may not get responses to e-mails sent to this person or indication that he has received them.
- Any communication you have with a narcissistic boss should be in writing and be very concrete. Keep written records of everything you do and back it up.
- Know that this boss will always want to be treated with awe, flattery, and admiration.
- Always try to say something truthful and complimentary to such a boss.

How to Speak to Someone with NPD

CHAPTER 18

Handling Interactions with a Narcissist

Whether it's a pleasantry or light and friendly chat in the office hall or in the mall, or even a serious conference or exchange of information, you typically know what is acceptable to say and know how to listen respectfully to another person and how to give appropriate responses. But when it comes to a verbal exchange with a narcissist, you can feel lost, bewildered, and aggravated because the normal rules don't always apply. The interactions may not come out the way you'd expect, or think, or want, because from the narcissist's point of view, it's all about the way that he interacts, regardless of you. But by knowing what to expect from a narcissist and some suggestions on how best to handle him, you will be able to better deal with narcissists anywhere in your life.

How to Speak to Someone with NPD

Normally when you say something to another person, you have an expectation of the general way that person will respond. But if he doesn't respond in the way you might expect, you can be visibly shocked, which means that you almost lurch backward as if from a punch. A response from someone with NPD can feel more like a punch. So it is helpful if you are prepared for those kinds of responses and what you might do to have better communications.

It is best not to react with fear, anger, or impatience. There are some neutral responses you can use to help reduce the kind of forceful control or intimidation the narcissist likes to have in communications. For example, speak with an attitude of patience or curiosity, using responses and questions such as: "That's interesting, can you help me with more explanation about that?" Or "I'm not so clear about what that means. Can you please tell me more or clarify?"

In one sense, these types of questions can give you an emotional boundary to avoid taking the narcissist's statements personally or to be thrown off balance. You don't want to fall into the trap of feeling responsible, feeling guilty, or letting the person with NPD control you as well as the conversation. You don't want the narcissistic forces to interfere and affect your own personal space.

If you are in a group situation with someone with NPD, the same types of questions are helpful to create emotional space for yourself, and to help the narcissist focus on accountability and responsibility for his statements or positions. The following types of questions can help both you and others in a group deal with the balance of power that the narcissist likes to control:

- How did you, or what helped you to, reach your position or decision?
- What things did you consider to make your decision or position?
- Can you help us by making your intent clear?

In general, know that these pointers will help when speaking to someone with NPD. The process is not automatic, but by concentrating on using deliberate language, you can be patient and stay focused both on what the narcissist may want from you at the moment, and on how you respond.

Other ways to engage with a narcissist include:

- Always listen carefully and think pleasant thoughts; smile.
- If the narcissist sees you as a good source of support, a source of recognition and acknowledgement, communication may be easiest.
- Pepper your communication with positive comments and recognitions that are truthful and sincere, anything that you honestly might admire. Don't make the mistake of being insincere in flattering.
- Keep in mind that the narcissist does not and cannot deal well with frustrations or challenges.
- Keep in mind that narcissists will probably not treat you as an equal or truly recognize your significance. Instead, they may have unrealistic and unreasonable expectations of you because they feel entitled to it.

Stay Strong and Don't Be Manipulated

Because someone with NPD usually has the need to be in control, to be correct, and to achieve the goals of his own agenda, he will often manipulate another person. Following are some suggestions on attitudes and communication strategies that can help to prevent you from being manipulated.

Generally, there are three rules to consider:

- Don't respond with any kind of argument; always be a kind listener. If your patience is tried to the point that you are no longer a kind listener, exit the conversation.
- Set a firm boundary to meet your own needs. Warn the narcissist if he is pushing too far, and make it clear what you will do if he infringes on your boundaries.
- If necessary, move away to take care of yourself.

ALERT

A person with NPD will usually see only himself as perfect and you as the one with a problem or the one who is wrong, and he will usually try to insist on that "truth." However, most often the problem is not with you.

People with NPD can often try to turn around or twist the reality of something they did to place the blame on you. They may continue to deny any fault and will blame you with whatever efforts it takes. You may be accused of the lie or accused of being mean, unfair, judgmental, or worse.

People with NPD may try to manipulate you if they suspect you have criticized them. First they will become defensive and angry, and then make demands with expectations of you, with consequent outrage when you are not able or willing to fulfill these expectations. But getting angry with the narcissist in return may help you to vent some of your feelings, but it will not help you to empower and protect yourself from further manipulation.

A narcissist can use finances as a way to get you to do things you don't want to do, or attempt to manipulate you into becoming a person you don't want to be. He may use finances to keep you dependent and obligated. It is a good idea to have your own means of financial support so that your narcissist cannot use money to manipulate you.

ESSENTIAL

Finding your inner strengths should help you to not allow any person to use inappropriate language or actions with you. If you allow this to happen, it is as if you give the person permission to tear down your self-respect.

If you do find that you have difficulty handling the strong words or strong emotions of a narcissist, you may want to work on developing greater strengths in your own self-esteem and self-confidence. Find ways to appreciate your own intelligence, creativity, and abilities. Hobbies and or clubs are great for personal involvement and for building self-esteem. Volunteer work also offers personal rewards that keep your own sense of self-worth positive and uplifted. The more you recognize what things about you have shown your strength—maybe it's how you always keep your word, or how you don't procrastinate about things—the better you will be able to resist manipulation by the narcissist, or by anyone else.

If a person with narcissism or NPD tries to manipulate you into any action that you don't wish to participate in, here are some suggestions to help you focus on holding your own ground:

- Sound sympathetic. You might say something like, "Yes, I can understand what you are asking, but I am afraid that won't be possible." And repeat as necessary.
- Be firm with a boundary that you set. You might say, "I don't want to take this on. I don't want to be in the middle of this." Or, you might just listen, nod, and then state clearly some particular thing you are going to do right at that moment such as, "I'm going to the store right now. Yes, I hear you. I understand but I have to go." Or, "I'm really not going to do that or take that on, but I have to go now."

Get What You Want from a Narcissist

If there is something you want from a narcissist, whether it is a smoother and more managable way of dealing with him, or some specific thing, the major key is that you first understand how his mind works. When you have a good idea in advance how the narcissist will respond to you, you will be better prepared to know how to approach him.

Know that the narcissist will want, need, and look for admiration and praise. The narcissist's drive will usually be directed toward either beauty, intelligence, power and influence, or independence. If you can figure out which one of these types of validation the narcissist likes most, use it in your compliments to him. Just make sure the compliment is about something that you truly do admire. Make sure he hears and accepts the compliment before you proceed. Showing the narcissist that, by doing something you want, he will get something significant, especially if it's along the lines of his interests, is also helpful. For example, if you know your narcissist is hung up on appearances and a sense of celebrity, and there is a movie you really want to see together, say, "I hear this is the movie for all the beautiful people and the in crowd. Anybody who is anybody is running to see it." Or, if your narcissist's particular hot button is a belief in his superior intelligence, you might say, "The reviews all said this is not a film for the weak-minded; only the quickest minds will figure out the twists and turns."

Be clear, concise, and precise in knowing and stating what you want. This makes for better communication with anyone in general. But with a narcissist you are hoping to get him to answer to you without his getting lost in what you are saying and then just turning the conversation back to himself.

You might feel that you yourself are being a little manipulative with this approach, and it may seem uncomfortable for you. But being more straightforward, such as simply asking for your own needs and desires, with a narcissistic partner has probably failed time and time again for you. As you start to use this technique and see that it can work to get things you want or need, it will get easier to use over time.

Being Assertive

Finding your balance of assertiveness will always be helpful to you to get what you want from any situation, as well as from a narcissist. Just know there is a difference between being assertive and being aggressive. A response or request made with aggression is similar to the response you may get from a narcissist: demanding, threatening, sometimes sarcastic, and maybe even violent. But assertiveness means to stand up for yourself while respecting other people's rights. Being assertive means knowing your own limitations and boundaries.

ESSENTIAL

One young woman explained that she always had behaved passively because she was afraid of being rejected. But this behavior led to her being victimized and she responded to that with aggression. Why? She didn't know how she could be assertive. With classes and counseling, she learned a better way for expressing herself by being assertive, not aggressive.

Here are some tips on how to be assertive in your communications:

- Use eye contact in conversation to both engage the other person and show acknowledgement to him.
- Your body language always tells a lot; there is a difference between a defiant angry stance and a relaxed, calm, and open posture.
- Use the 4Cs in your language: clear, complete, concise, and coherent language; that is, to the point without using words that are hurtful.
- Understand that you will perceive things differently than he does, and be prepared for that.

- Do phrase everything beginning with "I"—such as "I feel . . ." Never begin, "You make me feel . . . ." A narcissist will never react well to anything that resembles an accusation.
- Keep your mind flexible and open to looking for solutions, rather than being stubborn and inflexible.

The Power of Control

Most narcissists fear not being in control or a loss of control. Therefore the more you can allow him to believe he is in control, the better things can go for you. Additionally, this will add to your own self-confidence in that you have the underlying understanding of where the strength and power of the control really is—with you, rather than with the narcissist.

Getting What You Want Can Change

As your relationship with the narcissist goes on, you may begin to see someone who is different from the person you saw in the beginning. In the beginning that person was special, charming, unique, generous, and giving; but now you see a kind of arrested emotional development, perhaps lying, cheating, and mistreatment. When this happens, what you want from him may change. You may want to disconnect or to look into counseling. You may come to a realization that you may not be able to have an adult, fulfilling relationship with this person.

Stop Being Victimized or Abused by Narcissism

There is never a time when you should feel you deserve anything less than decent and respectful treatment. But due to the common behaviors that often result from narcissism, you could be a victim of abuse—from mild verbal abuse through physical abuse.

Being a victim of some incident or circumstance is nothing to be ashamed of because most people at one time or another unsuspectingly may become a victim. Since it is impossible to know and be aware of everything, innocence can bring about victimization. But everyone learns from these experiences, and it is the knowledge that prevents further victimization and/or abuse. Knowledge of potentially dangerous situations gives you the power to avoid or prevent them. And there are plenty of potential dangers to be aware of with those suffering from NPD.

ALERT

If you have gone through an abusive situation, you may feel traumatized by the incident or situation. You do need to be listened to and heard by friends and/or a good counselor. This will begin to validate what happened to you, and improve your own sense of worth to get yourself feeling in control and empowered.

Living relationships, work relationships—all relationships—have clashes in personalities at times. But normally, people have healthy ways of resolving them. With a narcissist, however, resolving clashes is an almost impossible challenge; he will fight to be right, and it can easily happen that you are victimized or abused in the process. You may let some things slide, but you should have zero tolerance for abuse.

Here are some further suggestions that can help you avoid being victimized in your relationships with narcissists:

- Be prepared in any communications for the fact that the narcissist's perceptions will be very different from yours, but he most likely will not be willing to consider your perceptions.
- Have a good support system of family, friends, and counselors.
- Have a life of your own of work, hobbies, activities, and financial independence, if possible.
- Remember when communicating with the narcissist not to take things too personally.
- Set realistic boundaries and have the confidence to enforce them. Be able to say no.
- Be empathetic and compassionate—something that narcissists have great difficulty with or are unable to do at all.
- Know yourself and be honest with yourself in your needs and goals.
- If you need or want to indicate a correction to the narcissist, try the "sandwich approach." You begin with a truthful compliment or praise,

then a gentle corrective statement, following up with more praise for a past real performance.

- If you have a problem where the narcissist is too demanding for a response from you, you can use these examples to buffer your response: "Can I have a little breather to think about that?" "I'm sorry that you feel that way." "What is it you are asking me, specifically?" "I see that you are angry, and that is okay, but maybe we can discuss this later when you aren't so angry." "I can see how that can be frustrating for you." "I know you are more than capable of finding a way to fix your problem."

- If you are getting a silent treatment from a narcissist, you may respond with "I'm not going to keep asking you when you want to talk, and I'm not going to follow you around. Why don't you just let me know when you want to talk, and I'll be here, okay?"

- If you do find yourself in a bad episode or one that is escalating, tell the narcissist in a calm, steady manner that you cannot deal with the anger right now, and then leave the room or house. Showing that you are visibly upset or very stressed may further fuel narcissistic behaviors.

ESSENTIAL

Don't be afraid to say "No" without any detailed explanations. Just, "No, because that's how I feel about it" is good enough. If you are not used to speaking like this, you might practice saying "No" until you can say it as easily as "Good morning," but in an assertive, and not aggressive, way. Many etiquette specialists say that "No" is a complete sentence of its own!

If you are trying to end a relationship with a narcissist because of abuse, it may be helpful for you to let friends, neighbors, employers, and counselors know that you may be having difficulty in ending it. But understand too that the narcissist who is abusive may try to contact or harass you through them. Do involve police if there is an indication of danger or violation of your rights. If the narcissist contacted you after ending your relationship, you might respond only with one firm statement: "I have decided to end our relationship so I need you to stop contacting me." If you have imposed a "no contact rule," do stick by it. Boundaries are not negotiable.

Dealing with the Lies

When dealing with a narcissist, one of the major problems is often the narcissist's attitude toward lying. Normally, when you communicate with others, there is an assumption of honesty, because there is no reason, no rational motivation, that the person should be or would be dishonest with you. So this typically allows you to trust the information the person is exchanging in communication. This is usually what makes the communication worthwhile.

Most people have learned and understand that lying can often create negative consequences, which are not desirable. However, the narcissist's attitude toward lying is often very different. For him, lying can be just a tool for getting what he wants. He may view it as being clever or being superior to others. Often the narcissist feels he is above normal consequences. If caught in a lie, he will probably see it as a threat and find a new lie to overcome this threat.

FACT

A narcissistic partner can even turn the act of lying back on you. He may lie repeatedly, but when caught, he will blame you, for snooping or doing whatever else it was that you did to catch the lie. Don't let him convince you that your discovery is worse than his lie!

Here are some helpful things to keep in mind when dealing with a narcissist who is or may be lying:

- If it is in a business relationship, take care to keep good documentation on events and conversations. Narcissists may and can use lies in order to set up people against each other. It may work like this, for example: The narcissist will lie to person A that person B doesn't like him, and then tell person B the same thing. Then neither party will speak to the other, and both can be manipulated at will by the narcissist. So put things in writing whenever possible. Follow up phone conversations and meetings with e-mails dictating everything that happened, and ask the recipient to simply reply and confirm that this information is accurate.

- If you suspect the narcissist is lying, it usually is not helpful to criticize or contradict him. Try repeating the last few words he said as though phrased like a question. This may encourage his disclosure.
- If you are a submissive person, learn assertive skills. Question the narcissist's accuracy in retelling of events. "Are you sure you said *ABC*? I remember you saying *XYZ*, and I asked you to confirm it twice. Is it possible that you're remembering incorrectly?"

Negotiating Skills in Handling Interactions with a Narcissist

In your interactions with narcissists, you already know that they don't necessarily respond and react in the ways most people do or in ways that one might expect. In fact, there may be more possibilities for arguments and inflamed interactions that just seem to escalate, with nothing but painful ends. But there are ways you can learn to identify the "hot buttons" in your interactions with narcissists—those things that will most likely lead to arguments—and to prevent things from going down that damaging path.

The word "conflict" has many historical roots in the word "contest." It is believed to be the idea that things are always in competition for a winner who takes all and a loser who loses all. Historically, people have developed and used tactics to win a competition by reducing, beating out, or annihilating the opponents. However, there are equally, or even more effective, tactics to use to avoid arguments, to negotiate, and to work on a path to connection.

To think about avoiding conflict, recognize that you want to have your share of power to balance the interaction. You can probably understand that

225

the opportunity for bullying that continues on and on happens when the victim of the bullying just cowers with no strength. You do have the right to keep your power. You do this by not placing the control of your life into the other person's hands, which happens when you make statements such as "You are making me miserable because you always do this to me." When you do this, you are telling the other person that he has total power over you.

Since you have learned that narcissists are more defensive than average, there are statements that should be avoided and phrased differently in order to avoid throwing narcissists into a defensive and aggressive mode. Narcissists have definite hot spots, and will fight with their usual weapons when these hot spots are opened, such as:

- Blaming a grievance on the other person.
- Stating that someone else's actions or inactions caused the problem.
- Using threats to try to get their needs met or their grievances understood.

Avoiding Hot Spots

Try to avoid jumping to conclusions—you probably have already seen that narcissists may do this often with negative consequences. At a point where you've jumped to the conclusion that the other person is not listening to what you're saying or what your needs are, or trying to fix behavior the way you'd like or expect it to be, it can feel to the narcissist that you are not allowing him to exert his influence, correctness, or power. Instead, take a place of space for yourself momentarily, drawing your own boundary, and remove yourself. Consciously put down any weapon of anger and try to think of connecting instead.

State your need as simply as possible without any threats or consequences. Always begin with two special words: "*I need* . . . more help with the children or the housework, or, *I need* a little more time for myself and we need to find a solution to this together." Then leave it at that to allow the other person a chance to digest it without any threats or consequences if he does not or cannot comply.

Partners do need to understand exactly what the other's needs are. Often one or the other just assumes knowledge of this, thinking it must be obvious. But usually things are not so obvious.

Do use humility and gentleness when you see that there may be an escalation, such as: "When you begin to look like that or say these things, I feel really scared. I just don't know what I should do or say; I am really lost about this." This centers you and although it may sound like you are being weak, you are not. By identifying your feelings and expressing yourself honestly, you are holding on to your power.

The Wisdom of Aikido

Aikido is a Japanese martial art that focuses on using your opponent's own strengths and power against him, defending yourself, and at the same time disabling your opponent without harm. Aikido literally translates into "the way of blending energy." The idea behind aikido is to redirect the force of an attacker's blow, rather than trying to oppose it head on. The way the practitioner does this is through keen observation of the attacker's movements and an almost spiritual connection to the "life force" of the attacker. This way she can find the rhythm of the attack and use the perfect counter technique. "Aikido negotiation" is a technique that applies similar ideas not in combat but in interpersonal relations or negotiations.

In using aikido concepts in personal interactions during conflict situations, the goal is not to destroy the other person or say or do things that could incite more struggle and put more strain on the negotiations.

ESSENTIAL

An essential aspect of aikido recognizes that conflict should not be viewed as a contest between winners and losers but as a natural part of life. By looking at your relationship with a narcissist as a part of nature, instead of as a constant power struggle, more like living in an area that is often prone to heavy thunderstorms, you can be better prepared to deal with it.

You can think about using aikido wisdom with narcissists who may not be able to settle fights because their narcissistic behaviors get in the way. But you can take the lead by redirecting their destructive energies into a better way of interacting. If the narcissist asks for something that you immediately feel negative toward, stop to think that this is not a contest, but see it instead as an opportunity to learn the difference between you and the narcissist. There is often going to be that difference of opinion and way of seeing things. You don't have to agree with him, but you do have to acknowledge him, and appreciate and respect his ideas. You do not have to believe that you are right and argue to prove you are right.

Maintaining flexibility in your interactions, in which you can move from your own point of view to a willingness to bridge a connection, can be essential in negotiating with the narcissist.

An analogy to Native American shape-shifting is a real negotiating skill that anyone can practice and learn. This means that you are flexible to be able to know when to speak and when to be silent, when to show your self-confidence and when to show your humility, and you can move from one to another quickly and easily.

Here is a physical exercise that illustrates the concept of aikido negotiations and how to change direction without inflicting harm on another:

1. From behind you, have someone put her hands on the back of your shoulders. Now, have her start walking, pushing you forward so that you have to start walking in the direction she is pushing.
2. As you start walking, start to resist, making her push harder and harder to move you ahead.
3. Now, suddenly spin to one side, in the same speed or rhythm of the pusher. Stay in contact and roll along the pusher's arm, so that you wind up behind the pusher and leading the direction of where you both walk.
4. See that as soon as you are willing to not push back against the controller, but instead to make a subtle change of direction, you have found yourself in control of the situation.

Forgiving Rather than Arguing

If a narcissist says or does something to you that you feel is unfair or unkind, you do have the right to be angry. And when this happens, it may be hard for anyone to think about forgiving right away. But forgiving does not have to mean that you let the behavior and the person off the hook. Forgiving can be the choice you make about how to judge and deal with this manipulative or intolerable behavior.

With an injustice, it may be natural to want to release that anger or frustration in a harsh way. But when you already have insights about a narcissist's behavior and you know you might respond by lashing out, with your knowledge you can feel centered in knowing and holding on to your own power.

The more you know about your own ideas, emotions, and preferences, the more you can be aware of the differences in the narcissist's preferences, and your awareness gives you the power to interact in even difficult situations that are about to erupt or escalate.

Handling an Argument

Arguing can happen in even the best of relationships with partners, spouses, or family members. But because of the behavior methods and patterns of narcissists, the potential for arguments is almost always there. Narcissists easily can bring on your anger and other strong emotions. But there are techniques and skills you can develop to handle the kinds of interactions that can lead to arguments, or escalate to fights and worse.

Dealing with the Anger

Getting angry is a natural feeling. But just as angry narcissists will act out with hurtful consequences to you, your responding to your own anger in negative ways will not help matters, either. If you are treated with disrespect, it is okay to let your partner know that you're mad; but it is important to regulate the way you react, and for you to remain calm and in control of your own negative emotions. Remember what it was that made you so mad, and think about it later when you are calmer.

Don't say hurtful things out of anger such as "I hate you" or "I'm leaving you." Instead say, "I feel angry and I am going to the other room to get calm, or outside to cool off." Then you can release your anger and wait until you are calm to come back and face the situation. Empower yourself by realizing that instead of acting out in anger, you can use this opportunity to express positive self-control. Then, after the anger subsides, try to be light in discussing it. Admitting that you are sorry or that you feel embarrassed showing your humility goes a long way to crossing the bridge to a positive connection with your partner.

If the argument is with a spouse or partner, or any person who is very important to you, focus on what is precious to you and on the things you still do agree on, even at the moment of a argument. Even if the narcissist crossed a boundary, there will be time later, after you have both cooled down, to figure out what to do better next time to stop that from happening again. Make time for dealing with angry feelings, to soothe yourself, and to think about redoubling your efforts to set the best boundaries for you. Do not rehash the reason for the argument before you have figured out how to defend the boundary that was crossed so it won't happen again.

Don't complain, or threaten angry punishments. Make sure to be fair when explaining your boundaries and consequences. Avoid "If you call me that name again, I am leaving!" But do say, "I do love you but you must stop calling me names and being so disrespectful. If you don't cut it out, this conversation will have to end." Don't say, "Stop saying that or next time I'll slap your face." Instead say: "The way you are speaking is not acceptable to me, and I don't wish to discuss this now; I need a breather so I can cool off." Threats only breed resentment and just inflame a fight. If your partner's behavior is unacceptable, you have to learn skills to set better boundaries for yourself to limit his unacceptable behavior. Don't forget what the argument was all about; make mental notes about what the hot spots were, and which of your boundaries were violated.

Decide what the meaning of silence is. Sometimes in an argument you or the narcissist may resort to silence and not answer. This can be just a moment of freeing that can happen when a person facing a conflict or criticism feels overwhelmed. Do give your spouse, partner, or family member a chance to collect and clarify his own thoughts. Don't ask, "Are you listening to me?" Instead say, "I think we both can use time to settle down. I know I will feel better if I take a break. Please understand that this is not an attack. Let's both take a timeout and then we can regroup and discuss this again later."

Your hurts because of what the narcissist said or did may cause you to feel like doing or saying mean things and to hurt back. But doing those mean things are all things you would probably regret later. Try to just look at what hurt you, and share it honestly. "I feel really hurt when you say that I am selfish and worse. I have to go cool off so I can come back fresh and we can move beyond this." Then look at your partner with kind eyes, remembering your love, even despite being furious. Try not to take personally the things the narcissist is saying.

Know that when you admit your hurts and vulnerability it takes great courage. Admitting your vulnerability is courage that is strength, and also brings your love into power. For example, say, "I am being hurt very much by the things you just said about me, and I'm really angry right now. Yes, I love you very much, but I need a little break to just walk away and get calm, so I don't say something hurtful that I don't really mean."

Sometimes if you really have blown your top and gotten real angry, it can take as long as two or three days to completely calm down and look at the situation more objectively.

ALERT

Research has shown that using a boxing bag or other aggressive physical exercise really does not help to blow off steam as much as doing some kind of soothing or relaxation technique to shift your attention away from your anger. Using drugs or alcohol may also just continue your anger and aggression rather than put you on a recovering path. Just give yourself a moment to concentrate on a beautiful and peaceful thing and you will get feel better.

Make sure to deal with the hurt that has been inflicted on you. If you are a parent, you have to let your children know that everything is all right with you, that everything is okay. You want to make sure you feel safe, and make sure your children also feel safe.

Try to think of patience and time. Rome wasn't built in a day. Just look for your own inner place of happiness, no matter what is going on with your partner.

CHAPTER 19

Ongoing Controversies

Narcissistic personality disorder is a confusing condition for its sufferers, as well as for people living with a narcissist. But narcissism is equally misunderstood by the public, and sometimes even by the people who study the condition. That is why NPD often gets confused with other conditions, and why there are a lot of ongoing controversies and many myths surrounding NPD.

NPD Versus Schizophrenia

There has long been a controversy regarding whether or not there actually is a distinct emotional disorder to be called "narcissism" or narcissistic personality disorder. This controversy is echoed by the recent push to remove NPD from the diagnostic literature as a separate personality disorder. The thinking is that many, if not all, psychological disorders have a degree of narcissism in them. For this reason, many confuse NPD with schizophrenia, or believe that NPD is a type of schizophrenia, or vice versa.

However, there are distinct differences between the two conditions. A schizophrenic often has "delusions of grandeur," and that is the basis for its sufferers being labeled as having a kind of narcissism. But the schizophrenic actually develops a superhuman alternative personality, more closely related to multiple personality disorder than NPD. The "delusions of grandeur" of a schizophrenic could have him actually believing he is God, or Jesus Christ, or some other famous historical figure, as opposed to the inflated self of the narcissist, which he believes to be who he really is.

When looked at more closely, there really is no controversy between these two disorders. The conditions have some other very clear distinctions.

In a study intended to show that NPD was a separate condition from schizophrenia, a group of patients who were hospitalized and treated with a diagnosis of NPD were compared to those hospitalized for a diagnosis of schizophrenia in terms of effective therapies and clinical outcomes. The results concluded that NPD is a valid diagnostic entity, distinct from schizophrenia.

Schizophrenia is a psychotic disorder, usually with a clear medical or clinical cause, as opposed to the environmental and developmental issues that usually lead to NPD. Schizophrenics not only have delusions of grandeur, but also suffer from other delusions, such as hearing voices and other hallucinations. The person with NPD may have a skewed view of reality, but not to the point of hallucinations. The bizarre behavior, paranoia, and other jumbled thought patterns of schizophrenia can often be treated and kept under control with medication. But there is no known medication that can control the symptoms of narcissism. Therapy, on the other hand, is what can help a person dealing with NPD. Therapy, without antipsychotic medication, is largely useless in treating the major symptoms of schizophrenia.

So what does all this mean to you when dealing with a person with NPD? Only that you might think it sometimes feels as if you are living with a schizophrenic, but technically you are not. But since the symptoms of schizophrenia are more easily recognizable, and more easily controlled than those of NPD, it's hard to say if that is better or worse.

NPD and Obsessive-Compulsive Disorder

Obsessive-compulsive disorder, or OCD, is another condition that often gets confused with, or lumped together with, NPD. But again, while there is some overlap between the two, there are some very distinct differences.

Both the person with NPD and the person with OCD may obsessively pursue perfection, but it is for far different reasons. For narcissists the perfection needs to be with themselves. All of their behaviors are targeted at perfecting their false self-image. For obsessive-compulsives, not only must their perception of their appearance be perfect, but they also try to make the world around them perfectly ordered. Narcissists, on the other hand, care little about the chaos of the world around them; in fact, they believe they are so far above it as not to be affected by it.

Both people with NPD and OCD can appear detached, emotionally cold, and machine-like, and can be described as "control freaks." However, people with OCD have been shown to have empathy; in fact they can be deeply compassionate, feeling sorry for the people in their lives who do not see the need to correct the chaos in the world as they do.

People with OCD can and do form lasting committed relationships, albeit with their own set of challenges. If you are not sure if you are living with a narcissist or an obsessive-compulsive, or someone who may be a combination of the two, you might also read *The Everything® Health Guide to Obsessive-Compulsive Disorder.*

Is NPD an Emotional Defensive or Offensive Strategy?

One ongoing controversy to which there really is no clear-cut resolution is whether psychologically narcissism is a defensive or offensive strategy. Most schools of thought believe that narcissism develops as an early defense mechanism to protect an infant's worldview. Adults that develop NPD somehow get stuck in this early or infantile defense mode, and never grow out of the basic narcissism we are all "preprogrammed" with to survive.

On the other hand, if you live with a narcissist, you know how truly offensive they can be. NPD is also an offensive strategy used to both attack and generate narcissistic supply. It seems that NPD has aspects of both offensive and defensive strategies. At its core, narcissistic behavior is a defensive strategy to protect the narcissist's fragile false self-image. However, narcissists also have some very aggressive behaviors, such as the way they react to the slightest criticisms.

FACT

When making decisions, narcissists more than non-narcissists are "approach motivated." This means that their approach to life is more about gaining success than avoiding failure.

Whether your narcissistic spouse or partner, relative or friend, is attacking you aggressively to feed her own needs for superiority or to protect her true underlying vulnerability really makes little difference to you, the one who has to endure it. However, understanding that the way a narcissist lashes out may have some basis in what they see as self-defense may help you have a little sympathy for them. And if you can feel compassion for your partner with NPD, you may be better able to help her. You are able to feel genuine empathy—something that the narcissist cannot feel.

Is There a Gender Difference?

There are both male and female narcissists, and for the partner, relative, or friend dealing with their negative behaviors, each can be equally destructive but in different ways. This is because both male and female narcissists have the same needs, such as craving adoration, feeling grandiose, and lacking—they just get their narcissistic supply in different ways. Male and female narcissists express their narcissistic needs differently, although the goals are the same.

Female narcissists tend to concentrate more on issues of body image for their feelings of superiority and adoration from others. They flaunt their physical charms and sexuality to achieve positions of power more so than do their males counterparts.

Male narcissists, on the other hand, become almost comic book exaggerations of male gender roles. They focus on intelligence, power, aggression, money, and social status to feed their false self-image of superiority.

Unlike male narcissists, who may rely on sources of narcissistic supply from outside the home, such as work, business associations, or social clubs, female narcissists draw supply from the more traditional female gender roles: the home, their children, or as the "perfect wife." Female narcissists tend to be less exploitive of their sources of narcissistic supply than do males with NPD; females tend to draw others in and keep them close.

ESSENTIAL

It is easier for females with NPD to think of their children as emotional extensions of themselves because indeed they once were their physical extensions in the womb.

Female narcissists will tend to play the role of the victim, using the "why me?" attitude to get narcissistic supply more often than male narcissists. Female narcissists tend to be more self-destructive and more likely to self-mutilate or attempt suicide than do male narcissists.

Another major difference seems to be in the likelihood of getting help. Women, in general, are more likely to ask for help or admit they have a problem than are males. The same seems to be true of female narcissists, who are more likely to seek treatment for NPD than are male narcissists.

Narcissists will use any relationship in their lives to draw supply from. Since women generally are closer to children, narcissistic mothers tend to be more common than narcissistic fathers. Male narcissists, for the most part, consider their children more of a nuisance than as a good source of narcissistic supply. Of course there are exceptions.

Narcissists need to be able to function in society, to keep up their false self-image, and to get what they need. Since the condition of narcissism is basically the same in terms of the disorder itself in men and women, the differences in expression are probably based more on what is the acceptable behavior for men and women in society.

Male narcissists tend to concentrate their efforts on being aggressive and assertive to gain their superiority over others. This kind of dominating, self-centered behavior is usually more socially acceptable for males, especially in western society.

Although it occurs, this kind of overbearing behavior by females would gain fewer benefits. Female narcissists more often have to meet their narcissistic goals through more subtle, indirect, and often flirtatious means that are more traditional of female roles.

As with all men and women, female and male narcissists have their differences. The point is, whether male or female, any narcissist can be very difficult to live with.

Healing, Changing, and Recognizing a Breakthrough

There is the range of opinions and controversy about whether or not a person with NPD can be cured, have a breakthrough, be healed, or have a fully functional life. The answers to this, of course, depends on each unique circumstance—what the particular narcissist's behaviors are, what potentially are the roots of it, what is the support system for him like in the present, will he be ready or willing to work for change, will there be any type of counseling involved, and will that therapy mesh with the individual. With all these different factors, opinions vary from extremes—"there is no cure," or "run away from a narcissist," to written testaments from renowned psychotherapists and other counselors about successful breakthroughs, healing, and recoveries in individuals with narcissism—through and including middle-of-the-road hopefulness.

ESSENTIAL

There are many psychology therapists and experts who believe and have found that even though recovery from narcissism is a difficult process, as with other personality disorders, it is mainly something that is learned; it is not inherent. And that the behaviors and coping defenses of narcissism that have been learned can thus be unlearned. This gives hope to anyone who wants to continue in a relationship with a narcissist, or who wants to change narcissistic tendencies he may see in himself.

Breakthrough Work in Therapy

Therapists and counselors have seen progress made in patients with narcissism and NPD. The opportunity for this to occur most often happens when the client and therapist can make an emotional connection, which can open the door for the client to have the courage to look at his fears, pains, hurts, the way his life affects himself and others, and can begin to work on regulating behavior patterns and destructive patterns. This point is considered to be a breakthrough.

The late renowned psychotherapist Alexander Lowen saw breakthroughs with narcissists, having developed and practiced a therapy called bioenergetic analysis. Bioenergetic analysis therapy uses the body to heal the problems of the mind. Lowen described in detail his work with clients with narcissism, of using his methods that resulted in breakthroughs, and the recovery of more fulfilling lives for people with narcissism.

One of Lowen's descriptions illustrates how he helped a patient to a breakthrough to release his inner pain. Dr. Lowen instructed the patient to lie over a bioenergetic stool in a stressful position that forced the patient to breathe deeply, charging the body with oxygen, which in turn activated the sense of feelings. Lowen encouraged the client to make a sound while letting out air from the body, again allowing feelings to be released rather than being held in and repressed. Lowen noted that a client's letting out air with a vocalized sound resembling a cry or sob can result in the breaking point, much like a pump being primed, that allows the flow of tears, hurts, anger, pain, and sadness from long ago to be released. Lowen found, however, that the patient must be ready and willing for this type of breakthrough to happen.

The next step in this breakthrough was for the client to fully express his anger in the therapist's office—an important step to rid the client of his fear that his inner rage is craziness or madness. When clients can see their anger and be free of it, having found a safe place to give up control, they can accept their feelings and end up with newfound self-possession and self-acceptance. This provides an important realization for the client—that what is really crazy is their false smiles, their false poses and images to be the good girl or good boy, and their denial of true feelings. One of Dr. Lowen's methods used to reach this second breakthrough point is to have the client lie down and twist a towel, shouting out words of rage, sadness, and loss he feels.

Inner Child Work for Recovery

Many studies on narcissism and therapists talk about healing the inner child as a major step to breakthroughs in recovery. From one point of view, you can think of inner-child therapy not as work but as a mystery to solve the questions about the cause-and-effect dynamics in one's life. This is a healthy start, and these types of questions are healthy ones: Why am I always attracted to the type of people that I am? Why do I react the ways that I do in certain circumstances? Where did I get these ways of acting? Why do I sometimes feel so alone, scared, angry, helpless? By asking these questions, one can put a halt to letting past experiences be the dictator of present behaviors as though a reprimanding parent were still there causing shame, creating threats, blaming and criticizing—causing whatever present reactions you have without being conscious of those old parental influences. Over time a person can go from having simple guilt, such as "I did something wrong" or "I made a mistake," to internalizing and believing there is something inherently wrong with *me*, that I myself am a mistake. But by looking at that inner child, letting it come out, knowing that it is safe and okay, a suffering person can finally put the power of a critical and shaming inner voice to rest.

This process can help to change the narcissist's relationships not only with others but with the world around him. It can mean the difference between just going through life and *living* life—and that is a breakthrough no matter how you look at it.

The Narcissist's Self-Knowledge Breakthrough

Although some ex-spouses and even counselors may say categorically that narcissists can never change, many have found that people suffering from NPD really do have times when they realize the weight of their illness. These sufferers can recognize that their quality of life could be better; that it is causing others who are close to them pain or harm; that their relationships, friends, and work are not as fulfilling as they could be and that loneliness and depression, failure, and anxiety are issues for them.

From the Narcissist's Point of View

There are a number of self-proclaimed narcissists or sufferers of NPD who are prolific writers and lecturers on the subject of their illness. They can offer some valuable insights, even though both the insights and the persons themselves may be controversial.

The common factor among these self-proclaimed and often diagnosed narcissists, who seem to be, if not cured, at least able to function well, is a recognition and acceptance of their condition. They tend to see the condition as a plus, an asset, a possibility that can be transformed into a great opportunity to teach, warn, and be helpful to other people. In a way they are what can result when a narcissist learns to have empathy. His condition can now be seen as a blessing to others, something that gives him purpose, self-worth, confidence, and reassurance. By believing that he is helping others, he is also helping himself. Many conventional counselors also find one way to work with narcissists in therapy is to use their condition as a plus rather than as a minus.

Such speakers may be controversial, however. It is not all that different from the proven idea of recovering alcoholics helping other alcoholics.

Some of the other suggestions that "recovered" narcissists recommend in books, lectures, and online forums include:

- That narcissists know and accept themselves as intelligent and inquisitive, and understand that their narcissism may be dysfunctional, but that it saves the narcissist from even more dysfunction.
- That narcissists note which of their behaviors are self-defeating and which are productive, in order to suppress the counterproductive ones and promote those that are productive.
- Use negative and positive feedback and reinforcements as conditioning to work on dysfunctional behaviors.

Are Narcissists Aware of Their Reputations and of Themselves?

Research studies of narcissists have found that those who scored high in narcissism also tended to rate themselves as better than others—as more intelligent, more physically attractive, more likable, and more humorous than others. Interestingly, they also rated themselves with negative aspects of narcissism at higher levels than others, such as being arrogant, impulsive, more oriented to power, and exaggerating their abilities.

In another study on how narcissists see themselves, the findings revealed that narcissists do have self-awareness of themselves and know that other people see them as being narcissists. The study also showed that the narcissists thought of themselves with a much greater self-inflated image than the way others saw them.

Possibilities of Change for a Narcissist—Negatives and Positives

There are many who describe themselves as authorities, or as having had relationships and experiences with narcissists, and many in online chat groups, who find the need to vent their painful experiences. Many of them describe narcissists as "terminal"—terminal to themselves and to others, totally unable to see their painful ways, totally uncaring, totally unable to take on any responsibility. But actually that in itself is a very narcissistic view, to see things as being so absolute.

In truth, for years narcissism was thought to be untreatable. But during the past forty years, as the disorder became more prevalent, studied, and better understood, more effective therapies were found to aid in this disorder. Today it is understood that narcissists can and do learn to relate to others, just not the way you may like them to. However, they can learn to react in more positive ways with the right kind of therapy designed specifically for them.

Leaders in the field today believe that there are many normal aspects to narcissism, and that most of us use them as a defense in stressful situations from time to time. People with NPD just use them way too often and to extremes. But they can be taught other, more productive ways to handle those situations when their self-esteem feels threatened. One way this can be accomplished is in a group therapy setting where narcissists can be made to interact with other people with the same problems and recognize it in each other. They can understand more about themselves through others who are not too different.

The main reason why many narcissists fail to see any breakthroughs is that they fail to seek or continue treatment. They will usually only seek treatment at a crisis point. It is at this point that the narcissist is vulnerable and most open to help.

Elimination of the Diagnosis of NPD

A very loud and recent controversy about narcissism is the talk that there is a strong possibility that NPD, along with some other personality disorders, may be dropped as a distinct diagnostic category in the next updated edition of the *Diagnostic and Statistical Manual of Mental Disorders*, the DSM-V. The DSM is the clinical bible of the American Psychiatric Association.

The current volume, DSM-IV, recognizes narcissistic personality disorder along with nine other personality disorders:

- Paranoid Personality Disorder
- Schizoid Personality Disorder
- Schizotypal Personality Disorder
- Antisocial Personality Disorder (ASPD)
- Borderline Personality Disorder (BPD)

- Histrionic Personality Disorder (HPD)
- Avoidant Personality Disorder
- Dependent Personality Disorder
- Obsessive-Compulsive Personality Disorder

The committee working on the next DSM edition proposes eliminating five of these, with NPD probably the best known of the five to be tossed out. As of the writing of this book, no decision has yet been finalized.

However, whether or not the official diagnosis of narcissistic personality disorder is dropped from the DSM or not makes very little difference, in one sense. If the diagnosis is dropped, that will not mean that all of the narcissists in your life will instantly disappear. In fact, part of the controversy over the proposed DSM change is that what may disappear is the narcissist's ability to get the kind of help they need.

ALERT

The move to possibly eliminate NPD from the DSM is not without precedent. For example, there was a disorder called passive-aggressive personality disorder in the third edition (DSM-III), but it was removed from the fourth (DSM-IV) and current edition (DSM-IV-TR), because women's groups felt the diagnosis unfairly labeled women, who were practically the only ones ever diagnosed with the condition. This doesn't mean that this kind of behavior ceased to exist; it's just that the APA decided to yield to political pressure and hide it in the "Personality disorder not otherwise specified" (PDNOS) category.

Many well-known clinicians have voiced very strong and vocal objections to eliminating half of the current diagnoses of personality disorders, and are particularly upset over the proposed NPD cut. The rationale by the American Psychiatric Association has to do with diagnosis, insurance regulations, and the fact that so many of these personality disorders overlap, or co-occur. The way the system works now, if a clinician is seeing a client who meets the diagnostic criteria of more than one of the conditions, and she wants to treat that patient for more than one of those conditions and expects to get paid by an insurance company for that treatment, the clinician must submit a dual diagnosis. Insurance companies do not like paying for dual diagnoses, so the response by the APA is to collapse the diagnoses where they overlap. But this would be as if health insurance companies stopped recognizing "high blood pressure" as a separate illness from "heart disease," and despite the real existence of the illness, the American Medical Association were to decide that hypertension doesn't exist!

Under the changes proposed at this writing, the five new classifications recognized would be:

- Antisocial/Psychopathic Personality Disorder
- Avoidant Personality Disorder
- Borderline Personality Disorder
- Obsessive-Compulsive Personality Disorder
- Schizotypal Personality Disorder

What you need to realize from all of this is that if these changes do happen, just because the current members of the DSM committee are thinking about eliminating NPD in the Manual doesn't mean it no longer exists. It may mean you just might find it harder to understand exactly what your loved one's problem is, or at least to get an official diagnosis of it. In a very real sense, if the diagnosis of NPD is indeed eliminated from the DSM, it may be seen as a grave insult by narcissists, because they will not even get their own category in the literature.

On the other hand, some say that *not* labeling narcissists with an official "condition" or "disorder" might actually encourage more narcissists to seek help—that their false sense of perfection and entitlement may actually encourage more of them to seek treatments. The bottom line is, narcissism and narcissists have existed long before "NPD" entered the *Diagnostic and Statistical Manual* and they will continue to do so. Long after this controversy dies down, and long after the next edition of the DSM is published, no matter what you call them, you will still be finding dependent, schizoid, paranoid, histrionic, and narcissistic personalities in the world.

CHAPTER 20

Where Do You Go from Here?

You have already shown that you are a person who cares to take stock of your situation and gather information, because it prepares you for making the most sensible decisions about where you are going. As you have discovered, narcissism has its broad range of pros and cons. Throughout this book you've seen how narcissists or people with NPD have definite charms, abilities, personalities, and positions that anyone would find desirable in a person. But you have also discovered that there are plenty of real, negative behaviors. How you will deal with these behaviors and these people will be your personal decisions, and not easy ones. From here on, you are already on a path prepared with good reasons, explanations, tools, and suggestions that you've already hopefully taken to heart.

Narcissism and the Concept of Self

When you think of the narcissists in your life, a few words probably come to mind: They are "full of themselves," they are "selfish," they only think about "themselves" and are "self-serving." These are all very true, because narcissism and NPD are all about the "self," or at least about the narcissist's often warped perception or concept of "self."

If it's true that most, if not all, of your narcissistic partner's, friend's, or relative's behavior is tied into their false view of themselves, it is also true that for a lot of that behavior, they cannot "help themselves." This is because development of narcissism is anchored in early self-concepts. The self is everything to a person with NPD, so narcissists spend an awful lot of their time on "self-regulation"—doing things to make themselves look or feel better. If you live with one, then you know that this is most often at the expense of others.

Narcissists lie to everyone, about everything, but the very first person they lie to is themselves. For all of their seeming self-centeredness, the sad truth is that narcissists can never really see themselves, at least not in the way that others truly see them. But whether the concept of self that a narcissist has is true or not, if you live with one, you know one thing that is all too real: His world revolves around that self. With such an exaggerated image of self-importance, every aspect of the narcissist's life—work, home, school, simple everyday existence—is approached as though there is nobody else even around.

But it still may be hard to understand how this overinflated concept of self takes hold. It may be easier to see by looking at an example of the narcissistic behavior that often develops in a person who is suddenly thrust into fame and celebrity.

More often than not, if you take an average person, push him into the limelight, lavish him with fame and admiration, surrounding him with people who suggest that whatever he does is perfectly okay even if it's not, this individual will start to possess inflated self-views. As the saying goes, he starts to believe his own press.

It then becomes a growing kind of "fame monster." This inflated sense of self increases the once-regular person's social confidence. Now he can "hobnob" with the elite, and establish relationships with other famous individuals. Having relationships with and being seen with other celebrities and high-status individuals only serves to further inflate his concept of self.

But eventually, he must be careful that this overinflated balloon of self does not pop. He must protect this highly inflated self-concept by always blaming others for his failures and by taking credit for things that he really had nothing to do with.

Parents can often do many of these exact same kinds of things, producing the same kind of cycle just when a child's sense of self is forming, which can lead to narcissism later in life.

FACT

More than one clinical study has found that narcissists, who do not exhibit a clear definition of who they are, as opposed to non-narcissists who do, are more likely to react to feelings of failure with anger, aggression, and other negative emotions.

Why is any of this important to your ongoing interactions with a narcissistic partner? Because if you can change your perceptions of people with NPD by understanding how they are deceiving themselves as much as they are you, perhaps you can better help both of you to heal.

Consider this: Everyone is always trying to find "himself," to know who he "really is." But your narcissistic partner was robbed of this opportunity at an early age. Something or someone has wounded him very deeply, which has had the result of separating him from his true self, without help.

In order to protect himself from pain, rejection, and abandonment early in life, the narcissist has had to learn how to pretend to be something he is not. And for many who develop full-blown NPD, the charade has gone on so long that they no longer know it's an act.

The road to recovery can be made a little easier, if you can find it in your own heart to express the compassion and empathy for your narcissistic partner, relative, or friend that they cannot show you. Instead of looking at that person who has made your own life so difficult as a "narcissist" or some other negative label, simply look at him as a wounded soul—as a human being whose negative behaviors are the result of his being cut off from his true, or better, self, often through no fault of his own.

Evolving Knowledge Base about NPD

Through controversy, study, and the development of better ways to cope with the condition, understanding and knowledge of NPD by professionals and the public continues to grow. A lot of progress has been made from a belief that narcissism is just healthy self-esteem necessary to succeed, to its recognition as a damaging personality disorder. That is good news for its sufferers and their friends and families.

There is still a lot to be learned about narcissism, but every day brings new insights into NPD, and knowledge is power. As you continue to evolve your own personal understanding of the narcissists in your life and what makes them tick, remember these things from the evolving knowledge base of narcissism:

- Narcissists can appear charming, and it can even be fun, exhilarating, and exciting to be with them in the short term. But in the long term, life with a narcissist can be very difficult.
- Narcissists form relationships with people based only on what they need and can get from the relationship. Others' needs will always be secondary, if considered at all.
- Narcissists spend most of their time dedicated to making themselves look and feel better, usually at the expense of others.
- Narcissists must have the best of everything, live in the best homes in the best neighborhoods, have the best jobs, and drive the best cars, as much as possible.
- Despite their outward bravado, most narcissists have very low self-esteem.
- Many narcissists use lies and deceit very easily and often.
- Narcissists are emotionally immature, stuck in an infantile defense mode.
- Narcissism is on the rise in America, some say growing to epidemic proportions, especially among college-aged men and women.
- Digital technology, cell phones, and particularly social networking on the Internet are suspected to be largely contributing to narcissism, especially among teenagers.

There is no "cure" for narcissism, no medication to treat its symptoms. However, there are effective therapies that can help narcissists and their partners or family members live better lives, if they are willing to work at it.

Power of Love and Loving in Relationships and Narcissism

If you are hoping and planning to stay in your relationship with a narcissist, you must have some very good reasons. Although there is controversy about whether a narcissist does, can, or can learn to love, as with everything else about narcissism, there are many varying degrees, and every situation is unique. So, if you believe in, and want to improve, a love relationship, you are already on that path just by what you have learned through this book.

You know you already have the courage to put in the effort needed and you can already say to yourself and your narcissist, "Sweetheart, I am realizing so much about you, and I want to keep on learning and realizing more and more about you." This is part of loving, something that not just narcissists but everybody wants: to be recognized as being special. And this helps to allow feelings of safety and calm for more love to flow.

ESSENTIAL

If there is love in your relationship with a narcissist, you have a lot of power because you already are the most influential, important, and powerful person in his life. When you recognize that, it can help you avoid your own threatened feelings and negative reactions, such as yelling or shaming that just lead to the narcissist defending himself more and more.

In general, there are well-established and well-documented ways of communicating love to a partner or spouse with narcissism:

- Use gentleness and kindness often and in special moments every day. When speaking, use eye contact with a kind expression in your eyes.

- At least once a day say to the narcissist, "Today, I appreciate you for . . ."
- When listening to him, say, "I want to hear what you are saying better, I want to listen better." The reassurance of your interest in his words, that you are paying attention, is important. Try to restate what your partner said, and ask, "Did I get that right?"
- Smile in a special gentle way at a special time every day.
- Saying a person's name in a loving way with a gentle tone is a welcome thing.
- You must know a gentle playful thing that your partner or loved one really likes. Don't forget about it; do it often, or at unexpected times. Many times it is the soft and subtle things that bring a loving connection closer.

FACT

Studies have shown that people's health is actually in danger without support and relationships. Loving relationships, intimacy, being cared about, being connected—all make for better all-around health. In fact, health studies show that a feeling of isolation is a predictor of heart disease.

Loving and Commitment

There are thought to be two general ways that love relationships are held together. One is through a type of obligation, such as the respect for vows and for giving one's word of honor, constraints of welfare of children or finances, or religious and moral beliefs. The second is an active dedication and devotion that believes in involvement and a feeling of enthusiasm. Marriage and relationship experts have described that when both of these conditions are present, it creates the strongest bond in a love relationship.

Commitment and vows for loving are often thought to just be about feelings both people are feeling at the time of the first vows and what they are as you progress into the future. But commitment is actually not only about feelings but about the work to be done when things are not going so well, when that picnic gets the rain, the ants, and the mosquitoes.

What Happens to Love?

People search for love and for being in love, which always begins with a feeling of everything being perfect. Too many relationships that begin as "perfect" do collapse, however. That is because this state cannot stay sustained without work to keep it alive and growing. You need to develop and use an ability to deal with balances of love and resentment, both powerful emotions, and of conflicts of needs and satisfactions, and dealing with life's circumstances. But that initial enamored stage is an opportunity to glimpse the kind of love that is possible, and knowing that, you can learn to sustain or rekindle it as necessary.

The positives of love are overwhelming at first: feeling that life is meaningful, special; feeling whole and complete; feeling wanted and needed; feeling power in life and in the world because of your unique twosomeness, a completeness and freedom from any deep fear, or lacks or needs. It is intense and intensely satisfying.

The negatives in love relationships are usually the ones most easily spotted and felt and spoken about, however, especially when that includes a narcissist's negatives, such as jealousy and possessiveness, rage, anger, and the need to be always right. Add to that the terrible emotional wounds inflicted in childhood, probably by narcissistic parents, and a relationship with a narcissist can seem like a challenge that even the Power of Love cannot overcome. But it can; it just takes work.

Loving a Narcissist

Narcissists or people with NPD are usually carrying around with them a lot of pain inside—whether they recognize it or not. Like everyone, they deserve and want to be loved.

If you do love a partner or spouse with narcissism or NPD, and you don't want to give up on him, you have courage. It does take courage to keep your heart and your love there when things are abusive and hurtful. It does take endurance and patience to accept that you just can't make someone else happy, and you can't go on believing that another person is the source of your happiness. But when you see how to build good support for yourself and stand up for yourself, and set the boundaries that are important for you in your life, you will build on your love.

Most likely in the beginning of your relationship with a narcissist you were the center of the world, even though this phase did not last. For a time, most likely the narcissist seemed to truly care about you, seemed to be attached to you and to love you. For many narcissists, this is an idealization phase that he may get bored with, and then look for another person or other sources. For narcissists, the idea and accomplishment of long-lasting commitments, with continuing feelings of happiness and love, are most difficult.

ALERT

Not everything about a narcissist is 100 percent false all of the time. There can be moments, especially in a person with just narcissistic tendencies and not full-blown NPD, that he is truly feeling what he says. However, it still may be that he is not experiencing those feelings of love, compassion, or other positive emotions to the degree that his partner is.

As a relationship goes on, there is bound to be threatening situations. You know the expression, you always hurt the one you love. That expression came about because whoever the person is, narcissist or non-narcissist, people care most about the people who are closest to them. And narcissists care about what those people close to them think about them. They just do not like to be wrong or to make a mistake, to feel that they are bad. It is often too shameful or too fearful for them. They want and need approval. Maybe it does go back to a child who didn't get seen or was passed over, who didn't get enough eye contact, and who didn't feel recognized—and maybe the child thought it was because he made some kind of mistakes. For many narcissists there is a constant quest of getting approval, of being good enough, which never does have a resolve. There is never enough outside approval to help the narcissist feel good enough inside. And if he hears a complaint, that panic, fear, and shame can come out by twisting the situation to blame someone else—that close one, that loved one.

However, one downfall of a love relationship with a narcissist is the balance and level of emotional investment. There can be a definite imbalance in what is being given and what is received. You may not notice it for a long time when things are going well, and you may be investing your own deep capacity for giving and caring about satisfying needs. But when you finally have a need to express something to change or develop about the relationship, there may not be that willingness to listen and indicate a reciprocal emotional investment in caring about your concerns and needs.

ESSENTIAL

Lack of empathy is one of the characteristics or behavior difficulties that usually describes a narcissist or person with NPD, and is often given as a reason narcissists have difficulty loving or even cannot love. There are many degrees of narcissism, however. Still, many therapists, recovered narcissists, and partners will confirm that often the narcissist's lack of empathy that the books describe is not calculating but is really a reaction to the kinds of pressures he has the most trouble dealing with. So during times when those types of pressures are not happening, there can be a much greater connection between people.

Unconditional Love

Love is something inside you. It is you and does not depend on anything else or anybody else. You have to experience it, to grow it, and to give it. When you give it unconditionally, you do not expect to get a reward, a reaction, anything in return. So that even if you get some kind of negative reaction, you don't feel you expected something else. Of course, this is the ideal, the perfect, the idea of the infinite source of love that can flow from one person to another and back with no conditions. But it is possible to come as close as you can to this ideal.

Because love is in you, you don't have to plan for it or wait around for the knight or queen, you can just feel it anywhere, anytime, about anything. You don't have to find a relationship to look for and find love; you can think of yourself already in a space of love. This love is your reality, not a fantasy, because it exists just because you say so.

An Ayurvedic myth explains an interesting idea about love. In the story, a king cobra snake used fierce and frightening ways to rule. This worked, and people and animals went out of their way to avoid any confrontation with him. One day, the snake hid to listen to a saint speaking about unconditional love and peace. The snake liked what he heard, and decided to change his behavior to politeness and warmth toward all. But he was amazed that these people and animals did not react with equal politeness and love. In fact, he was rejected and stoned. The saint happened to see him lying there crying and bruised, and heard his story. The saint explained that before you can have and show unconditional love, you must know who you are first, and who you are loving. Why are you changing your behavior? Make that decision and state it out loud to your partner: "I am going to make an effort to change how I speak to you, because I know when I'm mean, it hurts you. I don't want to do that."

In order to give and receive unconditional love in your mind, you need to first know your own "conditions." If you are lacking in self-esteem or dignity, you first need to heal your own history, who you are, and be aware of the person you are loving. Otherwise, like the snake, you may be shocked, battered, and left alone in misery.

When you are in the process of standing up for yourself, you may be relating with conditions, but if both parties understand this in the process of building a love relationship, they can have the vision of unconditional love.

The Narcissism Epidemic

If there is a narcissism epidemic in the United States, as many speculate there is, how did we get there? There is not one single cause for it, but rather a convergence of many contributing factors over the last few decades. It started in the so-called "me decade" of the 1970s, when admiring yourself came to be equated with success in life.

This idea swelled to something of a movement with the dawn of self-help gurus and motivational speakers in the 1980s and 1990s, which become the age of entitlement. This "me first" attitude is just taken for granted as part of American culture today, when even preschoolers sing welcome songs with lyrics that say, "Hey look at me, I'm special!"

Add to this mix enabling technologies such as cell phones and the Internet, and you have a recipe for increased narcissism. Narcissism at its most basic level is a belief in a fantasy world in which you are better than everyone else in it. The Internet not only makes such fantasies literally possible, it encourages the use of false identities and gives everybody the opportunity to be a "viral celebrity." Social networking is the narcissist's dream, where success is gauged by the number of "followers" you have.

There are other factors of modern American society that have also allowed people to buy into a fantasy that they are better than they really are. Easy access to credit allowed people to live in fancier houses and drive bigger cars, and appear to have greater social status than they really did—until the bills came. Giving trophies out in Little League to all players, and inflating kids' grades and other over-the-top feedback, all lets them feel they are smarter or better athletes than they really are. And finally, we are a culture that has become celebrity-obsessed—so much so that stories about celebrities now lead on mainstream news programs.

The statistics that have led some to say narcissism has reached an epidemic are based on changes in averages. The level of change in narcissistic traits in the population today as opposed to ten or fifteen years ago represents a classic bell curve, with small changes at the average, or middle, and much greater changes at the ends. At the top of the bell, the average person is only somewhat narcissistic, yet noticeably more so now than ten years ago. But at the high end of the curve—those diagnosed with NPD—there are now three to four times as many people with that diagnosis than there were ten years ago. Which means that there are a great many more highly narcissistic people now than there were just a decade or so ago.

Will He Ever Change?

So with all that has been learned regarding narcissism and NPD, the big question in your mind probably still is: "Will my narcissistic partner, relative, or friend ever change?" The answer is a definite "maybe." A better question than "*Will* my narcissistic partner ever change?" is "*Can* my narcissistic partner ever change?" And the answer to that is resounding "Yes!" But it will take work on both of your parts.

The truth is if you expect your narcissistic partner, relative, or friend to ever stop being narcissistic, that is very unlikely. Fundamentally, narcissists probably never do change—once a narcissist, always a narcissist. However, what you can hope is for them to become "better narcissists." This means that they can add some positive, even loving behaviors to go along with their narcissistic ones. This is a very effective avenue of therapy for the narcissists, because it does not try to dispel their hyperinflated sense of self, but tries to get them to add compassion, warmth, and empathy into that personality. And there is growing evidence that it can be done.

FACT

One study of married couples who were dealing with a narcissistic spouse found that after therapy, when the partners with narcissism learned how to express more feelings of warmth and caring, they actually became better partners over time.

An approach to healing that is designed not to rid individuals of narcissism, but to get them to better live with themselves and others, *as* narcissists, can be the most effective. It takes a very good therapist, who can in a completely nonjudgmental way get the narcissist to re-evaluate his negative behaviors as they relate to real-world, even narcissistic, goals. For example, if the narcissist had an issue at work, and became angry and hostile toward a coworker because of a perceived threat to the narcissist's ego, the therapist would say, "But how did screaming at Annie in front of everyone help you reach your goal of being supervisor of the department?"

The narcissist's response would likely be that it felt good to scream at her, "but I see that it probably may have affected my reputation with the boss." When the therapist can get the narcissist to see that, the therapist can then ask the client to come up with an alternative way of handling the situation, one that would still serve the client's narcissistic goal of becoming the leader of the department. With this kind of approach, over time, the narcissist will learn to shape his behaviors to be consistent with his goals, but at the same time become increasingly aware of the detrimental and damaging effects of his narcissism.

How Far I Have Come, and Why Has It Been Worth It?

Knowledge is power, and certainly from reading the information in this book, you have gained both knowledge and power. And in your dealings with a narcissist or person with NPD, you have cared about understanding, making wise choices, and empowering yourself in order to make your decisions. You will have gained the best of self-empowerment to deal with and/ or stand up to the narcissist with the best possible words and actions that you can.

ESSENTIAL

When you are able to feel solid and whole within yourself, this feeling gives you protections from situations where a narcissist tries to manipulate you. Most often a narcissist can sense a person who is vulnerable or one who is strong.

These are the steps you have taken already as you read through this book:

- The step of recognition and realization. You probably already feel some relief in recognizing a first step, in accepting that narcissism is a disorder that affects people's personalities. Narcissists are usually not aware that they are acting this way, nor is it their usual intention to cause harm to people; it is just the way they operate. Realizing this has probably already given you some relief from your own feelings of responsibility and causation.
- The step of removing yourself a little, to not take personally this other person's disorder. Once you understand this, you can see that his actions have nothing to do with you or your actions. At any time, he may be accusing you or indicating that he acted out because of something you did or did not do. But you now know that you can step back from this and not take it personally.
- The step of moving yourself forward, to not sit back and accept things the way they are but to seek and want changes for the better.
- The step of thinking about your personal boundaries, your personal requirements, your needs and rights, so that you take steps to refuse to accept abuse.
- The step of processing your feelings based on your understandings and realizations. This is the way to healing. An important step to

emotional and physical health is to be able to express your feelings, especially anger or fear, by sharing your story. This is the path to getting yourself unstuck and moving forward in healing toward health and feeling good.

- The step of putting plans into motion, expressing yourself in creative ways, your outlets, your support system. You have already begun to organize in your mind any chaos and trauma, making sense of it, and realizing you are not alone in your struggle with people in your life who are narcissists.

- The step of avoiding consequences and having the courage and strength to open yourself up to the learning and work that leads to growth.

- The step of giving yourself the opportunity to live your life with unconditional love for yourself, because you are striving to be honest with yourself.

- The step of being in the present, looking at what you are doing now that is creating your future.

- The step of realizing the importance of a support group, whether that means counseling, a type of therapy, turning to friends and relatives, or any combination of these things.

- The step of becoming aware of ways in which a person with NPD can be helped. These include help by a professional or loved one who can create for the narcissist an environment where it's emotionally safe to accept personal faults and failures, and to tolerate mistakes in other people. Communicating unconditional positive regard can help teach a person with NPD alternative ways of getting narcissistic supply without having to resort to destructive behaviors.

- Finally, the step of feeling that you are back in control. You are back in the driver's seat because you are not waiting for things to get better, you're not waiting for the narcissist to change; you are working on changing yourself.

At this point you probably are feeling better about the level of love and respect you command and have in your life. And you are probably more certain about the direction you plan to take in the relationship(s) you have with a narcissist. Hopefully, reading this book has been helpful to you in several ways. If your situation is one in which you have previously thought about ending a relationship or ending contact with a narcissist, going through this book has helped you to have concrete reasons for your decision. If your situation is one in which you needed to know how to better handle interactions with a narcissist, you now have the knowledge, ideas of what you are up against, and the tools for yourself to begin practicing. If your situation is one in which you want to learn how to continue your relationship with a narcissist and work on bringing the relationship to a better level, you now have knowledge and ideas of how to do that.

ALERT

One client who had recovered through therapy after ending two traumatic relationships with narcissists said she realized that her pain from feeling betrayed, abused, and rejected by the narcissist was more about herself as a hurt child. Trying to get a narcissist to love her was like trying to get her aloof, emotionally unavailable father to love and approve of her. So she continually chose men who really could not love her and tried to make them change, because she hoped they would save her wounded little girl. Recovering from those unhealthy relationships enabled her to heal her painful past with her father. She now makes healthier choices in whom she picks for intimate relationships.

Both you and the narcissist do want the gifts, the rewards, of intimacy and love that people can give to one another. Both you and the narcissist really want to be seen and loved for just the person you are. The challenges of working on relationships to achieve that are not easy for anyone. Most people do find it easy to sometimes slip into a place of wanting to protect any good image. It's not always easy to admit to making mistakes, to being foolish, to having a shortcoming or problem. These kinds of admissions are especially difficult for a narcissist. Getting to a place of feeling safe enough to look at oneself honestly does take patience, time, and work. But the rewards of being able to have a loving intimacy are worth it, for a narcissist and for anyone.

Whatever your situation is, you can recognize the benefits of counseling or therapy for yourself to have a trustworthy and knowledgeable person for support and to encourage your inner strengths as you work with the challenges a narcissist presents.

Tooting Your Own Horn

If you have been going overboard to try to deal with a narcissist, or spent too much worry and energy on it, you have to recognize that you have already taken a great step forward at this time. You already have put a dividing line between your past losses of energy and comforts, and are easing into a new way of seeing what is going on and how you are dealing with it.

You deserve a congratulatory note to not be so quick to worry and care about the narcissist's needs and pleasing him, but instead putting yourself and your needs and pleasures in the limelight. You deserve congratulations for knowing the difference between selfishness and excessive self-absorption; you recognize a healthy attention to the self.

You are now aware of how and where you can be taken advantage of, and how you go about strengthening your position and protecting yourself from being taken advantage of. You now see just what should go into an equal relationship rather than one that is unbalanced.

You deserve the recognition of a diploma for the wisdom you have gained about the types of illusions, lies, and distortions the narcissist puts forth. With this knowledge you already have a protective shield from these types of distortions affecting you personally. If you have been suffering from anxiety or depression as a result of not feeling in control of yourself in your dealings with the narcissist, now you can see you are on a path to letting anxiety and depression fade away as you gather your means of control over the situation. And this is your path to feeling happy.

Throughout this book you have been checking on your own values in life for survival, for power, for authenticity, for rules, for sharing, for improving, for learning, and for flowing. Your lists, your thoughts, your decisions with each of these values make you stronger and should allow you to take pride in your ability to wrest some control of your own life back from your narcissistic partner, relative, or friend.

Putting What You Learned and Know into Your Life

After reading any book or taking a class, all that great information, all those ideas are in your head. Some people take notes, write a thought or two down, or tell another person what they read or learned about, and that helps to remember it. But then, how do you take this huge amount of great information and put it into a practice, especially in dealing with your feelings and emotions?

Most counselors would agree that the best way to merge what you learn into how you live your daily life experiences is to begin healing your inner child. This goes for both you and the narcissist. Usually people are not aware of how much of our lives are being run by the child within us. Things just go on year by year, with the same kinds of reactions and actions, which unconsciously relate to old childhood hurts and attitudes without most of us ever realizing it. It just seems your natural behavior. And this pattern of what you know as natural for you is what goes on in your most intimate relationships. Most counselors will agree that one of the best ways to put what you learn into your daily life is to put that learning and understanding of your own child and the child of your partner into your present-day mature self.

There are many teachers, books, and so on these days that will tell you that the goal is to learn to love yourself—but no one really tells you how to do that. One way is to learn to love, understand, and embrace your inner child.

Putting Fear, Shame, and Guilt to Rest with Your Adult

Parents do have to discipline their children. Within the levels of what society accepts, that can often involve a fair amount of shame, fear, and guilt to set limits, to teach, to show consequences, and to correct children. But now that you're aware of more inner processes and outer processes that go on, you can start to understand your own triggers and patterns and those of your partner. You can see where those patterns might have come from by checking in on that child within who knew about the causes.

Whenever you have a strong reaction to something or someone, this often can signal a hurt, a wound from that child in you that somehow didn't get healed or soothed or understood. When you have this strong reaction, try to think back to when you felt like that as a child. Probably you will recall a situation in which you, as a child, felt terror, panic or rage, hopelessness, or loneliness. And you might recall a parent who caused you to feel ashamed or guilty or fearful because of what happened. But now, your mature person sees it, knows it, and puts it to rest with your own love and tenderness for that child who suffered. This method can help to prevent a critical parent voice in your head that makes you feel there is something wrong with you, that you should feel ashamed, or frightened of the consequences, or judgment that you are unworthy. Now as the adult you can speak not only to that hurt child but also to the critical parent voice in your head and tell that voice to stop, it's time to zip it!

Here are questions to ask yourself when you feel a button being pushed:

- Where is this feeling coming from?
- Why am I reacting this way?
- When did I feel like this before and what is it actually reminding me of?
- Do I feel like an adult or a child right now?

It does happen that in this process of seeing and understanding your inner child in the present, you also become more aware of your partner's reactions by realizing that he shares a similar experience. And this helps to further along a positive relationship connection.

ESSENTIAL

Decisions and choices are the way you live your life. One good way to think about making your decisions and choices is to ask yourself: "Is the outcome of this choice or decision going to make me stronger or weaker?"

How to Be Glad for the Rain, the Troubles, the Madness

One positive way to deal with things going wrong and feeling strong emotions is to think of it as a dark madness; then use this madness to bring in the light around it. Whether you are feeling jealousy, anger, or defensiveness, know that there is a child inside demanding some kind of attention or protection in recognition of that feeling. And when you see that child, it can help you to feel more loving. Doing this can give you an important space to be able to see yourself, even watch yourself, and certainly love yourself.

Staying Focused and Moving Forward

You know how to keep focused to keep your eye on the road ahead while driving. It is something that you have done millions of times without even thinking about it. But staying focused on establishing new habits, on learning new things, is something you have to think about and then apply yourself to the task.

Moving Forward with a Narcissistic Partner

Now you know how to stay in control of how you react and you know how to act in the present. You have a deeper awareness of why you do the things you do and think the thoughts you do, and all of this is helping to build bridges between you and your spouse or partner.

Now, try to look at things through his eyes. See what he sees, mirror what he feels. If you are "not getting it," don't fall back on old habits of reacting negatively. Instead, ask him to better explain what he means.

You need to find the common ground between you. Make time for planning sessions, where you both can envision the things you would like to do and accomplish together. There must be ways to spend more quality time together. Think of the hobbies or things that you both enjoy—the kinds of things that brought you together in the first place. Plan a special vacation for the two of you, and choose places to go and things to do that will really make you both happy. Find more ways to share the common tasks of everyday life, and finds ways to make each of your lives easier and more rewarding.

Doing these things can help to bring a specialness to your partner's life. But do not forget about your own happiness, because bringing your happiness into the relationship is a gift you give yourself and your partner.

Making Room for Healing

Moving forward, as the two words imply, is a process of movement that continues. And, of course, that's the direction you want to be moving with your life, whether that includes the narcissist in your life or not. To keep yourself moving forward, you want to always be doing some emotional healing. Healing is something that your physical body systems are always in the process of doing to keep you well. But emotionally, you need to put your own forces into the process, because emotional healing is not something you only need occasionally or for one major crisis. People are so emotionally complex that it really is an ongoing exploration of learning to know oneself, and to know and understand the loved ones in your life. Here are a few tips for everyday emotional healing.

- Always share positive feelings. One can never hear enough of them.
- Let your partner be the priority often enough, and let him see that indeed he is the priority.
- Keep something exciting and passionate going in one small way each week, something that the two of you really used to love together and still could.
- Let your partner know that he is the one that you are the most interested in and most want to listen to and hear from.

Important Parts of a Good Relationship for Partners

The good and the bad, the sun and the rain, the yin and the yang. They always do exist, side by side, and you know that both of you are responsible for the good and for the bad, too. Here's the time to take responsibility for a problem, take ownership of your part in it, and leave the blame behind you.

Take hope in the belief that good will win over bad. When bad things have already happened, it's hard to be hopeful. Keeping hope alive can seem like a big risk to take. But there is great power in hope. Science knows that it is in the right-brain hemisphere that a person's empathy and compassion are involved. Interesting studies using brain imaging have indicated there is a relationship between shortcomings in the emotional connection of children with their mothers and development patterns in the right-brain areas that will affect empathy and compassion.

In other studies with talk therapy and patients with personality disorders that included narcissism, brain scans showed that the therapy did create changes in the right-brain areas. A study like this offers some amazing physical evidence to support the fact that there can always be hope for change and a better life for narcissists with the proper support and work.

Studies on recovering patients have found that those who described themselves as hopeful recovered much more quickly and with a more complete and effective recovery than those who didn't.

When you think about being hopeful for the narcissist in your life, with the difficulties you have had, it is natural to feel worried, to fear that what you want may not happen. But if you are already on this path, you probably have more hope than you realize; it's just hidden by your fears. Hope keeps love going and helps you believe you will have the kind of enjoyment in your relationship you want.

The trick of being able to walk in your spouse's or partner's shoes will give you another view from his perspective. And it's bound to be different than yours. It's like not only visiting another country but living in it for a bit. This is no easy feat, because with your sensitivity you can feel your partner's pain. And you can be there to help find solutions to problems with your thinking.

What your own family role models were like may have influenced the standards you look for in your partner, and they are most likely different from your partner's role models and his standards. It's a good idea to explore them together, just like a home movie.

Being able to say "I'm sorry" and offer forgiveness usually helps to break through bitterness, distance, and the self-serving traps of blaming tit for tat. It's a brave thing to be able to say, "I am sorry. Can you please forgive me?" Make sure you're not giving a "nonapology" like, "I'm sorry you think that," or "I'm sorry you feel that way." This puts the blame back on your partner for his thoughts or feelings. More appropriate are "I'm sorry if I did something to make you think that," or "I'm sorry if my comments hurt your feelings." Realize your role in the situation and acknowledge it.

If you have made vows to each other, keeping them, not just saying them, and making good on your promises keeps love alive. You might even want to think about renewing them in an official ceremony—it is a great way to tell your partner that he is still "the one" despite any difficulties you may be working through.

Establishing Healthy Habits and Boundaries

In order to ensure your own mental health and happiness, it is essential to establish your own lifestyle habits and firm boundaries first.

Boundary Necessities

Everyone began establishing boundaries as far back as they can remember: Labeling a door "My Room, Keep Out." Closing a bathroom door for privacy. Telling Grandma not to pinch your cheek. Boundaries are always important to protect and ensure one's needs and interests. There are many boundaries that you have already established in your everyday life that you don't even think about because some are not as crucial as others. But here are some boundaries that are important for you to maintain, especially if there is someone with narcissism or NPD in your life.

ESSENTIAL

You can create an emotional boundary to protect you from your narcissist's negative energy. Envision an invisible shield totally surrounding you from head to toe—but this is not a "force field." It is a bubble of love and happiness, more like a womb or a cocoon, wrapping you in love. It is a warm and friendly blanket protecting you from the negativity of others. Increase the strength of this barrier by asking your Higher Power—whatever you believe in—for protection.

Decide which things you will allow and which things you will not tolerate. List them so you make it a pact with yourself. It may even surprise you to see written out what things are important to you for your personal space and well-being.

You need to note what areas to protect for yourself: your health, your financial situation, your social and family connections, the things that make your life's daily schedule easier. What do you need to do to protect your self-esteem? If a person with narcissism or NPD is having an effect on your self-confidence or your self-esteem, list what statements you will not take personally, which ones will be unacceptable. Take whatever steps you need to be kind to yourself and to support your self-confidence.

1. List any emotional outbursts that are disrespectful or abusive, and do not tolerate them. Decide what methods you will use to maintain your self-respect, perhaps by insisting on apologies or walking away.
2. Decide how much you give and what your limits are for giving. Just because a narcissist demands something from you does not mean you must do it. Enforce your own powers of judgment.
3. Decide what your energy zappers are and how to protect yourself from behaviors that do zap your energy.
4. Decide what rules you want to create for yourself, and for you and the narcissist, for more acceptable behavior and a better relationship.

ESSENTIAL

You are able to control your own emotions and actions, and you don't have to allow the negativity of a narcissist to affect you. Try this technique to give yourself a boundary of protection before your next meeting with the narcissist: Visualize the person, but think of him specifically with a good wish for his best interest.

When you feel yourself reacting to something negative or feel your energy draining, try this method. Think of the occurrence or the event inside yourself with each one of your senses. Where do you feel it, where do you see it, where do you hear it? Then close your eyes, take a few deep breaths, and let out all that badness in each large exhale. Picture it leaving your body as dark and then changing color to clean, bright, light.

Healthy Habits

It may be easy to think of habits as those unfortunate glitches that are troublesome, or the things you think have to be overcome—someday. But some habits can be healthy, too. And the more healthy habits you have in your life, the less likely that the bad ones will be troublesome for you.

Healthy habits work to continually build and strengthen the parts of you that go into feeling good and happy. Healthy habits are like magnets: They attract even more healthy and happy events into your life.

FACT

Aristotle, the famous Greek philosopher, said almost 2,400 years ago that healthy habits lead to happiness.

- **One blessing a day counts.** At least one time each day, maybe first thing in the morning, last thing at night, or even over a special cup of tea, think of something good about your day. If it's in the morning, think about the day ahead; if in the evening, think about the day's events. Gloss over any problems just for now—hurts, resentments, anger—just say, for now, all is forgiven just for this moment, and then find one thing that made you feel good or joyful or happy. Make that your blessing for the day, and know that your day is or was a good day, because that one thing counts when it comes to blessings.
- **Thank you.** Thank you is not just for special holiday gifts, but one thank-you a day brings gratitude and appreciation into your life. Think of one thing that you can appreciate for that day, something a person said or did, and tell that person what it is that you appreciate. Gratitude and appreciation can act like magnets to bring more appreciation and goodness into your life.
- **One kind word or deed.** Each day, make sure to do one good deed, something kind to somebody else to show that you cared or were concerned. Acting on kindness creates a wide path of glowing goodness that does bring back more kindness and fairness to you.
- **Budge from a grudge.** Think for one day that you can forgive the grudges, the hurts, the burdens of the past, and just for that day, act as if things were solved. Imagine those burdens thrown into the wind, just for that day. Letting go of these heavy negatives will give you a feeling of relief, of openness to let happiness and goodness into your life.
- **A powerful memory picture.** When one thing happens during your day that lets you feel good, proud, powerful, or special, breathe in that

moment and say, wow, yes, this is my good moment. Doing this will make a memory for you that will stay with you.

- **Go and do.** Make sure a week does not go by without going out and doing things, especially with close friends and family. Include social events that you enjoy, as well as finding some new ways to interact and give to people through volunteering or clubs. When you share happy times and good efforts with others, it deepens your own happiness, like a sponge of happiness.

- **Uniquely you.** Each day think about and recognize something strong about your unique personality. You know inside what it is you are—are you funny, fair-minded, curious, playful, down to earth? You don't have to worry about skills and abilities; just think about the uniquely wonderful person you are and focus on these aspects of you because these are your real strengths—the things that bring more positives and happiness to your life.

- **Practice makes for power.** Practicing something every day makes it a habit in no time at all. You can think of it in the way you might exercise a muscle to strengthen it. You can think about positive thinking as a muscle, the happiness muscle—with daily exercise, that wellness and happiness muscle will work for you, and with it you will have the strength and power to cope with or overcome anything, even the narcissists in your life!

APPENDIX A

Symptoms Checklists

Are you living with a narcissist? Do you think your friends or relatives may be narcissists? Are you afraid that you may be showing some signs of narcissism yourself? Use these handy checklists.

- Do you or someone you know have trouble putting things in perspective, or blow things way out of proportion?
- Do you or someone you know show little or no empathy or compassion for the feelings, thoughts, or opinions of others?
- Are you or is someone you know preoccupied with your own or his own problems?
- Do you or someone you know show little or no respect for authority and have little concern for morals?
- Do you or someone you know feel inferior, but want to be seen as superior by others?
- Are you or is someone you know extremely sensitive to any kind of criticism?
- Are you or is someone you know an exhibitionist and need sexual admiration?
- Are you or is someone you know exploitative, vain, and/or not self-sufficient?
- Are you or is someone you know using drugs and alcohol to provide feelings of power and well-being?
- Are you or is someone you know using drugs and alcohol to try to "feel whole?"
- Are you or is someone you know taking drugs and abusing alcohol to be selfish and self-indulgent?
- Are you or is someone you know abusing drugs and alcohol because you require a high level of stimulation?
- Do you or someone you know try to cut people off from others, or limit contacts with friends and relatives?
- Are you or is someone you know extremely jealous? Do you or he often invent relationships and suspect others of infidelities with friends, coworkers, or acquaintances?
- Are you or someone you know constantly belittling?
- Are you or someone you know often resorting to verbal or physical abuse?
- Do you or someone you know seem to enjoy punishing people?

❏ Are you or is someone you know seeming to suddenly withdraw emotionally?

❏ Do you or does someone you know seem to lack the ability to admit when wrong?

❏ Do you or does someone you know seem overly controlling and manipulative?

❏ Have you or has someone you know ever resorted to self-mutilation?

❏ Do you or does someone you know threaten, or otherwise try to intimidate others?

❏ Do you or does someone you know purposefully destroy others' possessions?

❏ Do you or does someone you know claim to know the feelings and motivations of you "better than you do"? Or, of others, "better than they do"?

❏ Do you or does someone you know believe you, or he, is better than everyone else?

❏ Do you or does someone you know constantly fantasize about power and success?

❏ Do you or does someone you know lie about achievements and/or talents?

❏ Do you or does someone you know demand constant praise and admiration?

❏ Do you or does someone you know believe that you are or he is special and beyond legal or moral consequences?

❏ Do you or does someone you know expect others to always go along with your, or his, ideas and plans?

❏ Do you or does someone you know set ridiculously unrealistic goals?

❏ Do you or does someone you know think emotions are a sign of weakness?

❏ Do you or does someone you know form relationships with others based only on what they can get back in return from them?

Risk Factors

While considering the signs and symptoms of NPD, it may also be helpful to have a quick guide to potential risk factors. Risk factors for the development of NPD include:

- ❏ Parents who ignore their child's fears and needs.
- ❏ Parents who belittle childhood fears, or say they are signs of weakness, especially in male children.
- ❏ General lack of affection, and not enough positive praise during childhood.
- ❏ Neglect and other kinds of emotional abuse in childhood.
- ❏ Inconsistent or unreliable caregiving from parents.
- ❏ Imitation of manipulative behaviors learned from parents.

What NPD Isn't

Even recognizing the signs and symptoms of narcissism, NPD is often confused with other conditions.

- NPD is not the same thing as obsessive-compulsive disorder.
- NPD is not the same thing as schizophrenia.
- NPD is not the same thing as borderline personality disorder.
- NPD is not the same thing as bipolar disorder.
- NPD is not the same thing as dissociative identity disorder.
- NPD is not the same thing as histrionic personality disorder.
- NPD is not the same thing as antisocial personality disorder.

APPENDIX B

Resources

Find a therapist or treatment for NPD in your area
www.medicinenet.com/narcissistic_personality_disorder/city.htm

An open guide to links, discussions, and resources on verbal, psychological, and emotional abuse by narcissists and others
www.dmoz.org/Health/Mental_Health/Psychological_Abuse

A Yahoo! group for recovering children of narcissistic parents
http://health.groups.yahoo.com/group/Adult-ChildrenOfNarcissits

Another online support group for families coping with narcissists
http://npd-family.livejournal.com

A comprehensive guide to mental and emotional resources for sufferers and their families, featuring hundreds of links and informative articles
http://psychcentral.com/resources

National Institute of Mental Health (NIMH)
The mission of NIMH is to transform the understanding and treatment of mental illnesses through basic and clinical research, paving the way for prevention, recovery, and cure.
www.nimh.nih.gov

National Alliance on Mental Illness
Founded in 1979, NAMI has become the nation's voice on mental illness. As the nation's largest grassroots mental-health organization, it is dedicated to improving the lives of persons living with serious mental illness as well as their families, through advocacy, research, support, and education.
www.nami.org

Mental Health America (MHA)

MHA is one of the country's leading nonprofits dedicated to helping people live emotionally healthier lives. Following is a link to their information and resources on personality disorders, including NPD.
www.nmha.org/go/information/get-info/personality-disorders

National Institute on Alcohol Abuse and Alcoholism (NIAAA), part of the National Institutes of Health

The mission of NIAAA is to support and promote the best science on alcohol and health for the benefit of all by increasing the understanding of normal and abnormal behavior relating to alcohol use; improving the diagnosis, prevention, and treatment of alcohol use disorders; and enhancing quality health care for abusers and their families.
www.niaaa.nih.gov

American Psychological Association (APA)

Based in Washington, D.C., the American Psychological Association is a scientific and professional organization that represents psychology in the United States. With more than 154,000 members, APA is the largest association of psychologists worldwide. Its mission is to advance the creation, communication, and application of psychological knowledge to benefit society and improve people's lives.
www.apa.org

EMDR International Association (EMDRIA)

EMDRIA is a professional association where eye movement desensitization and reprocessing (EMDR) practitioners and researchers seek the highest standards for the clinical use of EMDR. Find out more about EMDR, and find a practitioner using the techniques in your area.
www.emdria.org

International Society for Mental Health Online (ISMHO)

ISMHO is an international community exploring and promoting mental health in the digital age. Its members include students, teachers, researchers, clinical practitioners, and others interested in using Internet technologies to sustain positive mental health. ISMHO was formed in 1997 to promote the understanding, use, and development of online communication, information, and technology for the international mental health community.
www.ismho.org

Brain and Behavior Research Foundation (formerly the National Alliance for Research on Schizophrenia and Depression)

NPD is often confused with schizophrenia, and sufferers of NPD often also suffer from depression. An excellent resource for information about both of these conditions is the Brain and Behavior Research Foundation, previously known as the National Alliance for Research on Schizophrenia and Depression (NARSAD). As it was then, the renamed organization still is committed to alleviating the suffering of mental illness.
www.narsad.org

National Association of Cognitive-Behavioral Therapists (NACBT)

The NACBT is the leading organization dedicated exclusively to supporting, promoting, teaching, and developing cognitive-behavioral therapy and those who practice it; however, laypeople can also have many questions about CBT answered and find information on how to find a CBT therapist in their area on the site.
www.nacbt.org

Treatment Facilities for Narcissistic Personality Disorder

Treatment for NPD is not usually conducted in an inpatient setting, unless it is compounded by other conditions such as drug or alcohol abuse. However, there are two facilities in California that specialize in the treatment of all types of personality disorders, including NPD, that take patients from all states.

Psychological Care and Healing Treatment Center

PCH Treatment Center, while located in Los Angeles, offers psychological care and treatment to clients from all over the United States. If you or your loved one is suffering from narcissistic personality disorder, bipolar disorder, depression, psychological trauma, anxiety, or any other personality issues, PCH Treatment Center offers a safe and healing treatment environment.

www.pchtreatment.com

888-724-0040

Clearview Treatment Programs

Clearview Treatment Programs, with several locations in southern California, is a nationwide leader in mental health treatment. Clearview provides highly individualized treatment programs for people with various personality disorders, including NPD, as well as alcohol and drug addictions, and dual diagnosis.

www.clearviewtreatment.com

866-713-7948

Worth Reading—Books on NPD

Why Is It Always about You? The Seven Deadly Sins of Narcissism by Sandy Hotchkiss. New York: Free Press, 2003.

THIS BOOK USES EASY-TO-UNDERSTAND LANGUAGE TO EXPLAIN WHAT NARCISSISM IS, HOW UNHEALTHY NARCISSISM DEVELOPS, AND HOW TO ARM ONESELF AGAINST IT.

Narcissism: Denial of the True Self by Alexander Lowen, MD. New York: Touchstone, 1997.

LOWEN USES REAL PATIENT CASES TO DEMONSTRATE WHAT NARCISSISM FEELS LIKE FOR SUFFERERS. HE FOCUSES ON THE DENIAL OF FEELINGS, WHICH MAKES NARCISSISTS APPEAR "INHUMAN," THEIR OVERINVESTMENT IN THEIR IMAGE, AND CRAVINGS FOR POWER AND CONTROL.

Emotional Vampires: Dealing with People Who Drain You Dry by Albert J. Bernstein. New York: McGraw-Hill, 2001.

EMOTIONAL VAMPIRES TELLS READERS HOW TO SPOT A "VAMPIRE" IN THEIR LIVES, WHICH DEFENSE STRATEGIES TO EMPLOY TO PREVENT ONE FROM STRIKING, AND WHAT TO DO IF AND WHEN THEY FIND THEMSELVES UNDER ATTACK.

Enough about You, Let's Talk about Me: How to Recognize and Manage the Narcissists in Your Life by Les Carter. San Francisco: Jossey Bass, 2005.

PSYCHOTHERAPIST DR. LES CARTER OFFERS PRACTICAL TIPS AND EFFECTIVE STRATEGIES FOR MANAGING RESPONSES TO MANIPULATIVE BEHAVIOR, AND INCLUDES PROVEN APPROACHES TO HANDLING NARCISSISTS, THEIR DEMANDS, THEIR ANGER, AND THEIR LACK OF BOUNDARIES.

The Wizard of Oz and Other Narcissists: Coping with the One-Way Relationship in Work, Love, and Family by Eleanor Payson. Royal Oak, MI: Julian Day Publications, 2002.

FROM THE FINANCIAL BARONS OF WALL STREET TO OUR ELECTED OFFICIALS IN GOVERNMENT, WE ARE CONFRONTED DAILY WITH NARCISSISTS AND THE SELF-SERVING SYSTEMS THAT ENABLE THEM. HELPING PEOPLE RECLAIM THEIR LIVES FROM THIS SINISTER EXPLOITATIVE FORCE IS THE MISSION BEHIND PAYSON'S BOOK.

Narcissistic Lovers: How to Cope, Recover and Move On by Cynthia Zayn and Kevin Dibble. Far Hills, NJ: New Horizon Press, 2007.

IN A REVEALING STUDY OF RELATIONSHIPS WHERE PARTNERS LOVE THEMSELVES FIRST, LAST, AND ALWAYS, ZAYN AND DIBBLE HELP READERS DETERMINE WHETHER THEIR PARTNER IS OVER THE LINE AND HAS NARCISSISTIC PERSONALITY DISORDER. THE BOOK DRAWS ON THE AUTHORS' RESEARCH AND INTERVIEWS WITH A VARIETY OF MEN AND WOMEN WHO'VE BEEN "NARCISSIZED."

Children of the Self-Absorbed: A Grown-Up's Guide to Getting Over Narcissistic Parents by Nina W. Brown. Oakland, CA: New Harbinger Publications, 2001.

BEING A PARENT IS USUALLY ALL ABOUT GIVING OF YOURSELF TO FOSTER YOUR CHILD'S GROWTH AND DEVELOPMENT. BUT WHAT HAPPENS WHEN THIS ISN'T THE CASE? *CHILDREN OF THE SELF-ABSORBED* OFFERS CLEAR DEFINITIONS OF NARCISSISM AND NARCISSISTIC PERSONALITY DISORDER TO HELP YOU IDENTIFY THE EXTENT OF YOUR PARENT'S PROBLEM.

The Narcissism Epidemic: Living in the Age of Entitlement by Jean M. Twenge and W. Keith Campbell. New York: Free Press, 2009.

TWENGE AND CAMPBELL, PSYCHOLOGISTS AND AUTHORS OF PREVIOUS BOOKS ON SELF-ADMIRATION, TEAM UP FOR A THOROUGH LOOK AT A TROUBLING TREND THAT HAS BROAD CULTURAL IMPLICATIONS.

Index